NONVIOLENCE FOR THE
THIRD MILLENNIUM

NONVIOLENCE FOR THE THIRD MILLENNIUM:

ITS LEGACY AND FUTURE

Edited by

G. Simon Harak, S. J.

MERCER UNIVERSITY PRESS
MACON, GA

ISBN 0-86554-660-6

HM
1281
.N65
2000

MUP/H203

The paper used in this publication meets the minimum require-ments of American National Standard for Information Sci-ences—Permanence of Paper for Printed Library Materials, ANSI Z39.48-1984.

Library of Congress Cataloging-in-Publication Data

Nonviolence for the Third Millennium: Its Legacy and Future/ edited by G. Simon Harak
    p. cm.
ISBN 0-86554-660-6 (all. paper)
1. Nonviolence. 2. Nonviolence—History. 3. Nonviolence in literature. I. Harak, G. Simon, 1948-

HM1281.N65 2000
303.6'2—dc21

99-086084

CONTENTS

PREFACE

The year 1998 marked three impor-
tant anniversaries for people committed to nonviolent peacemaking.
That year marked the thirtieth and the fiftieth year since the
assassinations of Martin Luther King (April 4, 1968) and Mohandas
Karamchand Gandhi (January 30, 1948), and the fiftieth anniversary
of the UN Declaration of Universal Human Rights. In commemora-
tion and in hope, the authors in the following pages have contributed
their efforts to reconsider where the movement of nonviolence has
come from and to project its future into the third millennium.

At the close of his classic study of medieval millennialism,
Norman Cohn observes that though "[t]he story told in this book
ended some four centuries ago . . . it is not without relevance to our
own times"; that the hope for a "perfect world from which self-seeking
would be forever banished" still animates much of our thinking and
our hopes, especially for oppressed societies.[1] In this volume, we are
inviting the reader to walk with us on a nonviolent journey into the
third millennium. The word "walk" has a special significance in the
peace movement. Often nonviolent campaigns involve walking or
marching. We can recall the great U.S. civil rights marches led by
King in the 1960s and his Poor People's March on Washington. We
know about how often Gandhi walked around the villages of India,
preaching nonviolence, and about his famous "Walk to the Sea" to
make salt in defiance of the British monopoly.

A successor to Gandhi, Vinoba Bhave, was called "the walking
saint." He walked for twelve years and covered tens of thousands of
kilometers, asking for and receiving "land-gifts" from the rich to the
poor, eventually receiving pledges of some four million acres. When
the same Bhave thought to revive Gandhi's concept of the *shanti sena*

---

[1]Norman Cohn, *The Pursuit of the Millennium: Revolutionary Millenarians and Mystical Anarchists of the Middle Ages* (New York, NY: Oxford University Press, 1970), 285, 286.

(an unarmed peace army), he called for a conference in the city of Ajmer in 1959. After the conference, on March 2nd, 850 volunteers walked fifteen kilometers to Gagwana where the Peace Army began. Among the walkers was Martin Luther King Jr.[2] In his wonderful book, *Revolution from the Heart*, Niall O'Brien writes about how the growing dignity, power, and universalism of the basic Christian communities was expressed by walking together. He even understands walking as a spiritual discipline akin to that of monasticism.[3] The reader will forgive me if I call upon my Christian heritage and recall how much Jesus, whom we call "The Prince of Peace," walked from place to place in ancient Palestine, offering healing, forgiveness, and love in place of violence, and preaching the good news of liberation for those oppressed by the power that kills.

When we read or experience how the dominant powers resist these walks—sometimes by obstructing, sometimes with fury, too-often with violence—we can begin to suspect that the powers themselves perceive something very powerful and threatening about walking in nonviolence. As Stanley Hauerwas colorfully puts it, "[N]onviolence cannot help but appear as a terrorist tactic by those who want to make the world safe for war."[4]

For those engaged in nonviolence, however, the strategy of walking expresses a centrally important realization of nonviolent peacemakers: that the "end" is the unfolding of the "means." Just as one cannot make oatmeal cookies with the ingredients for rice pudding, so one cannot make peace by violent means. Understanding that intrinsic relationship between ends and means, we can see that walking is such a good means for nonviolent ends because it shares so many of the characteristics of nonviolence—in its gradual approach

---

[2]For a fuller account of this, and the whole "Peace Army" movement, see Thomas Weber's important and thoroughly researched work, *Gandhi's Peace Army: The Shanti Sena and Unarmed Peacekeeping* (Syracuse, NY: Syracuse University Press, 1996), esp. 75.

[3]Niall O'Brien, *Revolution from the Heart* (New York: Orbis, 1991), see especially chapter 46.

[4]Stanley Hauerwas, "The Nonviolent Terrorist: In Defense of Christian Fanaticism," Address to the Catholic University in Leuven, February 17, 1997.

to things, in its time for reflection, in its building of community, in its communion with the earth, and in its making the walker available, even vulnerable, to others on the road to peace.

In this volume, we will walk with many courageous men and women as they struggle to bring peace. We will walk back in time to meet the young Gandhi as he began his commitment to nonviolence. Soon we will find ourselves in Sri Lanka, in Tibet, in Cambodia, reflecting on the path to peace. We will travel to Iraq and Palestine, to Latin America and the Caribbean, meeting those who suffer persecution for the sake of justice. We will come back to the United States, and meet, as one of our authors has put it, "some of the finest people in the world" as they struggle to live out their commitment to active nonviolence, and to prepare the next generation to take up the cry of the poor for peace.

As I write, some thirty Nobel Peace Prize winners are petitioning the UN that the year 2000 be the beginning of a decade of education in nonviolence. It is our hope that, as you walk, you find with us, with them, and with so many others, a deeper sense of community, and an even deeper inspiration to continue to nonviolent struggle in your own world.

THE LEGACY

1

WHO INFLUENCED GANDHI?

Arun Gandhi

We begin our walk on a personal note, with stories of the young Mohandas Gandhi, struggling to overcome his fears from childhood and adolescence. In "Who Influenced Gandhi?" we find that Mohandas's early teachers in the life of nonviolence were his mother, Putliba, and his nurse, Rumbha. The one taught him the religious discipline and the other the religious narratives that formed his life. Later, when he had married Kasturba Makanji (both were thirteen years old), he found he had to surrender his strategy of dominating his wife, and admit that he was impressed by her courage in the face of things of which he himself was frightened. If all that sounds somewhat like a family portrait of the future Mahatma, it should: the author, Arun Gandhi, is the grandson of Mohandas and Kasturba. Arun spent long months with his grandfather in India discussing the nonviolent lifestyle after suffering a particularly painful childhood as a victim of racism in South Africa. These are some of the family stories he heard.

One summer evening, Gandhi's ashram in Ahmedabad, western India, had many visitors who wanted to talk to him about important issues that faced the country. That night in 1919, Mohandas was exhausted from his well-known fast. But the visitors could not be turned away. Kastur, his wife, compromised. She spread out a straw mat under a shady tree on the banks of the River Sabarmati and asked Gandhi to lie down while he talked with his guests. She spread a light sheet over him.

Soon it became dark. The evening was still pleasant and cool so the discussions continued out in the open. Gandhi had turned on his side. A while later he felt something crawling along his back. Instinctively he knew what it was. Panic would create chaos. In a calm voice he told two of his guests to slowly pick up the four ends of his shawl and carry the creeping intruder across the fence. It was only when they saw the snake slither away that they realized it was an eight-foot cobra. Mohandas continued talking to his guests, dismissing the interloper as though it were just a pesky fly.

This story surely indicates Gandhi's fearlessness and his nonviolence toward all living things. Yet Gandhi was not always so fearless or so nonviolent. How did he come to be the person that we hear about in this story? Who were the people who influenced Mohandas Karamchand Gandhi to achieve the greatness he eventually did?

It is an interesting question, but we need to be careful: often we place more emphasis than necessary on the *influence*, and not enough on the *commitment* needed to make that influence meaningful. Scholars and followers often asked Mohandas about who influenced him in his life. He himself, however, always discounted the importance of "influence," believing as he did that good influence, like good education at an Ivy League university for example, is meaningful only if one has the commitment to make good use of it.

Not all graduates of Ivy League universities are successful in life. Those who are morally successful must attribute their accomplishments as much or more to their desire and commitment as to their good education. Gandhi believed it was the same with influence.

Historically, there are several instances of people with profound influences having utterly failed in life. Harilal, Gandhi's eldest son, might be considered a case in point. Harilal was raised by the same extended family that raised Mohandas, with one exception: Mohandas's father was no longer alive, and Mohandas was away studying law in England.

Harilal received the same love and influences that Mohandas himself received while growing up in the midst of the whole family in Porbandar, India. In addition Mohandas and his wife, Kastur, gave him all the parental love and understanding that one could hope for. Yet, unlike Gandhi's other sons, Harilal drowned his life in alcohol and all the evils attached to intoxication, presumably because he did not have the commitment and/or the desire to use these influences to make something out of his own life. We surely sympathize with people who suffer from the disease of alcoholism. We must also admit, however, that each active alcoholic began by making choices to drink. Further, we are impressed with the number of recovered alcoholics among us who have made the commitment, with the help of a Higher Power, to stop drinking after they became addicted. Harilal's unfortunate life suggests that love and influence, while important in helping shape the life of an individual, do not add up to greatness without desire or commitment of the individual himself

For his part, Mohandas Gandhi had several bad influences that could have led him to grief. He had the innate wisdom, however, to understand that any action that made him feel guilty and uncomfortable was an influence he did not need. For example, fellow Indians studying with Gandhi in England convinced him that the eating of meat was necessary in the struggle for liberation from British colonialism. They were convinced that the British were stronger than the Indians because the British ate much more meat than the Indians. Gandhi was at first swayed by this argument. For almost a year he deceived his parents in order to eat meat, grow tall and strong and help overthrow the British imperialist administration. Showing his all-too-human weakness, the young Mohandas rationalized his immoral act by assuming lofty objectives. But let the reader note the true nature of the conflict within Gandhi about the eating of meat.

Those who eat meat would see nothing immoral about it and they may find it difficult to understand why one would make so much fuss over a person's choice of diet. It is not as though eating meat is prohibited by Hindu religion. There are many devout Hindus who do eat meat. However, the Gandhis belonged to a sect that abhorred killing animals for any reason, most of all for human consumption.

In ancient Indian civilization, social, cultural, and moral laws were rooted in religion to imbue them with more power. Such laws also become family tradition and each succeeding generation is expected to uphold these traditions. Thus the law prohibiting this sect of Hindus from consuming animals was, for the Gandhi family who chose to obey it strictly, a highly sacred tradition. Viewed in this context, when Mohandas consumed meat he transgressed a moral law which, in addition to breaking a long-standing family tradition, incurred religious opprobrium as well.

The choice before Mohandas was either to lead a deceitful life and continue eating meat, or to come out in the open, break family tradition, and leave the family home to live alone.

What troubled Mohandas was not so much the act of eating meat, but that he had to lie endlessly to his parents in order to do so. He realized it was not good to take liberties with moral and ethical values that have come down through the ages. Lying for little things today would lead to bigger things tomorrow. Then gradually, almost imperceptibly, that will lead to moral degeneration ultimately destroying the individual.

Another reason why Gandhi discounted the importance of influences was because he did not want people to think they cannot aspire to greater moral heights because they do not have the necessary influences. He believed that such a perceived lack becomes a convenient excuse for inaction. One of the problems of elevating people like Gandhi to sainthood is that we then excuse ourselves from imitating them in our own lives. We take comfort in the unfounded belief that it was because the saints were exceptionally endowed that they were capable of achieving moral and ethical heights. We create for ourselves a myth that saints are somehow born great.

Ever since Mohandas was given the title of "Mahatma," a "saint" or "Great Soul"—a title he detested but could do nothing about—he was certain the people were going to use this as an excuse for not accepting or practicing nonviolence. "They will follow me in life, worship me in death, but not make my cause their cause," he said during his prayer discourse in 1948, days before his assassination. He used every opportunity to impress on his audience that he was just an ordinary person with unflagging commitment to rise above the ordinary and a determination to achieve his goal. "If I can achieve it, anyone can achieve it," he would say.

One reason that Gandhi could espouse this philosophy was because of the Eastern view of death—so different from most Western philosophies of death. In the ancient Eastern cultures, life is a continuous, never-ending process. The cycle of birth and death is quite simply equivalent to the daily routine of changing clothes. In the long journey of life, death occurs when one body needs to be discarded to enter into a new one, just as in our daily routine we change one set of clothes for another, fresher set of clothes.

When one understands and accepts this theology, then the pursuit of excellence becomes a process that may not be attained in one lifetime but must, nevertheless, be undertaken. If nirvana or salvation is at the top of the ladder, it is difficult to climb it all at once. The eastern culture recognizes the weaknesses of human beings and believes that each of us must pass through various stages and learn to overcome those weaknesses. Often we don't. People become mired in all kinds of problems. Some spend their whole life in pursuit of sex, others in pursuit of material wealth; still others in acquiring power and distinction and so on. All of these, according to eastern culture, are essential stages of life and each of us must pass through and rise above.

In western popular culture the perceptions are oftentimes different from those I have just outlined. We are encouraged to view the world as a constant war between good and evil with good and evil seemingly as clearly defined as black and white. Such attitudes lead to sad but predictable results. Many people in the United States believe that if a person is a murderer we can destroy the evil by destroying him or her. Or take, for example, American attitudes toward Iraqi leader Saddam Hussein. We think that by removing Saddam Hussein, we will resolve—or to a significant degree remove—the problem of evil in the region. As a result, the United States maintain sanctions on Iraq that, according to the UN's own reports, have directly caused the death of over one million Iraqis, the majority of them children under the age of five. Thus, in our ignorant seeking to prevent evil, we perpetrate unimaginable violence and evil ourselves.[1]

From an Eastern perspective, we would say that such reasoning and action ignores the fact that good and evil are generated by the senses much in the same way as one becomes hungry. When we feel hungry some of us will go and eat junk food while others may seek healthy foods to eat, while still others may ignore the hunger until a little later. Whatever our reaction to hunger, it is dictated by the way we are taught to approach it. We would go for junk food because our parents have encouraged us or because they have denied us junk food without explaining why. There are many reasons for our choices and most, unless we are enlightened, result from our own ignorance.

This Eastern philosophy holds true for our sexual passions, greed, desires for power and fame, as it does for our hunger. It even applies to our pursuit of "justice" in Iraq. So the saying is true: We do not see things as they are; we see things as we are. The Eastern concept is that evil is there, but we cannot fight directly against it; we have to grow out of it, much like the lotus flower that grows out of murky waters.

When we come to the enlightened realization that there is more to life than pleasure, power, and material wealth, that life will become more understandable and meaningful. In this sense Gandhi believed that we must constantly strive to reach greater moral heights. It means we must develop the wisdom to recognize good influences and the ability and desire to absorb them in our lives to facilitate our eternal quest for eternal Truth.

Having acknowledged what Gandhi himself said about "influences," why then should I write about people who influenced Gandhi?

---

[1]For a fuller discussion of nonviolent responses to Iraq and the sanctions, see Kathy Kelly, "Voices in the Wilderness: Nonviolence and the Ongoing War against Iraq" in this volume.

Because these stories will satisfy my grandfather's reservations about naming influences. First, it was not just the love of those persons, but Gandhi's appropriation of that love, that led him to greatness. Further, these special persons who influenced Gandhi would have no exceptional standing in the eyes of the world. The lives they led, the values they held—and so the values he appropriated—were simple, we might even say, homespun. Perhaps for the more educated they might even seem painfully naïve. All the better for our purposes. For then Gandhi will not accuse of us citing his lofty influences so as to excuse our "ordinary selves" from "taking up his cause." Finally, a focus on these influential persons will remedy a noticeable lack in our understanding of Gandhi's adoption of nonviolence: the influence of women in Gandhi's life and in the development of his philosophy. The remainder of this chapter, thus presents a brief overview of three persons who influenced Gandhi—three different women who, by all academic standards, would be considered illiterate and uneducated: His mother, his nanny, and his wife.

Gandhi's mother, Putliba [*poo-thili-bah*], laid a foundation of nonviolence for her children with her love, understanding, fearlessness, and spirituality. Putliba Gandhi was gentle, intensely spiritual, and so all embracing in her love that she was incapable of harming anyone. It is said about her love for life and nature that one day in Porbandar while she was entertaining some guests at home that someone noticed a deadly scorpion crawl over her bare feet. She simply scooped up the scorpion with her bare hand and dropped it out the window.

Although Mohandas had seen and experienced his mother's fearlessness, it was a long time before he came to the point of loving all living things. Not until he was an adult was he able to conquer his own fears of insects, reptiles, and the dark. That is the point of this chapter. The influence was there, in the person of Putliba, but Gandhi was still afraid. As a child when Mohandas recoiled in fear of imaginary (or real) insects and animals, his mother would say, "If we don't harm them, they won't harm us. There is nothing to fear." Nevertheless, Gandhi had to make a life-long commitment to make those words his own. His parents had by that time moved to a city, and the young Gandhi was thus never exposed to real-life snakes. His childhood fears came from within—from his own imagination.

While Gandhi was still in South Africa, he exchanged lengthy correspondence with the Jain philosopher, Rajchandra, on the question of nonviolence. Rajchandra claimed true nonviolence, according to the Jain philosophy, is when one is prepared to die rather than to kill a snake. Gandhi wrote that this was difficult to accept. To most people, such would not be an appealing point of view. Beginning in South Africa, however, Gandhi said that he would try to attain that goal in his life. He also said, however, that he would not recommend it to others, but would leave it to their own commitment.

Mohandas Gandhi's mother was a pious woman, very open and very inclusive. Her understanding of religion came through her willingness to listen, to understand, to evaluate, and to absorb. She was not educated. She could neither read nor write. Her curiosity and thirst for greater understanding of spiritual matters was genuine. She attended discourses in her own temple and heard discussions at home when scholars from different religions visited. Her mind was like cotton wool that absorbed everything. That genuine sense of respect and understanding for other religions is rare even among the most educated.

Gandhi wrote about how impressed he was with his mother's sense of spirituality and amazed at her capacity to fast and lead a very disciplined life. Like most Indian women, she fasted on several days of the week. In the Indian context a fast assumes many different forms. There are those who fast the whole day without eating or drinking anything; or those who eat just one meal in twenty four hours; those who fast by reducing the quantity of their food and those who consume only liquids.

The fast that Mohandas's mother had undertaken was yet another variation in the concept of fasting. Like the Muslims during Ramadan, she ate only when she was able to see the moon. There are a large variety of other fasts, each according to his or her own desires, undertaken as a matter of self-discipline. The concept of fasting emerges from the eastern concept of reaching "upwards" by being completely in control of one's senses and desires. By regular fasting one is able to control one's desire for food and learn to live with as little as possible. It requires mental discipline to be able to perform one's daily duties as always while fasting.

While fasting Putliba cheerfully cooked and fed the family, cleaned up, entertained visitors, and did many other household chores. She fasted almost continuously for one reason or another. On one occasion, Mohandas writes, he was anxious for his mother to see the moon so she could break her fast. These were the monsoon months when the skies were overcast. His mother went on doing her chores unconcerned about the moon. The young Mohandas would stand near the window and peer into the gray and gloomy skies praying for the moon to come out so that his dear mother could eat.

When Mohandas caught a glimpse of the moon he frantically called out to his mother to come and see it. But on this night, the moon disappeared before Putliba could get to the window. She simply shrugged her shoulders and said, "It looks like God does not want me to eat today."

What mattered to Putliba was discipline and her faith in God. She was more concerned about her spiritual nourishment than her physical nourishment. She would not seek excuses to break her fast. She said, and later Mohandas made this a part of his philosophy of nonviolence, that one must never become a slave of one's senses. Cravings are parts of every human being and if one submits to everything one craves for, then one goes down the ladder of spiritual growth. By constant awareness and discipline one rises above.

All the other Gandhi siblings experienced the same influences and saw their mother fasting and praying, but none was as moved as Mohandas. This again supports the contention that influences alone do not make a great person.

Mohandas and his siblings were never subjected to any kind of physical or psychological violence at home. When discipline was necessary it was achieved through penance together, usually fasting. That is, parents took equal responsibility for any wrong that the child may have committed. So if a child did some wrong, parents took the punishment themselves, undertaking some fast or other spiritual discipline. This was another family practice that Mohandas incorporated into his own life, but the other siblings did not.

There is the famous episode when Mohandas confessed in writing to his parents about stealing money from home to eat meat. His father, terminally ill, lay in bed alone when Mohandas worked up enough courage to hand over his confession. Tears streamed down his father's face as he read it. Mohan was moved to tears, too. Both of them embraced each other and allowed the tears to wash away the indiscretions.

When Mohandas was a rambunctious little boy always running after birds and butterflies, people or processions, his mother could cope with him no longer. Rumbha, possibly as old as Putliba, was retained to take care of the child. She became the second unlettered woman in Mohandas's life who had a profound influence on him. She told him stories from the scriptures and from Indian history. Since she too could not read, the stories were orally transmitted.

Mohandas records two of Rumbha's stories that made a great impression on him. The first was that of Shravan, the only child of poor peasants who, in their old age, had become blind. One day Shravan's mother said, "How I wish we could go on a pilgrimage of all the shrines before we die." Shravan heard his mother's lament and said, "I will take both of you, to fulfill your wish." "How can we do this," she asked incredulously, "The shrines are in four different directions and so far from each other."

Shravan made two large open baskets, tied them to two ends of a strong bamboo pole and one morning set off on foot carrying his parents on the long pilgrimage. Months went by before they were on the last leg of the pilgrimage. They had visited the shrines in the west, the south and the east, and were crossing a forest to go to the last shrine in the north. One day Shravan stopped near a brook to eat and rest. After the meal, while his parents took a nap, he went down to the river to wash and fill a pitcher of drinking water.

King Dasrath, an avid hunter renowned for his ability to shoot an arrow and hit the target by following the sound, was out hunting deer in the same neighborhood. On this day he was boasting about his prowess and his hunting companions challenged him to prove his claim.

While they were talking, King Dasrath heard a gurgling sound coming from the direction of the river. "There I can hear a deer," he whispered to his friends and promptly shot an arrow in the direction of the sound. Then they all stood stunned by a human cry of anguish. He had struck Shravan.

King Dasrath and his companion ran down to the river to see what had happened. They found Shravan face down in the water with the arrow through his back. He was pulled and revived for a moment, but the wound was fatal; Shravan was dying.

"Forgive me," King Dasrath said. "I did not expect a human to be here."

"I am dying," Shravan said, "But I am concerned about my parents. What will happen to them? They are blind, old and waiting for me under the tree yonder."

"I will take care of them," the King promised. "It won't be easy," Shravan warned. "They love me so much that if they know I am dead they too will die." The King promised, "I will do my best." Then Shravan breathed a deep sigh and died.

The King requested his companion to arrange for Shravan to be cremated according to Hindu rites while he took the pitcher of water and went in search of Shravan's parents. When he found them, he dared not utter a word to them, lest they recognize that he was not their son Shravan. For a few days he carried them along in silence. However, the parents became apprehensive and the mother asked in anguish, "Son," she said, "Are you tired of us? Why are you silent? Do you want to give up the pilgrimage and go home? Please say something," she pleaded.

Tears streamed down the King's face but he still could not utter a word. When they stopped for lunch Shravan's mother, out of sheer desperation, grabbed the King's arm. She knew then that this was not her son.

"You are not my son," she cried. "Where is my son? What have you done to him?"

The King now had no recourse but to tell them the truth. Both were so grief-stricken, that they refused to eat and died.

This story had a profound impact on Mohandas. The love and respect for parents; the desire to do everything for them, even to the extent of submerging one's own desires to fulfill the wishes of parents; the selflessness, the love, the tender bond between parents and children even in poverty—all this touched Mohandas at his core. That story from Rumbha his nanny stayed with him all his life. Mohandas never lost an opportunity to use Rumbha's stories as a basis for a sermon.

Her next story was the story of King Harishchandra. It is familiar because of its similarities with the Hebrew story of Job. Harishchandra was a God-fearing, upright King who never did anything wrong in his life. All his subjects loved him because of his faith in God. One day there was a discussion between God and anti-God. Harishchandra cannot stand up to adversity, said anti-God. He will remain faithful to you only as long as everything is provided. A wager was made and Harishchandra became the victim of mind-shattering hardships and adversity.

There was dissension in his courts and he was deposed. He was turned out of his palace with only the clothes on his back. When he and his wife and son walked through the streets of what was once his kingdom, the people stoned and tormented them. They could find no shelter, food or understanding although Harishchandra was until the day before the most loved and respected King. No one seemed to care for him and his faith in God was tested to the utmost.

The family was forced to break up. Harishchandra could find employment only in the crematorium to help dispose of dead bodies, while his wife and son were taken as slaves. Finally, one day his son was ordered to be killed in the most gruesome manner: he was to be cooked in a vat of boiling oil.

Through all these tribulations Harishchandra remained firm in his commitment to God, and his wife and son supported him. Finally, as in the case of Job, anti-God conceded defeat, Harishchandra was reinstated as the King and all was well in the Kingdom of God.

These stories have been told to generations of growing children by numerous baby-sitters, but how many are affected as Mohandas was? Mohandas pondered over the subliminal message and concluded that faith was more important than the concept of God. Everyone has a different vision or perspective of God. No one can truly establish the who, what, where and why about God. Mohandas felt that instead of trying to answer such questions, which no one really can, the best thing is to have faith in and an abiding respect for the eternal search for Truth. Mohandas was convinced no one possesses the Truth; we can only pursue it. Our success in ultimately finding the Truth would depend upon our honesty, humility, and commitment.

Rumbha gave the young Mohandas another talisman—one more reason to have faith in God or the power within. When she realized Mohandas was afraid of imagined or real dangers, she advised him that when afraid he should chant the name of the Lord Rama, the most popular deity in the Hindu world. This, she promised, would bring him the deity's comforting presence.

She told Mohandas to use the name of Rama as a mantra, to repeat it every time he was overwhelmed with fear. He found this extremely comforting and peaceful not because it was the name of Rama that he was repeating but because of ~~but because~~ the exercise of repeating the name of someone you have faith in distracts one's mind from the object of fear. As he grew and enlarged the scope of his faith he believed a mantra could be the name of anyone or anything in which a person had faith.

The third unlettered, uneducated woman to have influenced Mohandas K. Gandhi was his wife, Kastur. A soft-spoken but very determined young woman, Kastur was a member of the Makanji family that lived a block away from the Gandhis. Since both fathers were public figures—Mohandas's father was the Prime Minister of the State of Porbandar, and Kastur's father was the Mayor of the City of

Porbandar—the families knew each other well. While the adults socialized the children played together. There is, therefore, reason to believe that Kastur and Mohandas were childhood friends who grew up together. In fact it is believed that Kastur was a few months older than Mohandas. However, since no official records are available of her exact birthdate, one must depend upon the memory of those who knew that Kastur was born in April, 1869, while Mohandas was born on October 2, 1869.

Kastur and Mohandas were married when they both were thirteen years old. In keeping with the culture and tradition of the time, Kastur learned to play a secondary and supportive role in her married life. Although some say she sometimes teased Mohandas about being older and wiser than he was, she never mentioned it in public.

The eastern tradition encourages the "tilt relationship." That is, a relationship where one looks up to someone because of their wisdom, education, age, rank, social standing, or whatever other yardstick one chooses to use. The tilt relationship encourages humility and respect. Unless one has humility one will not recognize that someone can be wiser than we are and therefore command our respect. Without respect there can be no relationship worth the name.

When trying to understand relationships based in the eastern culture, it is essential to keep the "tilt relationship" in mind. Kastur looked up to Mohandas for direction not because she was submissive or enslaved. She did stand up for her rights when necessary. It was through her loving, active resistance to injustice that she taught Mohandas lessons in nonviolence.

A teenage Mohandas, who bought pamphlets on the role of husbands in Indian society, molded himself into a domineering husband who kept his wife in check. Consequently, he ordered her to do nothing without first consulting him. Kastur listened to him quietly, avoiding argument, but continuing her normal activities without defiance.

The Gandhi's lived in the eastern Joint Family System, which brought together several generations to live under one roof. The oldest member of the household was the doyen and everyone looked upon him or her for guidance. During the day the men and women kept away from each other. The women were mainly in the inner sanctums of the house busy with household chores while the men, when home, remained mostly in the outer section where they entertained visitors and guests. It was not right for the women of the house to face strangers.

Meetings between men and women during the day were not considered appropriate because in the hierarchy of an Indian household, based on age and status, young couples should not talk in the presence of elders. It was also considered inappropriate for a younger person to countermand the authority of an elder.

During the day, therefore, Kastur remained in the inner sanctum of the house with the other women. In the Gandhi household all the women were her seniors either by age or by status. The women often went out to the temple or to the market or to visit friends or relatives. Inasmuch as these elder women never asked their husbands for permission to leave the home, Kastur followed suit. Moreover, she accompanied them whenever asked to join them on such visits. When Gandhi learned about these visits he could not contain his anger, considering this an erosion of his authority as a husband.

That night he waited in the room for his wife. When she arrived, he lashed out at her brazen disregard of his injunction:

"Have I not told you that you are not to leave the house without my permission?" he stormed.

"Yes, you have," Kastur replied calmly.

"Then how do you explain going out this afternoon?"

"I was always told that I must obey the authority of my elders. Should I assume that you supersede the authority of your mother? Do you wish that I should tell her I cannot obey her until I have your permission?"

The young Mohandas was struck dumb. He could not tell his wife to disobey his mother. He realized the absurdity of his demands and pursued them no longer. Imagine what could have happened if Kastur had lost her patience and retorted in anger. It could have escalated into a major conflict. This happens every day in households around the world. Instead of anger, Kastur used tradition and wisdom to respond in a calm and collected manner so that Mohandas was able to see for himself the absurdity of the situation.

Gandhi was also frustrated by his wife's fearlessness, which showed up his own fearfulness. Not only was she not afraid of him, but she was not afraid of any of the things he feared—like darkness (He could not sleep without a night light.) and snakes. (Nightmares about them often kept him awake at night.)

It hurt Gandhi's ego to think that a woman exhibit more courage than he. As he often did, Mohandas sought advise from his Muslim friend, Sheikh Mehtab, who claimed to be absolutely fearless and adept in the art of controlling women. Mehtab attributed Mohandas's fears to his vegetarianism. Tellingly, he could not explain why Kastur, also a staunch vegetarian, could be possessed of a courage foreign to himself. Mehtab would flippantly dismiss it as a woman thing. Mehtab succeeded in making Mohandas eat meat, but not in making him visit prostitutes.

Mehtab was apparently determined to corrupt the morals of his Hindu friend. He had succeeded in influencing Mohandas's elder brother, now he wanted to do the same with Mohan. Mehtab once paid a prostitute and sent Mohandas into her boudoir, but Mohandas was so ashamed that he sat on the bed until out of sheer disgust the prostitute ranted and raved and threw him out, cursing his impotency.

Kastur had sensed that Mehtab's intentions were not good. She had never met him nor talked to him but she had a woman's intuition, which told her that he was up to no good. She suspected that Mohandas had started eating meat. There was no other explanation for Mohandas's periodic "upset stomach" and "loss of appetite" that prohibited him from eating at home.

However, Kastur also knew that confronting Mohandas would be counterproductive for what she wanted to achieve. Mohandas had to discover the truth for himself. She prayed for wisdom to dawn on him and when it eventually did, she told him she was glad that he got out of the friendship before he went deeper into a moral abyss. She did not adopt a "I-told-you-so" attitude. Nor did she give the impression that she was more worldly-wise than he was. There is a lesson in this for us, as there was for Mohandas himself. In similar circumstances, we would lose our temper, lash out, use "I-told-you-so" language, and exacerbate the problem rather than help the person overcome it. Kastur was no psychologist; she had never seen the inside of a school building. Yet she displayed greater wisdom than many of us would have in similar circumstances.

Knowingly or otherwise, Gandhi often put his wife through difficult times. He went alone to England for three years, leaving Kastur with a little child. Shortly after his return from England, he began a legal practice in far off Bombay. His practice eventually failed and he returned home for a few months. Soon he decided to leave his wife and now two children with family while he pursued his legal career in South Africa.

He did not live up to the expectations of the family who spent enormous amounts of money to educate him in England so that he would come back, find a lucrative job, and support them all. In England, Gandhi spent more money than he was expected to, so that his brother, already strained to the limit trying to run the household, was obliged to send him more money. Kastur must surely have suffered the barbs of her sisters-in-law and other family members who had to suffer financial constraints because her husband was living so lavishly in England. She suffered quietly, never bringing the matter up with her husband, except on occasion politely to remind him of his financial obligations to his family.

When Mohandas did finally reunite with his family, taking them with him to South Africa, he subjected Kastur to more pressures. Her modest, Eastern life-style was turned upside-down. She had to adopt western ways. Her simple eastern habits and all that she had learned since childhood had to be left behind in India, along with her friends and relatives. She was accustomed to a very informal life-style in a large home with shared responsibilities, where members of the extended family supported each other. Now life was going to be much more formal.

She was accustomed to squatting on the floor to cook hot meals off tiny coal stoves, while the family squatted around her. Now she was forced to cook on a strange stove that was as large as a furnace, sit at a table, and, most galling of all, learn to eat with eating utensils rather than with her fingers. She had to dress differently, wear constricting shoes even at home. In India she could walk around the house barefoot. She now had to live with strangers in her own home, while in India the women were insulated from strangers. Worst of all, she had to change homes almost every year. Every transformation in her husband's life created a change in her lifestyle as well. Yet she never complained.

What Kastur went through in her life was ground enough for any modern couple to declare incompatibility and even seek a divorce. It was largely due to Kastur's quiet patience and resilience that their bonds were strengthened.

She was able to reason with Mohandas, make him see the Truth from a different perspective, and bring about a change in his attitude and thinking. She achieved all of this through love rather than confrontation.

That is what impressed Mohandas most. He learned from Kastur that one can change even the most rabidly prejudiced person through love, never through conflict or confrontation. This, he concluded, had to be the basis of the philosophy of nonviolent action. If it could work so effectively between two people, why should it not work on a larger scale?

He began his experiments with Truth and the philosophy of nonviolence not only to use it as a strategy for resolving conflicts, but mainly as a strategy for building strong and sound relationships between people. His experiences under his wife's influence taught him that the stronger the relationship, the fewer the conflicts.

He acquired the humility to realize that even his unlettered wife had something to teach him. Once he was humble enough to accept this, he went through the logical steps of respecting her and strengthening their bonds. This in turn led him to appreciate that all the common people in India were more than capable of the practices of *ahimsa* (noninjury).

In the process of helping to build relationships between different people he always emphasized the need for humility, respect, understanding, acceptance and appreciation. We must have the humility to accept that there are others who are wiser that we, respect people for their innate wisdom, age and standing in life, understand each other through learning and inquiring, accept the differences that exist between us, and finally appreciate those differences.

It is as significant as it is unusual that the three persons who made an impact on the life of Mohandas K. Gandhi were all women who according to modern academic yardsticks were completely illiterate and uneducated. In many ways, Gandhi found that to adopt nonviolence meant to adopt the dispositions and practices of women. None of these three women could read or write, yet all had wisdom and the power to love—the *satyagraha* ("soul force") to influence the life of a man who may yet be considered the "Man of the Century."

2

GANDHI AND THE ORIGINS OF NONVIOLENCE: EDWIN ARNOLD'S *THE LIGHT OF ASIA*

Graeme MacQueen

Gandhi heard many stories of his Indian background. But he had to wait until his law studies in England to read the story of the Buddha. His friends had encouraged him to read Edwin Arnold's The Light of Asia, *and Gandhi was profoundly moved by it. Later, he was to write in his Autobiography that his "young mind tried to unify the teaching of the Gita,* The Light of Asia *and the Sermon on the Mount." Graeme MacQueen tells of the young Gandhi's engagement with this story of the Buddha, a man who "rejects the use of force . . . but does not grow weaker with this rejection."*

A young man is moving about a small, sparsely furnished room in London. He is twenty years old and the year is 1889. He has a little stove on which he has made himself a cup of cocoa and now he sits down, places the cup beside him and takes up a book. The book has been recommended by some English friends. It deals, say the friends, with spiritual matters—Indian spiritual matters. The young man is both interested in the book and somewhat embarrassed, for although he is from India he has read little about Indian religion.

He begins to read. The book is in verse. It tells the story of a prince filled with unsatisfied religious yearnings. Driven by his desire for knowledge and enlightenment, the prince leaves his home to go on a quest. The young man in the London apartment is drawn into the story. He too is filled with religious longings; he too is on a journey with an uncertain outcome. As the young man follows the story—the story of the Buddha, the founder of Buddhism—he feels a gradual shift in perception. Changes he has been going through since he arrived in England two years previously gather momentum. He becomes more confident of his direction.

Although we must respect our heritage, says the story of the prince, we cannot be content with it. We must make up our own minds about the great matters of life and death. What parents think, what the country thinks—none of this is good enough. We have to discover what *we* think. The Truth is the highest good, and a person must be willing to take great risks to discover and live in accordance with the Truth. The young man nods slowly. He has always valued Truth.

But the story has more to tell him. It addresses the issue of identity. Since his early adolescence the young man has been wrestling with the question of who he is. He is Indian, yes, and Hindu. He is definitely not English. The English are unjustly holding his country in bondage and they must go. This much is clear. But what sort of Indian is he, and what sort of Indian can make the English go? The English rule India with such a small number of soldiers and administrators. They seem so big and strong, so expert in all matters, so confident. How puny, demoralized, and weak the Indians seem in comparison. How can the Indians become stronger? When he was in high school the young man was persuaded that the way to become stronger was to become more like the English. The theory in the schools was that modern Western ways of behaving—wearing ties, drinking alcohol, and above all, eating meat—were routes to power. How could a nation of sheep-like, passive vegetarians, rooted in superstitions and taboos of the past, ever get rid of the English? But now, at this moment in his room in London, the story of the Buddha is suggesting something different. This hero, this prince who renounces wealth and royal power to become a religious leader, is not weak at all. He challenges his father the king; he challenges the intellectual leaders of his day; he challenges everyone who cannot come up with evidence and reason to support their position. He rejects the use of force ("My chariot shall not roll with bloody wheels/From victory to victory"[1]), but does not grow weaker with this rejection. As he gives things up he seems to grow more powerful. It is not necessary for the young man in the London apartment to be told of this power: he feels it. The story itself transmits it, fills him with it. Even the renunciation of meat-eating seems a movement from power, not weakness:

> There hath been slaughter for the sacrifice
> And slaying for the meat, but henceforth none
> Shall spill the blood of life nor taste of flesh,
> Seeing that knowledge grows, and life is one,
> And mercy cometh to the merciful.[2]

The young man puts down his book and begins to reflect. If the ancient traditions of India—vegetarianism and renunciation (giving up domination and possessions)—originated in acts of such conviction and clarity as this, he will need to rethink the high school theories completely. Maybe Indian traditions are not traditions of weakness and superstition. Maybe, if they can be grasped properly, they are close to Truth, close to strength as well. Maybe this is a clue to what sort of Indian can push the English out, and what sort of Indian can address the sufferings of the world. Maybe it is the sort of Indian he can become.

Sitting in his London apartment, the cup of cocoa now cold and forgotten, the young man is quiet. The story has taken him beyond

---

[1] Edwin Arnold, *The Light of Asia: Being the Life and Teaching of Gotama, Prince of India and Founder of Buddhism* (Chicago: Rand, McNally, 1890; originally published 1879), 150.
[2] Ibid., 194.

ideas and into experience. "I see, I feel/ the vastness of the agony of earth"[3] says the prince in the story, and the young man sees and feels it too.[4]

II

During his stay in London, Gandhi was greatly impressed with the legend of the Buddha. My account of his first reading of the story, although speculative in its details, is grounded in Gandhi's own testimony. The remainder of this chapter argues that from the story of the Buddha, Gandhi received a threefold model of spirituality that derived from the earliest period in the history of nonviolence and that he later carried forward in his own work. The story is thus a link between the origins of nonviolence and its manifestation, through Gandhi, in the twentieth century. Of course, this story was not Gandhi's *only* source of the threefold model; there were other texts and persons who presented it to him. Nor did the story provided him with the strategies and tactics of nonviolent struggle; these he got elsewhere. This essay, however, underscores the importance of the way this model was presented to Gandhi at this decisive moment in his life. It begins by noting some of the difficulties Gandhi was negotiating when he was in London and how the story addressed those difficulties.

Gandhi arrived in England just before his nineteenth birthday. He was to spend the next three years in London training to be a lawyer. He regarded England as "the land of philosophers and poets, the very centre of civilization,"[5] yet he had already decided while still a

---

[3]Ibid, 132-133.

[4]This fictional account has been put together on the basis of Gandhi's own words as recorded in his autobiography. See Mohandas Gandhi, *An Autobiography: The Story of My Experiments With Truth*, trans. Mahadev Desai (Boston: Beacon, 1957) Part I. I assume from his account that he read the *Gita* and *The Light of Asia* at around the same time (it is not clear which he read first). For help in dating his reading of these texts see also Raghavan Iyer, ed., *The Moral and Political Writings of Mahatma Gandhi*, vol. I (Oxford: Clarendon, 1986), 77-80, 480.

[5]B. R. Nanda, *Mahatma Gandhi: A Biography* (London: George Allen & Unwin, 1958), 24.

schoolboy that "I wished to be strong and daring and wanted my countrymen also to be such, so that we might defeat the English and make India free."[6] It is not surprising, in view of this complex relation to the English, that his three years in England included a good deal of self-searching, a grappling with the question of Indian and personal identity. Many of his reflections, recorded in his autobiography, mystify modern readers who are studying Gandhi to discover only his politics. Why all the talk about diet? Chastity? Why the concern about what he ought to wear and what his personal lifestyle ought to be? Such readers want to know his political analysis and his reading of history. Instead they find a discussion of his joy at discovering a good vegetarian restaurant! Rather than grow impatient with the young Gandhi, these readers should bear in mind four things.

First, it was a common perception on the part of many Indians that imitation of the English was a path that led both to power and to corruption. Gandhi's schoolmate had briefly converted him to meat-eating on the basis of the argument that to defeat the English one had to become like them: "We are a weak people because we do not eat meat. The English are able to rule over us, because they are meat-eaters."[7] Imitation, in other words, is the route to power. On the other hand, Gandhi's uncle had told him: "When I meet these big [Indian barristers who have trained in England], I see no difference between their life and that of Europeans. They know no scruples regarding food. Cigars are never out of their mouths. They dress as shamelessly as Englishmen."[8] The theme here is corruption through imitation, and the uncle means this as a warning to his nephew: Don't forget who you are and try to become English.

Second, these preoccupations with imitation of the English, which may seem odd to us, had a basis in English policy, and in European colonial policy generally. It was important for a country as small as England, if it wished to rule a country as vast as India, to create a

---

[6]*Autobiography*, 21.
[7]Ibid., 20.
[8]Ibid., 37.

body of Indians who would renounce their Indianness, identify with the English, and exert power on England's behalf. As Thomas Babington Macaulay had put it in 1835 in his famous *Minute on Indian Education to the Governor General of India*: "We must at present do our best to form a class who may be interpreters between us and the millions whom we govern; a class of persons, Indian in blood and colour, but English in taste, in opinions, in morals, and in intellect."[9]

So both the deep attraction felt by the schoolmate and the deep suspicions of the uncle had some justification in the English strategy for manipulating identity on behalf of Empire. Take, for example, the eating of meat. People whose religion prescribes vegetarianism violate a serious prohibition when they eat meat, and they become alienated from their own people. There is then no alternative for them but to go for solidarity and refuge to the group—the colonialists in this case—with which they now identify. As they are despised by their old compatriots they become increasingly loyal followers of their new friends. They become disgusted by, and openly mock, the superstition and backwardness of their old lifestyle and praise the realism, technological mastery and progressive spirit of the colonizer.

Third, the issue of diet had, well before Gandhi reached London, already proven its power to affect Indian history. The 1857-1858 uprisings in north India (called by the English the "Indian Mutiny" or the "Sepoy Mutiny"), which threatened British rule in the country, had been touched off by the East India Company's violation of Hindu and Muslim dietary regulations.[10] By Gandhi's time neither English nor Indians needed to be convinced of the importance of diet.

Finally, it was not merely Gandhi who was experimenting with lifestyle. The London to which he came was "the city of experiments in life-style, diet, creed, sex, clothes,"[11] a place where a great mingling

---

[9]Thomas Macaulay, *Macaulay: Prose and Poetry* (London: Rupert Hart-Davis, 1952), 729.

[10]The Company issued cartridges greased with pork and beef fat to the soldiers it employed, and these cartridges needed to be bitten off before insertion into the rifle.

[11]Martin Green, *The Origins of Nonviolence: Tolstoy and Gandhi in their Historical Settings* (University Park/London: 1986), 65.

of ideas was taking place, much of the stimulation coming from colonies and former colonies.

So in 1889 the young Gandhi was living in the belly of the imperial beast, trying to figure out his identity and his future. At this point he began to find books that helped him. Among the books he read were two traditional stories from India, both of which were new to him and had been cast in English by the poet Edwin Arnold. One of these books was Arnold's version of the *Bhagavad-Gita*, the Hindu scripture that would later become Gandhi's favorite text. In his autobiography he tells us that "the book struck me as one of priceless worth. The impression has ever since been growing on me with the result that I regard it today as the book *par excellence* for the knowledge of Truth."[12] The other book, whose influence on Gandhi has been less discussed by scholars, was *The Light of Asia*, Arnold's version of the legend of the Buddha. Of this book, Gandhi tells us that "I read it with even greater interest than I did the *Bhagavad-Gita*. Once I had begun it I could not leave off."[13] Gandhi does not tell us what his detailed thoughts were when he first read the book—I have let myself imagine these—but we have from him several testimonies to the deep impression the Buddha-legend made on him at this crucial time in his life.[14] The nature of the story and the precise sort of influence it may have exerted on him are crucial. It happens that another founder of twentieth century nonviolence, Leo Tolstoy, had reflected on the story of the Buddha during the great spiritual crisis he entered around 1879, shortly before Gandhi's arrival in England.[15] What is this story that seems to have carried such power for these modern prophets of engaged nonviolence?

---

[12] *Autobiography*, 67.

[13] Ibid., 68.

[14] Ibid., 68-69, 160-161; Iyer, *Moral and Political Writings*, 476-477; 479-483.

[15] Leo Tolstoy, *Confession*, trans. David Patterson (New York: W. W. Norton, 1983), 47-50. It is evident from his remarks on pp. 30-31 and 83 of this work that Tolstoy was also acquainted with the Buddha-legend in its Christian guise as *Barlaam and Josaphat*.

III

In a powerful kingdom a king and queen await the birth of a child. To their joy a son with all the signs of greatness is born. Shortly after his birth, sages predict that he will either become a powerful king or abandon his home and become a wandering religious teacher. If he chooses the second path he will open the way to liberation for living beings. The king is terrified that his son will become a reflective person, a person aware of the great problems of human existence. If his son develops this kind of critical consciousness, reasons the father, he might choose the second path predicted for him and, like religious and philosophical leaders before him, leave his home and family ("renounce the world") and go forth to search for the meaning of life. Then the king would lose both a son and a successor to the throne. So he keeps his son in the palace and gives him all sorts of material pleasures to keep him wrapped up in blind enjoyment. But one day the boy leaves the palace to visit the royal garden. Encountering an old man—he has never before been permitted to see anyone old—he says to his charioteer:[16] "Good charioteer, who is this man with white hair, supporting himself on the staff in his hand, with his eyes veiled by the brows, and limbs relaxed and bent? Is this some transformation in him, or his original state, or mere chance?"

The charioteer replies: "Old age it is called, that which has broken him down—the murderer of beauty, the ruin of vigour, the birth-place of sorrow, the grave of pleasure, the destroyer of memory, the enemy of the senses."

Shocked by the discovery of old age, and by the charioteer's explanation that everyone is subject to it, the young man says: "Thus old age strikes down indiscriminately memory and beauty and valour, and yet with such a sight before its eyes the world is not perturbed. This being so, turn back the horses, charioteer; go quickly home. For

---

[16]The quotations here are taken from Asvaghosa's poem, *Buddhacarita*, written in the first or second century CE. See E. H. Johnston, ed. and trans., *The Buddhacarita or, Acts of the Buddha* (Delhi: Motilal Banarsidass, 1972), Part 2, 37-38.

how can I take my pleasure in the garden, when the fear of old age rules in my mind?"

The prince goes home and broods on the fact of old age. In subsequent journeys from the palace he discovers the terrible facts of sickness and death. Unable now to take joy in the palace, he agonizes about the nature of existence. Finally, one day, having again left the palace, he encounters a religious ascetic who has left home to lead a life of integrity and spiritual searching. The prince knows at once that this is what he must do. He goes forth from home against his family's wishes, struggles for six years under a series of religious teachers, and finally wins a great spiritual awakening, becoming the Enlightened One or Buddha. He decides to spend the rest of his life passing on what he has learned to others.

Some of the more elaborate of the biographies then tell of key events in his four decades of teaching and to recount his final passing away in the village of Kusināra.

This story was retold, elaborated, refined, and changed over the centuries, but its inherent universality allowed it to travel widely and to be adopted in new regions as a key religious narrative, defining the problems of human existence and suggesting a way of dealing with them. From its original home, apparently in Northeast India, where it appeared sometime before the third century BCE, it spread gradually in all directions: one person told it to another; traders carried it by land and sea along the great trade routes; monks used it in their sermonizing as a way of communicating the essence of Buddhism. By 1,200 CE the basic story was known and revered in a huge portion of Eurasia, from Japan in the East to Portugal in the West, from Indonesia and Sri Lanka in the south to Scandinavia and the steppes of Central Asia in the north.

The story traveled to the West in two main waves. In the first case, it arrived greatly modified, with the Buddha transformed into a Christian saint who converts Indian pagans to Christianity. Called *Barlaam and Josaphat*, this retelling of the story enjoyed wide popularity in Europe from about 1000 to 1500 CE, arriving from the East in Arabic, being translated from Arabic into Georgian, from Georgian to Greek, from Greek to Latin, and from Latin to the various vernaculars of medieval Europe (Spanish, French, English, German, etc.).[17] In the second case, the story was encountered in Asia in the eighteenth and nineteenth centuries by Europeans busy with the work of colonialism. They translated and transported it to Europe. In this instance, although the story was certainly filtered, it reached Europe in a form much closer to that which it had had in Asia.

The Light of Asia belongs to this second wave. Missionaries, Orientalists, and colonial functionaries gathered together the elements of the Buddha-legend and published them, and by the time Edwin Arnold's work appeared, the story had already reached many of Europe's intellectuals and artists. (For example, composer Richard Wagner had decided some time earlier to create an opera based on an incident from the life of the Buddha.)[18] Arnold took the story out of the hands of this small group and gave it to a new and very large readership. The Light of Asia, was not a translation of an Asian version of the story of the Buddha but a verse retelling based on a handful of scholarly books that Arnold had read and on his three years' experience in India (1857-1860) as principal of the government college at Poona. When it appeared in 1879, about ten years before Gandhi arrived in London, it was an immediate success. Eventually, between half a million and a million copies would be sold in over eighty-three separate printings.[19] As Arnold's biographer has said, "it enjoyed a sale such as few poems have had since."[20] It was the most popular of Arnold's numerous works and was a main cause of his subsequent

---

[17]A good general account of the Barlaam and Josaphat transmission can be found in Philip Almond, "The Buddha of Christendom: A Review of The Legend o f Barlaam and Josaphat" Religious Studies 23:3 (September 1987), 391-406.

[18]The opera, which was to have been called Die Sieger ("The Victors"), was never completed, but ideas Wagner worked out for the Buddhist piece found their way into others of his works, especially Parsifal. See Robert Gutman, Richard Wagner: The Man, His Mind, and His Music (New York: Harcourt, Brace & World, 1968), 184-189, 452-455. See also Lucy Beckett, Richard Wagner: Parsifal (Cambridge/New York: Cambridge University, 1981), 11-13, 110-111.

[19]Brooks Wright, Interpreter of Buddhism to the West: Sir Edwin Arnold (New York: Bookman Associates, 1957), 74-75.

[20]Ibid., 75.

knighthood and of his nearly succeeding Tennyson as England's poet laureate in 1892.[21]

Nowadays it is customary to stress the "Orientalist" tilt of early Western presentations of Asian culture and religion—to show how Westerners created, in their writings, an Orient that reflected their own tastes and needs and that made it easier for them to justify their domination of peoples in the East.[22] To the extent that we take this approach we shall want to be aware of all that makes *The Light of Asia*, a product of English Orientalism of the Victorian period, and we shall be interested to see if and how it was used to justify English imperialism. We may, furthermore, wish to argue that when he read this work Gandhi was receiving not an authentic and ancient version of the Buddha-legend but a self-interested Western representation of the Buddha-legend, with the result that his mind became increasingly colonized and his relationship to his own tradition was weakened.

It is true that Arnold was in many ways, in thought and deed, a classic English imperialist.[23] It is true also that his success as a writer depended to a great extent on his evocation of an exotic Orient that appealed to the imaginations of his Western readers.[24] It is even true that he at times adopted the typical Orientalist view that, while the Orient offered "wisdom," the West was best suited for the practical realities of governing—and hence should be in a position of dominance. We can speculate that all of this may have confused Gandhi in two ways: first, it may have left him with the idea that India, however noble its traditions, was ill-prepared to govern itself and should rely indefinitely on the British; second, it may have lulled him

---

[21]Ibid., 129, 172-173. See also Philip Almond, *The British Discovery of Buddhism* (Cambridge/New York: Cambridge University, 1988), 1.

[22]Edward Said's *Orientalism* (New York: Vintage, 1979) has been the most important single work in this connection. Philip Almond's *British Discovery of Buddhism* carries the project further, into the reception of Buddhism by Victorian England.

[23]"Arnold was a frank imperialist, who believed that British rule was not only for the best interest of the Indians, but further justified on the principle that strong races ought to subdue the weak." Wright, *Interpreter of Buddhism*, 61. See also Wright's chapter 3.

[24]See Wright, *Interpreter of Buddhism*, chapter 6. Almond's *British Discovery of Buddhism* is also a crucial work on this issue.

into believing that the empire, peopled by generous souls like Arnold who were deeply interested in Indian culture and religion, was basically a good thing and was bound to become an even better thing as time went on. In other words, Gandhi's contact with Arnold, and with other members of the Orientalist and New Life tendencies in England, may have served to help keep him a loyal colonial.[25] It is certainly true that he did not fully turn against the British Empire until many years later.

There is more to the matter than this, however. Imperialism is a complex enterprise, and it frequently spreads ideas that ultimately subvert it. The French unwittingly spread Enlightenment ideas in French Indochina that helped destroy the French hold on that part of the world. *The Light of Asia* needs to be approached with a sense of this complexity, because here we have an English poet impressing an Indian colonial with the brilliance and power of the latter's own intellectual and religious traditions. The Buddha portrayed by Arnold is not, after all, a woolly-minded visionary but a first-rate thinker and a man of action. As Arnold wishes to portray it, Buddhism is a moral and religious system that deserves to take its place among the most dignified systems humanity has produced. This is not in any simple way the construction of an East that deserves to be dominated. Arnold is actually eroding claims of Western cultural and intellectual superiority, with serious long-term consequences for Western intentions to rule. This is why Arnold's work met with such strong opposition and even fury from some quarters in the West. Evangelical Christians such a William Wilkinson were convinced that Arnold was seriously hampering attempts to "christianize" the world by weakening Christianity's claim to unique truth and goodness,[26] while Monier Monier-Williams, one of the most eminent of English Oriental scholars, found it necessary to sneer at the idea that the Buddha could be thought of as "the light of Asia" and argued that the

---

[25]See Green, *Origins of Nonviolence*, 67-72.

[26]William Wilkinson, *Edwin Arnold as Poetizer and as Paganizer* (New York: Funk & Wagnalls, 1884), v-vi.

"extinct, the death-giving Buddha" ought to be abandoned for "the living, the eternal, the life-giving Christ."[27] Neither of these individuals thought Indians had the moral qualities necessary for governing themselves properly. Even those who claimed to sympathize with Arnold often distorted and domesticated his message. In an "explanatory" Preface to *The Light of Asia*, I. L. Hauser, commented that: "the East Indian, under an enervating climate . . . fixes his attention on the tip of his nose, and, in utter disregard of all claims, dreams his life away."[28] This is exactly the opposite of what the poem actually says.

Finally, in assessing the nature and impact of *The Light of Asia* we ought to bear in mind that the poem is merely one in a very long succession of attempts to tell the story of the Buddha. In many respects it is quite conservative and actually changes the received story less than some of the earlier Asian versions. Most importantly, whatever Arnold's personal character and views may have been, the poem preserves the ancient threefold model of spirituality and transmits it, through Gandhi, to the modern age.

The first of the three elements in this model of spirituality is *the religious goal is perception of the truth*. According to the old Buddhist texts, those who have reached the religious goal know things "as they really are."[29] Words and metaphors for vision, insight, and enlightenment abound.[30] The religious path is a path not primarily of obedience or faith but of increasing understanding. I believe Arnold is justified, therefore, in using the terms "truth" and "Truth" in his poem to

---

[27]Monier Monier-Williams, *Buddhism in its Connexion with Brahmanism and Hinduism, and in its Contrast with Christianity* (Varanasi: Chowkhamba Sanskrit Series, 1964; reprint of the 2d edition), 563. The lectures on which this work was based were originally delivered in 1888.

[28]*The Light of Asia*, 24.

[29]The term for this in the Pali language is *yathābhūtam*, which occurs repeatedly in the early Buddhist scriptures. See, e.g., Bhikkhu Kashyap, ed., *Dīghanikāya* I (Bihar: Pali Publication Board, 1958), 73.

[30]See, e.g., the famous first sermon of the Buddha where he says, speaking of his realization of the four noble truths: "there arose in me vision, insight, understanding: there arose in me wisdom, there arose in me light." F. L. Woodward, trans. *The Book of the Kindred Sayings (Samyutta-Nikāya)*, Part V (London: Luzac & Co. for the Pali Text Society, 1965), 358.

express the religious goal of the Buddha's striving. According to *The Light of Asia*, the attainment of this truth is worth great personal sacrifice. The prince leaves behind his wealth, his worldly power, his friends and family. He studies; he meditates; he undertakes experiments in diet that almost kill him. Gandhi's circle in England included many such seekers after truth, and his "experiments with truth" (part of the title of his autobiography) can be seen as the fulfilment of this model. Gandhi would later say that "My uniform experience has convinced me that there is no other God than Truth."[31]

The second element of this spirituality is the notion that the path to truth is one of renunciation and self-purification. Although the founder of Buddhism rejected extreme asceticism, establishing instead the "Middle Path" between self-indulgence and self-deprivation, by modern Western standards the Buddhist monastic path looks very ascetical indeed. This renunciatory path was supposed to aid in bringing about certain changes in the individual. Giving up the quest for wealth, dominance, and status was supposed to strengthen the will, clarify the mind, and purify the heart, and in these ways allow entry into the truth. The truth, in turn, gave access to power—not power that depended on domination but power derived from the moral and spiritual realities of the universe. Such power did not necessarily remain internal to the person: it could spill over into the world and into history.

Edwin Arnold's portrayal of this renunciatory path was apparently compelling to many readers in his day. In Gandhi's progressive and experimental circle in England renunciation and the simple life—sometimes inspired by Thoreau, sometimes by thinkers from India—were deeply attractive.[32] As for Gandhi himself, he tells us in his autobiography: "My young mind tried to unify the teaching of the

---

[31]*Autobiography*, 503.

[32]Useful works for understanding Gandhi's circle are Almond, *British Discovery of Buddhism*, Green, *Origins of Nonviolence* and George Hendrick, *Henry Salt: Humanitarian Reformer and Man of Letters* (Urbana: University of Illinois, 1977).

Gita, *The Light of Asia*, and the Sermon on the Mount. That renunciation was the highest form of religion appealed to me greatly."[33]

The third element is the idea that renunciation and the attainment of the truth require nonviolence. As an institutionalized system of thought and action, nonviolence appeared for the first time in recorded history among religious and philosophical groups in Northeast India around 500 BCE. (Further west, Pythagoras appears to have been developing a system incorporating nonviolence at about the same time.)[34] Violence was much discussed by the philosophers of the time in India, and nonviolence of a very radical kind was adopted by at least two of the schools of the day, Buddhism and Jainism. Of these two, Buddhism was more committed to missionary activity, and advocates of the Buddhist system spread in all directions. Nonviolence was diffused through personal example, monastic and lay rules, argument, and narrative. Stories incorporating nonviolence poured out of the sacred homeland of Buddhism for centuries. The Buddha-legend was one such story.

In this story, in renouncing kingship, the prince gives up conquest and domination. Looking for insight, he decides to live a life in which both force and ownership are reduced to the smallest amount compatible with a healthy life. The ascetic whose arrival prompts him to renounce household life and seek this insight is described, in the earliest version of the story that has come down to us, as *committed to peace and nonviolence*.[35] The adoption of nonviolence is seen not only as a sign of compassion, but as a prerequisite for the full vision of the truth.

Moreover, the prince's distress at the suffering of the world is not a mere egotistical agony (how sad that I will die!) but a suffering on behalf of all living beings. He is astonished at people's lack of

---

[33]*Autobiography*, 69.

[34]See W. Burkert, *Lore and Science in Ancient Pythagoreanism* (Cambridge, Mass.: Harvard Univ. Press, 1972).

[35]I regard the *Mahāpadāna Suttanta* as the oldest surviving version of the story. For the relevant passage in this piece see T. W. and C. A. F. Rhys Davids, trans., *Dialogues of the Buddha [Dīgha Nikāya]*, Part II (London: Luzac for the Pali Text Society, 1971), 4-41, at 22.

compassion for other beings. In some versions of the story the prince, shortly before his renunciation, sees a field being ploughed, and "when he saw the ground in this state, with the young grass torn up and scattered by the ploughs and littered with dead worms, insects and other creatures, he mourned deeply as at the slaughter of his own kindred."[36] This idea of the kinship of all life is one of the things that distinguishes Indian nonviolence from pacifism (the rejection of war) and that has made it a profound challenge to Western thought. Whatever its secondary effects, war is primarily intended as an interaction between human beings, but violence is an aspect of the interaction of countless species. If all life is interrelated violence toward other living things becomes problematic.

In the first wave of transmission of the Buddha-legend to the West, parts of the system of nonviolence—the critique of war, for example—were retained, but the idea of the kinship of life was obliterated.[37] No wonder: at the time *Barlaam and Josaphat* was making its way into Europe people were being severely persecuted for advocating the kinship of life via vegetarianism and the doctrine of the transmigration of souls through the bodies of animals.[38] How dare anyone suggest that the human soul, related to the divine in a unique way, could inhabit the bodies of beasts! What was standard fare in India was seen as poisonous heresy by the medieval Christian Church.

By the time of the second wave of narrative transmission, Europe had changed. By the early part of the nineteenth century there was increasing interest in all aspects of nonviolence, and the kinship of life

---

[36]*The Buddhacarita*, Part 2, 62. The incident is included in several other versions of the story as well.

[37]Evidence of the idea of the kinship of life can still be seen in the Ismaeli version in Arabic, but the Georgian version and subsequent Christian versions are silent. See Daniel Gimaret, trans., *Le Livre de Bilawhar et Būdāsf selon la Version Arabe Ismaélienne* (Geneva/Paris: Librairie Droz, 1971) and David Lang, trans., *The Balavariani (Barlaam and Josaphat): A Tale From The Christian East Translated From The Old Georgian* (Berkeley: UniversiEstate, 1966).

[38]See, for example, Malcolm Lambert, *Medieval Heresy: Popular Movements from the Gregorian Reform to the Reformation* (2d ed., Oxford: Blackwell, 1992), 27, and Colin Spencer, *The Heretic's Feast: A History of Vegetarianism* (London: Fourth Estate, 1993), chapter 7.

was regarded by many as part of the special "wisdom of the East" they most wanted to learn. Edwin Arnold seems to have regarded it as his duty to transmit the kinship of life to his country as a kind of sacred truth. He therefore stresses in *The Light of Asia* the Buddha's "wide love/For living things, such passion to heal pain."[39] "So are we kin," he says, "To all that is."[40] He adds that "All life/Is linked and kin;"[41] "all flesh kin."[42] These statements are given color by his treatment of specific episodes in the story, and he has no hesitation in emphasizing or even inventing passages that allow him to make the point. Arnold apparently took these ideas seriously in his own life. He is said to have given up hunting under the influence of Buddhist teachings,[43] and he accepted the young Gandhi's invitation to serve as Vice-President of a (short-lived) vegetarian club in London.[44] In fact, many in the English circle in which Gandhi moved were thirsty for such teachings. The vegetarian socialist Henry Salt, for example, whose book *A Plea for Vegetarianism* had a profound impact on Gandhi,[45] characterized his personal religious faith as "a Creed of Kinship," which looked forward to a day when "there will be no such barbarity as warfare, or the robbery of the poor by the rich, or the ill-usage of the lower animals by mankind."[46] India was one of the key influences on English thinking in these matters and Indian views on the treatment of non-human life had fascinated England from the beginning of colonial contact.[47]

---

[39]*The Light of Asia*, 63.

[40]Ibid., 152.

[41]Ibid., 192.

[42]Ibid., 207.

[43]Wright, *Interpreter of Buddhism*, 34.

[44]Ibid., 171, note 1; *Autobiography*, 58.

[45]*Autobiography*, 48; Hendrick, *Henry Salt* 110-112, 166-167.

[46]Hendrick, *Henry Salt*, 1-2.

[47]"Here be many Moors and Gentiles," wrote the merchant Ralph Fitch in the 1580s, in one of the earliest letters home to England from India. "They will kill nothing, not so much as a louse, for they hold it a sin to kill anything. They eat no flesh, but live by roots and rice and milk." Stanley Wolpert, *A New History of India* (3d ed., New York/Oxford: Oxford University, 1989), 140. Hendrick's book, *Henry Salt* makes it clear that India, via works such as the *Gita*, was a stimulus to thinking in England at this time.

The young Gandhi read both Salt and Arnold, and he appears to have met them both in London.[48] Through Salt he was led to see how nonviolence was compatible with modernity, while through Arnold he gained increased respect for nonviolence in its ancient Indian forms. In London he began to draw together the elements he would need to renew the ancient tradition of nonviolence and make it a living force for the twentieth century. He would eventually insist, in a way that directly parallels the Buddha-legend, that "To see the universal and all-pervading Spirit of Truth face to face one must be able to love the meanest of creation as oneself."[49]

IV

The Light of Asia has fallen into obscurity. Those who bother to read it today generally view Arnold as a minor poet who became popular by being in the right place at the right time. But perhaps we may turn this judgment around and say that he was appreciated by people in his time not just because he was good at making verses but because he had something to say that they felt they needed to hear at that moment in history.

What Gandhi heard was a voice from the deep past of his own culture. He stood, in London, at one end of a chain of storytellers that began in Northeast India more than twenty centuries earlier. He received through this story a quite specific model of spirituality.

Having gained confidence in his own religious tradition Gandhi could have become a reactionary. He could have chosen to construct a narrow national identity, to emphasize cultural and religious purity, to refuse any contact with non-Indian ways of thinking. But he did not. Perhaps it was not such a bad thing that he encountered the Buddha in London in the middle of a Victorian romantic poem. Perhaps the experience showed him that nonviolence cannot be

---

[48]For Arnold, see note 38; for Salt see Hendrick, *Henry Salt*, 111 and, for a much later meeting of Gandhi and Salt, 166-167.

[49]*Autobiography*, 504.

locked up in a culture or nation: it can and will travel. Gandhi went on to embrace a great variety of ideas that he encountered in his journeys, and his enthusiastic mixing of ancient Indian asceticism and English vegetarianism, Hinduism and Tolstoy, the Sermon on the Mount and the *Bhagavad-Gita* gave his nonviolence a universal rather than a national appeal. Once this set of ideas had passed through the furnace of his own struggles and become integrated and tested, it became a power for all cultures.

3

NONVIOLENCE: THE TOLSTOY-GANDHI CONNECTION

Anthony J. Parel

Anthony Parel reveals an underappreciated dimension of Gandhi's growth into nonviolence: his relationship with another storyteller, Leo Tolstoy. Tolstoy had insisted on nonviolence, especially in The Kingdom of God is Within You. *There he charged that the modern State was founded upon violence, and could never satisfy the Gospel call to nonviolence. Morally, then, the State had to be done away with. Gandhi acknowledged Tolstoy's insights, but changed them in his struggle for* Hind Swaraj *(Indian independence). His new understanding was a crucial step in presenting the relationship between nonviolence and the modern State.*

L￼eo Tolstoy and Mohandas Gandhi never met, but they corresponded with each other during 1909 and 1910. Of Gandhi's writings Tolstoy had read only one, *Hind Swaraj* (1909), the Mahatma's most fundamental work. "I read your book with great interest," wrote Tolstoy in appreciation, "because I think that the question you treat in it—the passive resistance—is a question of the greatest importance not only for India but for the whole humanity." He had also read *An Indian Patriot in South Africa*, Joseph Doke's 1909 biography of Gandhi (the first ever to be written).

However Gandhi had read far more of Tolstoy's work, and Tolstoy's writings influenced his early development. By 1910 he had read practically all of Tolstoy's moral and philosophical writings available in English translation. He thought so highly of these works that he listed six of them as supplementary readings to his own work, *Hind Swaraj*. These were *The Kingdom of God Is Within You* (1893) and *What is Art?* (1898), both of which he had his friends translate into Gujarati; *Letter to a Hindoo*, which he himself translated into Gujarati, and three short essays, *The Slavery of Our Times*, *The First Step*, *How Shall We Escape?*. The other works that he read included *The Gospels in Brief*, *The Four Gospels Harmonised and Translated*, *What to Do?*, *On Life*, *My Confession*, *Thoughts on God*, *The Relations of the Sexes*, *Christianity and Patriotism*, and a number of Tolstoy's short stories such as "God Sees the Truth, but Waits," "Ivan the Fool," and "The Death of Ivan Ilyich." Gandhi did not pay great attention to Tolstoy great novels such as *War and Peace* and *Anna Karenina*, not because he did not appreciate their artistic merits (he did advertise them in his weekly newspaper, *Indian Opinion*), but because Tolstoy himself had thought that, as far as the question of nonviolence was concerned, his moral and philosophical writings were more important than were his works of fiction.[1]

The Tolstoy-Gandhi legacy occupies a very important place in the history of the theory and practice of nonviolence. Martin Green has written three books on the subject (Green, 1979, 1983, 1986), and those who wish to go deeply into the subject may profitably avail themselves of these excellent works.[2]

---

[1]Leo Tolstoy, *What is Art?*, trans. Aylmer Maude. (Tolstoy Centenary Edition. London and Oxford: Oxford University Press, 1929); *The Kingdom of God is Within You*, trans. Aylmer Maude. Tolstoy Centenary Edition. (London and Oxford: Oxford University Press, 1935); "The First Step," in *Recollections and Essays*, trans. Aylmer Maude. (Oxford: Oxford University Press, 1952).

[2]Martin Green, *The Challenge of the Mahatmas* (New York: Basic Books, 1979); *Tolstoy and Gandhi: Men of Peace* (New York: Basic Books, 1983); *The Origins of Nonviolence: Tolstoy and Gandhi in Their Historical Setting* (University Park, PA: Pennsylvania State University Press, 1986).

This chapter will first outline Tolstoy's ideas on nonviolence, then discuss how Gandhi accepted, modified, and further developed those ideas. If Tolstoy put Gandhi on the path of discovery, it was Gandhi who showed how Tolstoy's ideas could be actually put into practice. Without Gandhi it is doubtful whether those ideas would have become part of a modern tradition of nonviolent political action.

I

Tolstoy's major contributions to nonviolence are the following: (1) he gave nonviolence a metaphysical foundation in the ethics of the Gospels; (2) he identified the modern state and modern social sciences as the major obstacles to progress towards nonviolence; (3) he emphasized the importance of virtue for the flourishing of nonviolence; (4) he pointed out that art and aesthetics had an indispensable role to play in the promotion of nonviolence.

The *locus classicus* of Tolstoy's thoughts on nonviolence is *The Kingdom of God is Within You*, which argues that nonviolence is ultimately an ethical problem, for which the Sermon on the Mount provides the best solution. This is how he posed the problem:

[H]ow [are we] to settle the conflicts between people who now consider a thing evil that others consider good, and vice versa. To say that evil is what I consider evil although my adversary considers it good, is not a solution of the difficulty. There can be but two solutions: either to find an absolute and indubitable criterion of evil, or not to resist evil by violence. The first course has been tried since the beginning of history, and as we all know has so far led to no satisfactory results. The second course—not to resist with violence what we consider evil, until we have found some universal criterion—is the solution proposed by Christ.[3]

---

[3]*The Kingdom of God is Within You*, 58.

Tolstoy saw two major obstacles as standing in the way of implementing the ethic of the Gospels. They were first, the theory and activity of the modern state, and second, the teachings of nineteenth-century social sciences. The latter did everything they could to undermine the effectiveness of the ethic of the Gospels.

The modern state, according to Tolstoy, rests on physical violence or the ability to use the threat of violence. Government has always been in its essence "a force that infringes justice." History from Caesar to Napoleon and Bismarck, he says, is witness to this fact.[4] The modern state recognizes no ethics higher than that of national interest. It glorifies war. It presses science and technology into its service and promotes the manufacture and diffusion of weapons of mass destruction. It is always in alliance with the rich and the powerful sections of society, which tend to exploit the labor of the poor and the weak.

Tolstoy believed that society would be better off without the state. He was never impressed by the argument that without the state society would fall into chaos. True, the state suppresses private violence, but he argued that it does so only to prepare society for war with other states. It introduces fresh forms of violence into the lives of men. The pacification of domestic society has not meant that humanity has made overall advance towards nonviolence. The state in other words has not solved the problem of violence, it has only shifted its focus from domestic society to international society.[5]

In the nineteenth century, as Tolstoy saw it, the more powerful a state was, the more belligerent it became, prone to initiate foreign wars and embark on foreign conquests. Colonialism, imperialism, and the oppression of the indigenous races became the hallmark of the nineteenth-century state.

So much for those who had states of their own. What about those who did not have a state of their own but aspired to have one? The reference here is to nationalities and their nationalisms, and the

---

[4]Ibid., 176, 199.
[5]Ibid., 203, 211.

various nineteenth-century nationalist movements. Not only did each nation aspire to have its own state, but it also justified and glorified the use of physical violence in the pursuit of nationalist ends. Wars of national liberation were given almost religious sanction and violence done in the name of national liberation was celebrated as heroism.

The general conclusion Tolstoy drew was not very flattering to the modern state. The state was necessarily an institution founded on and encouraging violence, that could do nothing to stop the scourge of war. Under these conditions, for those who wished to live the life of the Gospels there was no ethically acceptable choice but to withdraw from the state and to stop all cooperation with it.

Tolstoy thought that the state as an institution was beyond redemption. Between the ethic of the Gospels and that of the modern state there was no room for compromise. Under these circumstances nonviolent persons had no choice but to live in small, stateless societies.

Tolstoy's criticism of nineteenth-century social sciences was no less radical. Those who came under his wrath included such figures as Charles Darwin, Auguste Comte, Herbert Spencer, Karl Marx, and Ernst Renan.[6] Common to them all was the belief that humans were only embodied beings, that the soul as a spiritual substance had no scientific status, and that human welfare should be understood solely in terms of the external conditions of life. Consideration of the soul and its welfare had to be excluded from all calculations of human well-being. Religion as a spiritual reality, they held, had very little to recommend itself. Religion in their eyes was basically a social phenomenon, whose significance varied with the evolution of the external conditions of life. Accordingly they held that human condition could be improved by improving just the external conditions of life. All human efforts had therefore to be directed to a general modification of the political, social, and especially economic conditions. This was to be brought about by the intervention of the

---

[6]Ibid., 108.

state, by legislation, by the introduction of modern industry, increase of commerce, and diffusion of scientific education.[7]

Needless to say Tolstoy was thoroughly skeptical of the position taken by these thinkers. For he held that humans were both embodied and ensouled beings. To treat them only as the one, not the other, was to distort the truth about them. Ignoring the soul was a major catastrophe that the social sciences had brought upon humanity. For it was in the soul that the fundamental truth about human welfare was being revealed. To the social sciences Tolstoy retorted:

> Let all those external alterations be realized and the position of humanity will not be bettered. So long as people pretend, that is, conceal the truth from themselves, no improvement of men's condition is possible. That improvement can only take place when they recognize that their welfare lies solely in the union of all men in the truth, and are therefore ready to put above everything else the recognition and profession of that truth which has revealed itself to them.[8]

Christ's teaching, observes Tolstoy, differs from other teachings in that it guides human beings

> not by external rules but by an inward consciousness of the possibility of reaching divine perfection. And in man's soul we find not moderate rules of justice and philanthropy, but the ideal of complete, infinite divine perfection. Only a striving towards that perfection deflects the direction of man's life from its animal condition towards the divine, in so far as that is possible in this life.[9]

---

[7]Ibid., 402.
[8]Ibid., 410-411.
[9]Ibid., 118.

He added that "Christian teaching consists in indicating to man that the essence of his soul is love, that his happiness comes not because he loves this or that man but because he loves the source of all, God, whom he recognizes in himself thorough love, and so this love will extend to all men and all things."[10] Tolstoy believed that "human life is an asymptote of divine perfection towards which it always tends and approaches, but which can only be reached by it in infinity." He further argued that the meaning and end of human life lay in promoting the Kingdom of God in the service of humankind. Such service could only be accomplished by each individual person's "recognition and avowal of the truth."[11] Nineteenth-century social sciences, Tolstoy concluded, were opposed to a spiritual understanding of human well-being. They were therefore not capable of promoting the cause of nonviolence.

Granted that nonviolence required a basis in the ethic of the Gospels, how is one actually to embark upon the new ethical path? Tolstoy gives a general outline of his response in a short essay entitled *The First Step*. The argument is that the cultivation of the four moral virtues—temperance, courage, wisdom and justice—is necessary for a nonviolent life. But the cultivation is not to be a haphazard affair; there is a certain order to be followed in the acquisition of these virtues. Only then will their cultivation be successful. Only then will progress in virtue be possible. As a Chinese proverb says, noted Tolstoy, the ascent on the ladder to heaven begins with the first step. This is also the teaching of all ancient moral philosophies. In Plato's philosophy, for example, the acquisition of temperance had to precede that of courage, wisdom and justice.[12] Tolstoy wanted to reinstate temperance as the first step in the ethical life of modern people. Temperance is the virtue that introduces moderation in the enjoyment of bodily pleasures—sex, food, and drink. Without temperance

---

[10]Ibid., 129.
[11]Ibid., 117, 444.
[12]"The First Step," 92.

it is not possible to lead a normal virtuous life. Without a normal virtuous life, nonviolence has no chance of succeeding.

In *The First Step*, Tolstoy bemoans the fact that modern culture is an intemperate culture, a culture of excesses neglects if not despises the virtue of temperance. For modern culture inculcates in people the idea that everyone has a limitless right to satisfy desires, that to put a moral limit on desires is tantamount to putting a limit on individual freedom. In modern culture there is a fatal alliance between desires and wealth. The struggle for wealth becomes a struggle to satisfy as many desires as possible. And violence lurks beneath this complex of desire-satisfaction and wealth-acquisition. The reader is invited to examine how relevant such an analysis remains for our society as we approach the third millennium.

The conclusion is not far to seek: a nonviolent culture needs the support of moral virtues, and first of all, of the virtue of temperance.

It is also interesting for our present study to include what Tolstoy had to say about art, aesthetics, and the ethics of nonviolence. One of his major contributions to the cause of nonviolence was to point out that there was a theoretical link between these three. He makes us think of art, aesthetics, and nonviolence in a new way.

Tolstoy develops his philosophy of art in his classic work, *What Is Art?* It is hardly possible to do justice to this great book here. All I can do is to identify what he means by art, and then to point out, why, according to him nonviolence must look for an ally in art.

Tolstoy defines art in terms of feelings and the capacity to evoke feelings through artistic symbols:

> To evoke in oneself a feeling one has once experienced and having evoked it in oneself then by means of movements, lines, colors, sounds, or forms expressed in words, so to transmit that feeling that others experience the same feeling—this is the activity of art. Art is a human activity consisting in this, that one man consciously by means of certain external signs, hands on to others feelings he has lived

through, and that others are infected by these feelings and also experience them.[13]

For Tolstoy, art includes poetry, drama, literature generally, music, paintings, sculpture, architecture, folklore, religious liturgy, and the like.

He held that all genuine art expresses deep feelings about the true meaning of life. It will distinguish between what is good life and what is evil life. He further argued that "what is good and what is evil is defined by what are termed religions."[14] Religions, according to Tolstoy, have a great deal to do with genuine art. They are the "exponents of the highest comprehension of life accessible to the best and foremost men at a given time in a given society—a comprehension towards which all the rest of that society must inevitably and irresistibly advance." That is to say, all great art, insofar as it expresses feelings about the meaning of life, has a religious quality to it. Thus Christian art evokes feelings of equality, solidarity, compassion, of "humility and love in place of any kind of violence."[15] The parables of the Gospels, the story of Joseph in the Old Testament, these and similar stories are, according to Tolstoy, are examples of great art.

Large sections of *What Is Art?* are devoted to the analysis of the character of modern art from the sixteenth century onward. Art gradually lost its moorings in the religious perception of the meaning of life. This, according to Tolstoy, was because art become more and more a means of pleasure separated from goodness. Art became the preserve of the rich and the powerful, something to be kept in museums or performed in expensive theaters. Art established an unholy alliance with wealth, business, and profit. "The art of our time and of our circle," Tolstoy bluntly asserted, "has become a prostitute."[16] It progressively lost its capacity to evoke feelings of human solidarity, compassion and nonviolence.

---

[13]*What is Art?*, 123.
[14]Ibid., 127.
[15]Ibid., 130.
[16]Ibid., 266.

Thus in *What is Art?* Tolstoy urges that art should cease to be meretricious. It should once again attempt to evoke feelings about the true meaning of life. And the true meaning of life, in our time, according to him, is revealed in the consciousness of human solidarity. He argues that

> The religious perception of our time in its widest and most practical application is the consciousness that our well-being, both material and spiritual, individual and collective, temporal and eternal, lies in the growth of brotherhood among men—in their loving harmony with one another. . . . In our age the common religious perception of men is the consciousness of the brotherhood of man—we know that the well-being of man lies in union with his fellow-men.[17]

That being the case, one of the functions of genuine art is to promote nonviolence. Tolstoy further writes:

> The task of art is enormous. Through the influence of real art, aided by science, guided by religion, that peaceful co-operation of man which is now maintained by external means—by our law courts, police, charitable institutions, factory inspection, and so forth—should be obtained by man's free and joyous activity. *Art should cause violence to be set aside.* (Emphasis added). . . . The task for art to accomplish is to make that feeling of brotherhood and love of one's neighbor, now attained only by the best members of society, the customary feeling and instinct of all men . . . The destiny of art in our time is to transmit from the realm of reason to the realm of feeling the truth that well-being for men consists in their being united together, and to set up, in the place of the existing reign of force, that kingdom of God—that is, of love—which we all recognize to be the highest form of human

---

[17]Ibid., 234-235, 286.

life. . . . The task of Christian art is to establish brotherly union among men.[18]

II.

Like Tolstoy, Gandhi also saw the modern state as posing a major problem to the cause of nonviolence. However, unlike Tolstoy, the Mahatma did not reject the state as such; he rejected only those features of the modern state that enhanced its violent character. In his view the modern industrial civilization was mainly responsible for this state of affairs. True, it enabled the state to improve the standard of living of its own citizens. At the same time, it also enabled the state to encroach on the territory of weaker nations, to conquer and colonize them. That is to say, as the industrial civilization gradually improved the living standards of the industrialized nations, it also encouraged the predatory tendencies of the modern state in many parts of Asia, Africa, and Latin America. Gandhi believed that violence was an inherent tendency of modern industrial civilization. Colonialism, imperialism, and the shameful treatment of indigenous populations were only the more obvious manifestations of this tendency. Gandhi had first-hand experience of the violent nature of the modern state in South Africa and colonial India. At the same time, he had a deep understanding of the nature and function of the state. He understood its strengths as well as its weaknesses.

As for its strengths, he was convinced that no society could survive or prosper in modern times without the ordering agency of the state. Without the state there could be no internal order, no protection against external threat, and no pursuit of the common good. In fact, Gandhi determined that it was the absence of a well-ordered state that opened India for colonial domination by outside powers. Gandhi's entire political life was devoted to fight colonialism, that is to say, to establish a well-ordered state in modern India.

---

[18]Ibid., 286-288.

At the same time he was perfectly aware of the weaknesses of the modern state—its tendency to concentrate power in fewer and fewer bureaucratic hands, to favor the rich and the powerful, to mistreat minorities, to place the national interest above *dharma* or natural law as the highest principle of national conduct. He was afraid that even if the modern state shed its imperialistic and colonial masks, it could assume new ones suited to the post-colonial conditions.

The conclusion he reached was fairly simple: the state is to be resisted as well as supported, depending on whether it served or dominated its citizens and whether it lent it support to the economic exploitation of the weaker nations. Accordingly Gandhi paid much attention to the task of taming the modern state, that is, to making it less and less violent. Of the many ideas that Gandhi developed in this regard, three deserve special attention. They are the ideas of *satyagraha*, *swaraj* and constructive program.

Gandhi's name is universally associated with *satyagraha*. Its basic principles are too well-known to require restatement here. In short, the concept emphasizes the use of nonviolent "soul force" against unjust governments. Joan Bondurant's *Conquest of Violence* still remains one of the best studies on the subject.[19] From our present perspective we need to emphasize that *satyagraha* was Gandhi's response to the modern state. It was both a way of resisting by nonviolent means the violent abuses of state power, and of securing the legitimate rights in a nonviolent manner. It was therefore a method of purifying the state of its excesses, and ultimately a technique of strengthening the state as source of order and public service.

Historically, Gandhi used the technique of *satyagraha* against the colonial state, which by definition lacked moral legitimacy. The question arises as to whether it could also be used against a state that has moral legitimacy. Gandhi's answer would be that *satyagraha* may still be used against such a state, if and when it abuses its powers. In

---

[19]Joan Bondurant, *Conquest of Violence: The Gandhian Philosophy of Conflict* (Berkeley: University of California Press, 1967).

other words, *satyagraha* is a moral weapon that the citizens may keep in reserve. It is Gandhi's solution to the problem of the modern state. It marks an advance on Tolstoy's position of total withdrawal from the state.

Turning now to the idea of *swaraj*, this too was a part of Gandhi's solution to the problem of the modern state. It is assumed that the state will become less violent if the citizens become more nonviolent. But how can such a state of affairs be brought about? Through the idea of *swaraj*.

Gandhi used the term *swaraj* in two distinct but related senses. In one sense *swaraj* meant rule of the self by the self, or internal self-rule; in the other sense it meant rule of the nation by the nation, or political self government or what we commonly know as "independence," bearing in mind that for Gandhi it always had an ethical dimension. The one was a personal moral achievement, the other a politico-moral achievement. Gandhi's thesis is that there can be no genuine, less violent political self-government without there being citizens who enjoy internal self-rule.

Here Gandhi's thesis marks an advance on modern political theory. Modern political theory is satisfied with political self-government: with a good constitution, a good executive, a good legislature, division of powers, etc. Modern political theory does not require as a condition for good, less violent government, the internal self-rule of citizens. Gandhi does, however, and he does so through his theory of *swaraj*. That is why he links the two notions of *swaraj*.

One cannot hope to build a less violent society unless more and more citizens learn to rule themselves, that is, unless they learn how to regulate their aggressive instincts and possessive appetites. The law and the constitution cannot by themselves make society less violent if individuals who constitute society do not undergo an inner transformation, however slight. Coming to terms with one's aggressive instincts and possessive appetites, i.e., making the necessary moral self-reform had to become part of good citizenship

Gandhi first outlined his theory of *swaraj* in his book, *Hind Swaraj*. He put it into actual practice when he took over the leadership of the

Indian nationalist movement in 1920. His minimum demand from fellow Indians was that violence may not be used to obtain political independence. He met with opposition from within the Indian nationalist movement on this point. His opponents wanted to be allowed to use violent means. Gandhi consistently refused to accept their demand: a person who cultivated inner *swaraj* could not at the same time use violent means to attain political ends. By and large Gandhi succeeded in his mission without having to resort to violence, eventually winning Indian independence without having to wage a bloody war. For this one has to thank the theory of *swaraj*.

The third major solution that Gandhi offers to the problem of the modern state is what he called the constructive program. The basic idea here is that if one wishes to build a less violent society, it is not reasonable to expect the state to bring this about by its own initiative. Voluntary, non-governmental organizations should be encouraged to deal with specific wrongs that afflict a given society. What these programs should include would depend on time and place. It is for the groups concerned to form the appropriate organizations. By shifting the focus from the state to voluntary organizations, one makes the former less bureaucratic and the latter more flexible in dealing with the ills of society.

In 1941 Gandhi himself drew up a list of constructive programs for India. It included nineteen different items, including the Hindu-Muslim problem, the evil of Untouchability, alcoholism, village sanitation, cottage industry, adult education, social and legal disabilities of women, rural poverty, etc.[20] These items reflected the needs of the time. The point however, is that reduction of violence is not possible unless voluntary organizations do their share in the form of constructive program. Satyagraha alone could not do the work. Neither could *swaraj* be enough. As Gandhi put it, without constructive program *satyagraha* and *swaraj* "will be like a paralyzed hand attempting to lift

---

[20]Anthony J. Parel, ed., *Mohandas Gandhi: Hind Swaraj and Other Writings* (Cambridge: Cambridge University Press, 1997),170-181.

a spoon."[21] Constructive program, in other words, energized society at the local level, and dealt with problems that otherwise might erupt into destructive violence.

By dealings with the problems of the modern state, Gandhi attempted to improve on Tolstoy's negative position. What of Gandhi's reaction to Tolstoy's insight that nonviolence must have a spiritual foundation? Tolstoy had discovered that foundation in the Gospels. Gandhi accepted that foundation, but he also broadened it to include the *Bhagavad Gita*. He considered this classic work of Indian philosophy to be the dictionary of his ethical life. He translated it from Sanskrit into Gujarati and supervised the translation of the latter version into English. He also wrote a commentary on it for the use of the ordinary people, people who had no scholarly background. In other words, he gave his own interpretation of the *Gita*.

According to Gandhi, though the teaching of the *Gita* is timeless, it had to reinterpreted from time to time, and adapted to the needs of a given time. In our present time, what was needed was a heightened awareness of the need for human solidarity and the reduction of violence in human relations. One had therefore to see what the *Gita* had to say to our age. As he saw it, the great lesson it had for our age was nonviolence. Though the teaching of the *Gita* is set in the context of a fratricidal war, its actual purpose, according to Gandhi, was to demonstrate the futility of war and the need for nonviolence. It taught that the roots of violence lay within the human psyche, in the uncontrolled state of its inner drives for power, pleasure, and possessions. The ego became the focus of this threefold drive. From this arose the conflict between the natural ego and the spiritual soul. The soul was a unitive faculty, whereas the unreformed ego remained a divisive inner force. The soul longed for spiritual unity between itself and God and all other human beings. By contrast the ego sought its own satisfaction irrespective of the requirements of the soul and the needs of others. There was, in other words, an inner war being waged between the ego and the soul, between self-interest and duty. The

---

[21]Ibid., 181.

basic task that each human being faced in this life was finding a solution to this inner war. It could be found, the *Gita* taught, if the moral agent acquired the habit of performing actions not in order to satisfy the selfish aims of the ego but in order to satisfy the require-ments of duty. Duty sought to harmonize the legitimate interests of the ego, the soul, and society. But the moral agent could acquire this habit only if it was prepared to keep egoism under reasonable control. It could do so, however, only if the person underwent a spiritual awakening. The person would also need divine assistance. For the *Gita* is a theistic work that exhorts the moral agent to commit himself or herself to the path of devotion to the Lord.

Gandhi's nonviolence then was built on a spiritual vision of life, such as the one outlined in the *Gita*. One ought to practice nonvio-lence not only for its societal and political benefits, but especially for its intrinsic value, its capacity to bring about inner peace, and to lead to the ultimate end of life, the union of all with the divine.

Gandhi therefore responded creatively to Tolstoy's insight that nonviolence needed a spiritual foundation. His response was equally creative to another of Tolstoy's insight, namely that nonviolence needed the support of the habit of virtue. The sources of violence being internal to human nature, a constant vigilance was needed for the gains of nonviolence to be stabilized. Here too Gandhi found support for this insight in Indian philosophy, in particular, in the philosophy of Patanjali's *Yoga sutra*.[22] Written in aphoristic style, this is the source book of Yoga philosophy. Gandhi was particularly influenced by aphorisms II. 30, and II. 35.

Aphorism II. 30 enumerates the five virtues necessary for an ethical life. The first of these is nonviolence, the others being truthfulness, non-stealing, chastity, and greedlessness. Those familiar with Gandhi's writings would recognize how fundamental these five virtues were to his philosophy. They formed the backbone of his

---

[22]Patanjali, *The Yoga Sutra of Patanjali, and New Translation and Commentary* by Georg Feuerstein (London: Dawson, 1979).

entire political practice. He wrote hundreds of pages of commentaries on each of these virtues.

Nonviolence, of course, occupied the pride of place in Patanjali's (and Gandhi's) list of virtues. However, Patanjali attached no political significance to it. It was left to Gandhi to draw out its political implications. In doing so, he showed great originality and independence of thought. Applied to politics, it meant that political opponents ought to resolve their differences in a peaceful manner.

Aphorism II. 35 ("When one is well-grounded in nonviolence, all enmity is abandoned in his presence") calls for special comments. It taught that true nonviolence has certain charismatic effects. In the presence of a person who sincerely practices nonviolence, hatred and enmity tend to subside. A diligent and faithful practice of nonviolence not only makes the practitioner peace loving, it also gives him or her an almost charismatic influence over others. Gandhi often said that he literally believed in this idea.[23] It was in the spirit of this aphorism that he undertook his famous tour of Bengal in 1946, when that province was ravaged by Hindu-Muslim riots. His mere presence pacified that province—which prompted Lord Mountbatten, the viceroy, to make the celebrated remark that Gandhi acting as "one man boundary force" did more for peace in Bengal than did ten thousand soldiers in the Punjab.

Gandhi also endorsed Tolstoy's views of the relationship of art and nonviolence. Unlike Tolstoy, however, he never wrote a book on art. Though invited to write one, he declined the offer out of humility.[24] But he had many pertinent things to say on the subject. Two great artists of the day, Rabindranath Tagore and Romain Rolland, both Nobel laureates in literature, were his devoted friends, the latter being also his biographer. With them he had serious discussions on the question of art and its relation to political action. It is, however, from Tolstoy's *What Is Art?* that he derived his basic ideas on the subject.

---

[23]M. K. Gandhi, *The Collected Works of Mahatma Gandhi*, Vol. 71 (New Delhi: Publications Division, Government. of India, 1958-1995), 225.

[24]*Collected Works*, 25: 250.

"The cause of the production of real art," Tolstoy had written, "is the artist's inner need to expresses a feeling that has accumulated. . . ."[25] Similarly, in describing his writing of Hind Swaraj, Gandhi asserted, "I have written because could not restrain myself. . . . Just as one cannot help speaking out when one's heart is full, so also I had been unable to restrain myself from writing the book since my heart was full."[26] By Tolstoyan standards, Hind Swaraj must be considered a work of art, a piece of literature, for it expresses the author's intensely felt feelings on the subject of swaraj, satyagraha, and nonviolence. All great art, as we saw earlier, had a deep "religious" source; it had the capacity to cause violence to be set aside. This certainly is true of Hind Swaraj.

In this regard one should also note of what Gandhi says in Hind Swaraj on the need to feel and experience inner swaraj: "The swaraj that I wish to picture before you and me is such that, after we have once realized it, we will endeavor to the end of our lifetime to persuade others to do likewise. But such swaraj has to be experienced by each one for himself."[27] Gandhi certainly experienced swaraj within himself: that is why his ideas had such power and authenticity. Thanks to this inner experience, he was also able to invent appropriate symbols, such as the spinning wheel, to corroborate his ideas, and to give them their emotional appeal. The spinning wheel became the symbol of Gandhi's nonviolent social revolution: it expressed the values of the dignity of manual work and the manual laborer, of self emancipation through the use of appropriate technology. Gandhi was a great communicator who knew the power of these aesthetic symbols to move people towards the goal of a nonviolent mode of life.

---

[25]*What is Art?* 266.
[26]Parel, xv.
[27]Ibid., 73.

III

Particularly pertinent to our times are the observations of Tolstoy and Gandhi on art and nonviolence. Today many complain about violence in the media, in the world of entertainment, in sports such as hockey and boxing. Yet many defend these manifestations of violence on the basis of artistic freedom. But what art? Genuine or meretricious? A re-reading of Tolstoy's *What Is Art?* will help us find some answers. We could also use a modern-day Gandhi to lead us in a new *satyagraha* against violence in the media, in sports, and the world of entertainment.

A careful reading of the writings of Tolstoy and Gandhi on nonviolence is a good starting point for a serious study of nonviolence in our times. Though a century separates us from them, their basic insights retain their freshness. They tell how deeply Western culture must lay the foundations of nonviolence in our ethical, aesthetic, and religious sensibilities, and how we ought to nourish these sensibilities with the aid of a personal spiritual life. In our external activities and our internal lives, both Tolstoy and Gandhi would say, lie the chief obstacles to our creating a nonviolent third millennium.

4

THE "GANDHI DIARY" OF RUFUS JONES

David W. McFadden

After journeying throughout the East, Rufus Jones, an important figure in American nonviolent history, met Gandhi on December 1, 1926. He kept a diary of that meeting, remarking on everything from Gandhi's physical appearance to his theories on Gospel nonviolence. Jones is so typically American in his observations that reading this diary is very much like having a visit with the adult Gandhi. I am the more pleased that my colleague has contributed to this volume, since this is the first time that Jones's "Gandhi Diary" has appeared in print.

> I am not coming as a tourist or out of curiosity. I am coming as a friend and as one who will be greatly helped by a contact with you at this crucial time when our main business is building a real spiritual civilization.
> —Rufus M. Jones to Mahatma Gandhi, April 20, 1926

> I will be pleased to meet you whenever you come. . . . I have always time to meet friends like you.
> —Mahatma Gandhi to Rufus M. Jones, May 28, 1926

Who was this Rufus Jones? Why did he think it was important to visit Gandhi? And what were his very frank impressions of the man known as "the great soul"? Let us look at these two men and examine this visit, a visit which had great implications for an understanding between western and eastern nonviolent philosophies.

Gandhi's long struggle for the transformation and independence of India began in the aftermath of World War I after his victory for Indian rights in South Africa. By this time he had many friends and contacts among progressive Christians, including Quakers, in both England and South Africa and was beginning to be known in the United States as well. From that time until his death in 1948, he was visited and interviewed many times. The records of these visits often reveal more about the visitor than about Gandhi. Occasionally, as in the case of the journal of noted American Quaker leader Rufus M. Jones, the interaction helps in our quest to understand the origins of twentieth century nonviolent movements and their relation to Gandhi's thought.[1]

Gandhi's interest in and reflections on Christianity and particularly the teachings of Jesus began during the time he was a law student in England in 1890. It was there, as he relates in his autobiography, that he met "a good Christian from Manchester" in a vegetarian boarding house, who urged him to read the Bible, particularly the New Testament. The Old Testament books following Genesis, reflected Gandhi, "invariably sent me to sleep. But the New Testament produced a different impression, especially the Sermon on the Mount which went straight to my heart. I compared it with the *Gita*. . . . My young mind tried to unify the teachings of the *Gita*, *The Light of Asia*, and the Sermon on the Mount."[2]

This religious quest continued for Gandhi throughout his life. He never lost his interest in unifying what he saw as the best of Christianity with the best of Hinduism and, later, Islam. In South Africa he first became acquainted with Quakerism and continued his exploration of what he saw as the shortcomings of both Hinduism and Christianity. "It was impossible for me to believe," he later wrote,

---

[1] I would like to extend grateful acknowledgments to the Quaker Collection, Haverford College, for permission to publish portions of this Journal of Rufus M. Jones.

[2] Mohandas K. Gandhi, *Autobiography, or My Experiments with Truth* (Washington, DC: Public Affairs Press, 1948), Chapter XX, 91.

"that I could go to heaven or attain salvation only by becoming a
Christian." On the other hand, Gandhi wrote:

> if I could not accept Christianity either as a perfect or the
> greatest religion, neither was I then convinced of Hinduism
> being such. Hindu defects were pressingly visible to me. If
> untouchabililty could be a part of Hinduism, it could but be
> a rotten part or an excrescence. I could not understand the
> raison d'etre of a multitude of sects and castes.[3]

Gandhi never lost his sense of the importance of many different,
yet equally valid, paths to the divine. In some very basic ways, as
Margaret Chatterjee has pointed out, Gandhi drew his approach to
the problem of religious pluralism from his own ancient Jain tradition
growing up as a boy in Gujarat. "This held that all religious awareness
is inevitably partial and incomplete, so that different traditions can
complement and enrich one another rather than being mutually
exclusive rivals."[4] As Gandhi wrote, reflecting on his reading in jail
in 1923,

> Only God is changeless and as His message is received
> through the imperfect human medium, it is always liable to
> suffer distortion in proportion as the medium is pure or
> otherwise. . . . I would therefore respectfully urge my Christian
> friends and well-wishers to take me as I am. I respect and
> appreciate their wish that I should think and be as they are
> even as I respect and appreciate a similar wish on the part of
> my Mussalman friends. I regard both the religions as equally
> true with my own. But my own gives me full satisfaction. It
> contains all that I need for my growth. It teaches me to pray
> not that others may believe as I believe but that they may

---

[3]MK Gandhi, *Autobiography*, Part II, 146.

[4]Margaret Chatterjee, *Gandhi's Religious Thought* (Notre Dame, IN: University of Notre
Dame Press, 1983), x

grow to their full height in their own religion. My constant prayer therefore is for a Christian or a Mussalman to be a better Christian and a better Mahomedan. I am convinced, I know, that God will ask, asks us now, not what we label ourselves but what we are, i.e., what we do. With him *deed* is everything, *belief* without deed is nothing. With him doing is believing.[5]

Rufus Jones, professor of religion at Haverford College, was co-founder and Chairman of the American Friends Service Committee, and the editor of the Quaker journal, *American Friend*. Jones was probably the best known Quaker in the world in 1925 because of his numerous publications and an increasingly important role in bringing together Quakers and other Christians in a growing and broadening ecumenical movement. Within Quakerism, Jones was particularly important in linking evangelical and quietist Friends in a commitment to a stronger, more activist faith. He was also one of the co-founders of the Fellowship of Reconciliation in 1917, the association of American pacifists from various denominations, determined to work within their respective churches to turn the United States away from war and toward nonviolence.

The touchstone of Rufus Jones's philosophy was the present reality of religious experience. He was utterly opposed to creeds or statements of belief—anything, in point of fact, that would tend to rigidly put into formulae the nature God's relationship with human beings, which he believed was a constantly changing, active encounter. He firmly believed that the nature of Friends' belief could not be captured in words but, just as George Fox originally saw, had to be experienced.[6]

---

[5] M. K. Gandhi, "My Jail Experiences, XI," *Young India* 4 September 1924 in Raghavan Iyer, ed., *The Moral and Political Writings of Mahatma Gandhi* (Oxford: Clarendon Press, 1986) I: 182.

[6] There are two biographies of Jones. By far the best, despite the nearly forty years since its publication, is Elizabeth Gray Vinings *Friend of Life: the Biography of Rufus M. Jones.* (London: Michael Joseph, 1958). Rufus Jones' daughter, Mary Hoxie Jones, has published

Jones always linked his belief in a vibrant spiritual life with the conviction of the importance of political action in the world. He was convinced that a very present awareness of the God within by necessity mandated individual action in the world. As he put it in one of his rare diary entries (his only sustained journal writing came on long trips abroad), "We must work in two directions: (1) for better political relations and ideals—for making war outlawed and (2) for deeper spiritual interpretation and comprehension."[7]

In an article in the *American Friend* in 1915, he inserted into the manuscript a handwritten admonition again expressing this fundamental conviction, "two things are absolutely necessary as conditions of leadership. The Church must have a living present experience of God, and it must be possessed by an overwhelming conviction that it has a definite mission to work out in the world."[8]

But at the same time, Jones always argued that any changes that Friends advocated in the world had to be accompanied by inner spiritual change. Political, economic, or social change devoid of the personal and spiritual could never last. As he noted in a letter to Charles Jenkins in 1927, "Our real mission as a Society of Friends in the world today is to help form the right spirit and the right atmosphere for the bringing of a better civilization for which we long . . . We must form the habit of sharing and cooperating. We must be as ready to sacrifice as we are now to compete. There is no substitute for this new spirit and this new way of life. . . ."[9]

Rufus Jones was in his mid-sixties when he was asked by the YMCA in 1926 to give a series of lectures celebrating its fortieth

---

an excellent biographical sketch, *Rufus M. Jones* (London: Friends Home Service Committee, 1955). Jones has left a huge corpus of published works, most of which are out of print, and a substantial manuscript collection well catalogued in the Quaker Collection, Haverford College.

[7]Diary of Rufus M. Jones, August 19, 1925, RMJ Papers, Box 63, Quaker Collection, Haverford College.

[8]RMJ mss insert, "Social Service and field activities," *American Friend*, December 2, 1915, RMJ Papers, Box 67.

[9]Jones to Charles Jenkins, June 14, 1927, RMJ Papers, Quaker Collection, Haverford College.

anniversary in China, in Shantung, Tientsin, Nanking, and Shanghai. He took the opportunity to visit Japan and India as well. At first hesitant to embark on a long voyage, he increasingly saw it as an opportunity to reflect on the ways in which spiritual renewal—east and west—could revitalize social change. On his voyage across the Pacific, Jones reflected on what he hoped he would find in Asia:

> I know only vaguely where I am going in this adventure. It is a new situation with new noises, new calls. The old, the customary, the conventional are overpassed and left behind. We must meet the unusual and speak to the age, to the eastern mind in fresh and creative ways. As soon as one gets down to the simple and elemental realities we humans are all pretty much alike and we shall understand each other. . . . I have been deeply impressed by the widespread interest that has been taken in this Eastern adventure of mine. Everybody feels that it is a real call. . . .There should emerge a unique type of Christianity for China, for Japan, for India, interpreted through their highest ideals and aspirations, absorbing into itself all that is truest and best, all that is most human and divine in their native religions, all that has been contributed by their extraordinary spiritual leaders of past ages. Christ is not jealous of rivalry. He is concerned only for truth and life. The spirit of Christ not only leads into all truth but gathers in all that is truth in the experience of the human race.[10]

In Calcutta, Delhi, Benares, and Allahabad, Jones had meetings with Indian Christians and missionaries, and discussed Quakerism and Hinduism. But the highpoint of his trip to India, and the discussions that filled his journal, were of his meeting with Gandhi. As Jones wrote in advance asking for a meeting, "I am not coming as a tourist or out of curiosity. I am coming as a friend and as one who

---

[10]The Journal of Rufus M. Jones, June 25, 1926, RMJ Papers, Box 74, Quaker Collection, Haverford.

will be greatly helped by a contact with you at this crucial time when our main business is building a real spiritual civilization."[11] Gandhi responded with an open invitation, "I shall be pleased to meet you whenever you come. However busy I may be, I know that I am by no means so much rushed as people in America are. I have therefore always time to meet friends like you.[12]

The two met for much of the day on December 1, 1926. The account that follows is taken directly from Jones's journal. Their meeting took place in Ahmedabad, in the Ashram where Gandhi lived, worked, and meditated. Jones began his story by recounting first the setting:

> When the time came for the visit we went to the simple hut where the Mahatma lives and works. A large number of native guests from the other parts of India were having an interview to discuss the problems of their sections with their chief. They all withdrew as we came in and we had our simple introduction.

Jones then continued by giving his impressions of Gandhi's physical appearance, and yet even then he could not avoid noticing Gandhi's spiritual qualities:

> Gandhi was sitting on a small matrass [sic] with a pillow at his back. He does all his work sitting on the floor this way with a little table in front of him. He wore a simple one piece cotton cloth draped over his body but much of the body showed through and revealed his tiny, thin physical structure in which the wonderful spirit has its habitation. His feet were in sight and he played with his toes with his pencil, somewhat as one plays with a watch-chain as he talks. He went on for a few

---

[11]Jones to Gandhi, April 20, 1926, RMJ Paper, Haverford.
[12]Gandhi to Jones, May 28, 1926, RMJ Papers, Haverford.

minutes talking with his secretary and asked us to excuse him while he finished some business which had to be attended to.

It gave me a good chance to study his face and head. His hair is closely cut and is turning iron gray. He has lost his lower front teeth and the gap is a good deal in evidence. The face is full of light and his smile which comes often is very fine and full of charm and gentleness. In fact his face well fits his character and his life history, the face is a faithful record of his life and spirit. There is tremendous depth to it and it reveals spiritual power, without showing lines of suffering and tragedy. He has consumed his smoke and translated his struggles into quiet strength of character and inward depth. A child would instantly feel at home with him and would run to him with perfect trust and confidence. He made us feel at ease at once when he turned and began to welcome our visit.

Jones began his questions of Gandhi by referring to their common friend, the Reverend John Haynes Holmes, a Unitarian minister at a large church in New York City and a committed pacifist dedicated to social justice and nonviolence. He then moved into his questions for Gandhi about the difficulties of the nonviolent path:

I asked him first about his friendship with John Haynes Holmes who had introduced me to him. He said we know each other very well but we have never met. I was much surprised. I supposed Dr. Holmes had been here and had seen him. I asked him whether after all his experiences of the difficulties of life and the complications of society he still felt that the way of love and gentleness would work. Yes, he said, it works better than anything else will. It has become the deepest faith of my being. It is built all through me—and he waved his hand gracefully over his little body—and nothing now can ever happen that will destroy my faith in that principle. Speaking of opposition and attacks he said that he learned early in his life to carry on his work without any hate or bitterness and lie above the spirit of hate and hardness.

Then Jones came to the question he may have wanted most to ask, to discover for himself and his Quaker and Christian friends in the United States the ways in which Gandhi was influenced by, or connected to, Christianity:

> I asked how much he owed his way of life to the influence of Christ and especially to the crucifixion. He replied very simply that so far as he was positively conscious there was very little direct Christian influence, but that the indirect and unconscious influence might well be an important factor. He went on then to relate his contacts with Christianity. He began with a hostile attitude toward it, for he supposed that to be a Christian meant to drink whiskey, to smoke a big black cigar and eat much beef. At the time he went to England he still held these crude views of Christianity. He made friends who were Christians and slowly discovered some of the deeper aspects of the Christian life.
>
> A friend gave him a Bible to read and he began at Genesis, reading straight on but much confused about what it all meant, until he got into Leviticus where he revolted and gave up his reading, quite disillusioned in regard to the Bible. It was only in 1893 that he came upon the N.T. and learned to love the sermon on the mount and the story of the cross. His reading of the N.T. has been frequent ever since and he reads it aloud and interprets it every Saturday to the students of Ahmedabad University which is his creation. The dear 'brother' who took us about said we all read the N.T. and we all love the sermon on the mount.

Jones then asked Gandhi about Quakerism:

I asked Gandhi if he knew much about Quakerism and he said that he knew little about it except what he got from his intimate friend Coates who was a Quaker. He has apparently read almost nothing of our Quaker books and seemed to know little of George Fox or John Woolman. I told him about our child feeding in Germany after the war and he was interested in the expression of love and good will, but he asked no questions and did not show much keenness of interest in it. I asked him if he had read the "Little Flowers of St. Francis" and he said he had not. I reminded him that in my first letter to him I had told the story of Brother Giles and St. Louis and he smiled beautifully and said that he remembered the story. He said that Hindu religion and literature was quite full of the principle of love and sacrifice and that his own faith in love as a way of life was born out of native sources rather than foreign sources, though he admitted the unconscious influences might have been much greater than he knew. He told me that a friend of mine had come to see him the day before and was still there, someone named Harrison. He sent out for him and I found that it was Tom Harrison who was spending two days in the brotherhood and speaking in the university. Tom says that Gandhi is lovely with little children who sit around him when he reads the lessons in the morning and evening from the *Bhagavad-Gita* or other sacred books (sometimes the Bible). He looks at them and smiles and tells them in simpler language what he has read and they smile at him and look very happy and gay.

This part of the conversation was revealing to Jones. It convinced him that while Gandhi had been touched by Christianity, he was still a Hindu and profoundly a man of India, with the transformation of India his top priority:

Gandhi's supreme interest is the reformation of India, the building of the new India. His ideals are all for practical ends.

I felt throughout our conversation that he was profoundly *Hindu*. His interests are not very keen beyond this boundary line. His religion is saturated with Hindu color and he clings even to the outgrown superstition of his racial religion. The *Gita* is his great sacred book.

At this point Jones began to learn, truly learn, from Gandhi. This at first expressed itself in his diary in negative ways, but in the process he reflected on what Gandhi was about and why he made the decisions that he did:

I expressed my regret to the brother who was my guide that the temple worship seemed so low and poor, expressing the feeling that it seemed too bad to encourage these types of religion. He said there are many rivers and all carry refreshing water. Some are great like the Ganges and some are tiny rills of water, but all are needed for a complete world. He felt that if Gandhi had taken a more exalted spiritual position in his religious life he could not have had the immense influence he has had over the common people. He is absorbed in his experiment to revive simple native industries. His Ashram is a place for growing cotton and experimenting in types of cotton, of ginning the cotton, spinning it and weaving various kinds of cloth. All the tools and implements are made there in the shops, including all the metal work. It was well done and gave work to about 150 persons.

The barns have many cows and the cow is an important part of the Ashram life. Everything is extremely simple—the life of the place is happy and full of the joy of creative work. The food is of the simplest but it is wholesome and probably adequate for the Indian system. Tom Harrison however seemed nearly starved and ate ravenously with us at the hotel. One would have thought he had not eaten for weeks!

Gandhi's simplicity is as natural as everything else about his life. There is no *pose* in his nature. He is thoroughly unspoiled and the most satisfactory thing about my visit was the conviction I brought away that here was a man who had attracted the attention of the whole world, a man who had controlled the thoughts of millions and influenced the destiny of an empire and who yet was still sincere and simple and unspoiled. It is the last test of greatness and nobility of soul. I was sorry to discover that Gandhi lacked the wider universal interests which are obviously lacking in him. He is first, last and always Hindu. He has very little of that universal mystical experience which is the ground and basis of a really universal spiritual religion. He is not quite the prophet type. In that respect he seems to me a lower type than St. Francis. In his own sphere however he is an extraordinarily great man and a beautiful character—a lover of men and an unselfish spirit. It is fine to have seen him just after the Taj Mahal. They are the greatest sights to see in India!

Gandhi discussed at considerable length with me his proposed visit to China next summer and asked me in detail about my visit, my lectures and my impressions of China. He was especially keen to know about interpreters and the necessity of translation. I spent considerable time telling him the general situation and the state of religion in China. He seemed greatly interested in the prospect of a visit to China and he will go if the way opens for his journey. . . .[13]

Gandhi never made this visit to China, and Rufus Jones never saw Gandhi again. But in many different ways this one visit with Gandhi left an enduring impression on Jones and his later work. He referred to the visit and his impressions of Gandhi in articles for Quaker publications. In an article in *The American Friend* in 1927, Jones discussed Gandhi's Ashrams as part of a strategy "for the redemption of India from the evils of materialistic civilization," claiming that the

---

[13]The Journal of Rufus M. Jones, December 1, 1926, RMJ Papers, Quaker Collection, Haverford.

life of the Ashram "would delight John Bellers and John Woolman" [British and American Quaker notables famous for their emphasis on simpler living].[14] A year later, in an address before the Five Years Meeting of Friends, Jones used Gandhi as his major example of the way of Peace to which Friends were called. "We must go the way of love that Gandhi has gone," he said. Jones recalled that he had asked Gandhi, "After all you have suffered, after all you have been through, do you believe that love will work?" And Gandhi answered, "I don't believe anything else in the universe as much as I believe that. . . . nothing in the world can ever take that faith in love out of me." Jones added: "We have got to learn to love that way—Love in the concrete."[15]

Jones continued to reflect on the deeper meanings of Gandhi's life and work, particularly his spiritual message and the ways in which Gandhi brought together Hinduism and Christianity. A scholar of Christian mysticism, and teacher and writer with a self-defined mission of helping American Christians, Quaker and non-Quaker, to add a more lasting spiritual dimension to their lives, Jones felt that there were other ways in which Gandhi was relevant to American Christians. Yet at first, as a confirmed western Christian with a clear and direct sense of a personal image of God, Jones struggled to see the relevance of Hinduism—even Gandhi's practice of it—to his own life. He confessed that he had not found in India what he had hoped to find—"the inward depth of life" or "moral and spiritual earnestness." Jones wrote, "I see nowhere any sign of a live mystical interest or a present mystical movement in India."[16]

But in his first major work after returning from Asia, *New Studies in Mystical Religion*, Jones concluded with a heartfelt tribute to what he had learned in India, "Perhaps some day we in the West will learn

---

[14]Rufus M. Jones, "Friends Have Sitting with Gandhi," *The American Friend*, January 13, 1927.

[15]Rufus M. Jones, "The Path of the Peacemakers," *The Friend*, December, 1928, 69.

[16]The Journal of Rufus M. Jones, December 11, 1926, RMJ Papers, Quaker Collection, Haverford College.

the secret which India has always possessed—that the Soul is the eternally important fact and its testimony the ground of all truth."[17]

Not until 1930, however, did Jones fully come to appreciate his Asia experience and his reflections on the spiritual contributions of Asian religions, and particularly his contact with Gandhi. In the spring of that year, John D. Rockefeller Jr., a friend of Jones for several years, asked Jones to be involved in the project of reassessing American Protestant Missionary work abroad. Jones had written a paper for a conference of the International Missionary Council meeting in Jerusalem in 1928 that expressed the sense he had then, freshly back from Asia, that Christianity's greatest challenge was not other world faiths, but rather "a world wide secular way of life." Jones instead called on world Christian leaders to encourage the deepening of spiritual directions in all faiths instead of trying to gain converts from them.

The challenge of this paper, and the vision and work of Rockefeller and John R. Mott of the YMCA led to what became the Laymen's Commission on Christian Missions. With Rockefeller funding, a commission of fifteen persons was formed from Baptist, Congregational, Methodist, Episcopal, Presbyterian, United Presbyterian, and Reformed Churches. The commission spent almost a year visiting India, Burma, China and Japan, meeting with missionaries and native Church leaders and drawing up a report and recommendations. At Rockefeller's urging, Jones agreed to be part of the appraisal group for six months and to assist in writing its report. As a preface, Jones wrote "a restatement for the present day of the fundamental content and programme of the Christian Religion." This short book, published separately as *A Preface to Christian Faith in a New Age* served as the starting point for the inquiry and kept Jones in particular grounded as to what the purpose of the commission was. After a semester visiting missions and indigenous churches in China, Japan, and India, the group met intensively on the voyage home, and Jones was asked to draft their report. As Elizabeth Gray Vining has noted, "determined

---

[17]Rufus M. Jones, *New Studies in Mystical Religion* (New York: Macmillan, 1927), 200.

though they were to produce a report which should satisfy everyone.
. . . their decision not to water down the final statements but to
include differing views added much to the value of the report and was
at least partly due to Rufus Jones's gift for seizing and expressing the
essentials of a conviction."[18]

The final report contained recommendations stunning in their
implications for Protestant missions, particularly in Asia. Jones himself
saw it as revolutionary. "It is quite an epochmaking piece of work and
will rattle dry bones for years to come," he wrote to Henry Cadbury.[19]

And rattle bones it did. *Rethinking Missions* was nothing less than
a call for a completely different approach to be taken by American
and British Christians abroad. It called for united action across not
only denominational boundaries but also religious boundaries. It
called for greater sensitivity of missions to the culture, religion, and
history of the countries in which they served, and a shift into
educational, medical, and agricultural work as the needs of the local
people dictated. All decisions over church government and finances,
and development of religious dimensions of missions should be given
over as quickly as possible to local people and indigenous communities. It was, in short, a call for disconnecting missionary work from
imperialism and colonialism, and the embracing of non-Christian
religious and cultural traditions of Asia. It would take decades, but
the new direction of American Protestant missions in Asia was clearly
marked, and bore the imprint of not only Rufus Jones but also of the
man he had met for only a day years before, Mohandas K. Gandhi.

---

[18]Elizabeth Gray Vining, *Friend of Life: the Biography of Rufus M. Jones* (London: Michael
Joseph, 1958) 236.

[19]Jones to Cadbury as quoted in Vining, p. 236.

5

WORLD WAR II AND THE ORIGINS OF THE COLD WAR: TOWARD A NONVIOLENCE HISTORY

Ira Chernus with Mark Elmore

In this intriguing chapter, Chernus and Elmore tell us of a different legacy that we have received from the past: a legacy of fear. They show us how fear has been used to underwrite policies that further promote violence. In laying bare this legacy of fear the authors show us how crucial it was for Gandhi and King—and for us—to overcome personal as well as community fear in order to promote nonviolence.

> The dominant impulse in India under British rule was that of fear. . . . It was against this all-pervading fear that Gandhi's quiet and determined voice was raised: Be not afraid. Was it so simple as all that? Not quite. And yet fear builds its phantoms which are more fearsome than reality itself, and reality, when calmly analyzed and its consequences willingly accepted, loses much of its terror.[1]

These words of India's first president, Jawaharlal Nehru, highlight an essential insight of

---

[1]Mahatma Gandhi, *Selected Political Writings*, ed. Dennis Dalton (Indianapolis: Hackett Publishing Co., 1996), 19.

Gandhian nonviolence: the indissoluble link between fear and violence. It is fear, above all else, that has triggered the violence that fills our history. The overcoming of fear is the portal to the culture of nonviolence. This article explores this basic principle of nonviolence and uses it to illuminate an important chapter in modern United States history.

The Idea of Nonviolence History

Nonviolence is a culture. More than just a political tactic or a religious force, it offers a total way of life to its followers. Nonviolence has its own values, its own organizations and forms of community, its own customs and rituals, its own publications, even its own songs. It also has its own rich past, which has created heroes like Gandhi and King. A number of well-qualified historians have studied that past. But the culture of nonviolence does not yet have its own way of telling of the world's past from the unique perspective of nonviolence.

Every culture needs to tell the story of the past—not just its own, but everyone's past—in its own way. The resulting version of history reflects the culture's particular biases, of course. But that is inevitable. History is always a matter of interpretation. Every historian begins with certain assumptions about human nature and the causes of historical change. For example, many of today's most influential historians assume that people are essentially motivated by their desire for wealth and power. They assume that nation-states operate as selfishly as individuals. These historians have become so influential because their viewpoint is shared by most politicians and other leaders in the United States. As their version of the past is told and re-told throughout our nation, their basic assumptions—their biases—are repeated so often that they are eventually mistaken for reality itself. In fact, these historians often call themselves "realists."

The nonviolence culture needs its own way of telling history, a way that can offer an alternative to the dominant "realist" version. This means seeing new things in "the same old history" because we are using a new vision, bequeathed to us by people like Gandhi and

King. This chapter offers an example of how such a nonviolence history might work, by looking at the Realists who led the United States into the Cold War and by illuminating the fears that motivated their words and deeds.

Although the Cold War is a thing of the past, it remains particularly important because of its continuing impact upon our current national discourse. The habits of fear that were learned in nearly a half century of Cold War are still very much with us. Going unquestioned, these habits create a self-perpetuating spiral of fear that continues to breed violence.

Only through the focusing lens of Gandhi, King, and nonviolence history are we able to lay bare the underlying patterns of a fear-driven discourse. Using their thoughts and words, we can gain new perspectives on human relations and the relations among nations that make up world history. We can see the truth of these matters more clearly than Realist historians themselves. This is not because nonviolence history is more objective. Since all history is interpretation, nonviolence history need not pretend to be value-free. It is not meant to be pursued for the sheer interest or pleasure of "objective" analysis. It is intended to serve the cause of promoting nonviolent alternatives to conflicts. The nonviolence historian pursues her craft to serve activists who are implementing nonviolent solutions. Just as the historian needs the activist, so the activist needs the historian: we must understand as clearly as possible the forces that generate violence, and the dynamic by which those forces operate, before we can intervene wisely to promote nonviolent alternatives. In what follows, we will examine the dynamic of fear both from the perspective of the Realist and from a nonviolent orientation, in order to begin to understand the dynamic forces that have operated during the Cold War.

Realism and Fear

Why did the Cold War begin? Some historians blame it on the aggressive designs of Josef Stalin, leader of the Soviet Union, who, they claim, wanted to conquer the world in the name of communism. Others attribute it to the aggressiveness of U.S. leaders and their desire for global political or economic domination. Still others suggest that no one was really at fault. Nations always strive for as much power as they can get, this argument goes. After World War II the United States and the Soviet Union were the only two nations strong enough to bid for world domination. Thus they inevitably fought with each other for that ultimate prize.

Most of these explanations take for granted the basic assumptions of Realism: First, all human beings innately want as much power and wealth as they can get; second, the world must be divided into nation-states who, like individuals, are inherently selfish; and, third, nations will use violence either to get more power and wealth or to prevent others from getting more. American leaders during the Cold War generally accepted this view (as they still do today). Most of the historians who tell the story of those leaders and their decisions share the viewpoint of the people they are studying. By calling themselves Realists they hope to deny the legitimacy of any other view of reality.

But the nonviolence culture must challenge this view of reality because, if it is accepted, fear and violence become inevitable, and national policy can never be based upon love. Reinhold Niebuhr demonstrated this convincingly in *Moral Man and Immoral Society*, his classic effort to refute Gandhian nonviolence. If selfishness is innate in every body politic, he argued, then all nations must be selfish. They must compete for power and wealth. The world must be permanently anarchic—a war of all against all—with every state trying to get as much control as possible. So every nation has enemies and faces violent dangers that are objectively quite real. No responsible national leader can ignore such dangers, Niebuhr argued. And since violent responses are innate in human nature, counterviolence is sometimes the most reasonable and effective response.

Nonviolence history can not be based on these premises, which make nonviolence impossible. It must see Realism as an interpretation, rather than a direct reflection, of reality.[2] It cannot take selfishness, greed, lust for power, and fear based-perceptions of danger as irreducible facts of human nature. Rather, those factors themselves must be explained.

Why do nations act selfishly and, in so doing, perpetrate violence? Most theories of nonviolence assume that the root problem is usually some kind of fear. Nonviolence therefore must involve overcoming our fears. Martin Luther King Jr. asked rhetorically: "Is not fear one of the major causes of war? We say that war is a consequence of hate, but close scrutiny reveals this sequence: first fear, then hate, then war, and finally deeper hatred."[3] Gandhi often addressed this theme:

> Active nonviolence necessarily includes truth and fearlessness. . . . Possession of arms implies an element of fear, if not cowardice. But true nonviolence is an impossibility without the possession of unadulterated fearlessness. . . . There is hope for a violent man to be some day nonviolent, but there is none for a coward. . . . As a coward, which I was for many years, I harboured violence. I began to prize nonviolence only when I began to shed cowardice. . . . Truth and nonviolence are, to me, faces of the same coin. . . . And if you want to follow the vow of truth in any shape or form, fearlessness is the necessary consequence. . . . Fear and love are contradictory terms.[4]

The day India gave up fear, Gandhi insisted, was the day it could begin a truly nonviolent struggle for independence.[5]

---

[2]For other interpretations (not based on nonviolence) of Realism as an interpretation see Francis A. Beer and Robert Hariman, eds., *Post-Realism: The Rhetorical Turn in International Relations* (East Lansing, MI: Michigan State, 1996).

[3]Martin Luther King Jr., *Strength to Love* (Philadelphia: Fortress, 1981), 112.

[4]Mohandas Gandhi, *All Men are Brothers*, ed. Krishna Kripalani (New York: World Without War, 1972), 84, 92; Ragharvan Iyer, *The Essential Writings of Mahatma Gandhi* (Delhi: Oxford University, 1993), 289, 243.

[5]Gandhi, *Selected Political Writings*, 71.

Indeed, for Gandhi genuine national freedom meant freedom from fear. His constant explicit assertion that nonviolence requires fearlessness implied an equally strong assertion that fear lies at the root of violence.

When individuals or groups are in conflict, each is afraid of something—and, most often, afraid of the other. So every act of violence is almost certain to elicit countervailing violence. Every story the historian tells is likely to be a story of a cycle of violence. This is the basic pattern of causation in human life that is central to nearly all nonviolence theories. As King put it: "Hate multiplies hate, violence multiplies violence, and toughness multiplies toughness in a descending spiral of destruction."[6] So a nonviolence historian will analyze the various forms of violence in the case being studied, will illuminate the particular kinds and processes of fear that generated and perpetuated the violence, and will explain the mechanisms by which fear and violence unfold and propagate themselves.

What kind of fear is most likely to be found? In his classic work, *The Power of Nonviolence*, Richard Gregg wrote that "fear is always a sense of impending or possible loss of something considered valuable."[7] Violence arises when people try to protect themselves against a loss, or to prevent any change that might portend a loss. As Gregg notes, greed, so often seen as the source of violence, is most often caused by fear of not having, or losing, wealth or material comfort.[8] King once called fear of loss the "soft-minded" attitude: "A soft-minded man always fears change. He feels security in the status quo, and he has an almost morbid fear of the new. The soft-minded person always wants to freeze the moment and hold life in the gripping yoke of sameness."[9]

King and Gandhi agreed that the fear underlying violence is ultimately fear of losing the most valuable thing of all: one's own individual life. As King put it: "Whenever a person lives with the fear

---

[6] King, *Strength to Love*, 53.
[7] Richard Gregg, *The Power of Nonviolence*, (Nyack, NY: Fellowship, 1959), 66.
[8] Ibid., 48.
[9] King, *Strength to Love*, 15.

of the consequences [of any action] for his personal life, he can never do anything in terms of lifting the whole of humanity and solving many of the social problems that we confront."[10] Theodore Koontz, in a recent summary of the principles of Christian nonviolence, has also found its root in a power that arises "when fear of being hurt or killed disappears, when one is no longer interested in defending oneself."[11] From a Hindu perspective, Gandhi saw fear for oneself as a result of ignorance—ignoring the truth that the individual self is a fiction, for only God has true, enduring reality: "There is only one Being Whom we have to fear, and that is God. When we fear God, we shall fear no man, no matter how high-placed he may be."[12] Nonviolence could only become a way of life when a person was no longer driven by fear of the loss of self.

Realist historians have uncovered plenty of evidence of the pervasive fear underlying public discourse and policy. They have not focused, however, on fear itself as the major force driving the decisions that make history, nor even as a topic worthy of independent study and evaluation. Perhaps this is because they live in what theologian Henri Nouwen calls "the house of fear" and, taking fear for granted, ask only "questions born of fear." As Nouwen says, "fearful questions never lead to love-filled answers. . . . Fear engenders fear. Fear never gives birth to love."[13] Once we step outside the "house of fear" we see that the Realists have it the wrong way around. It is not danger and violence that give rise to fear, but fear that gives rise to danger and violence. So the way nonviolence historians understand the past and the present will be quite different from the conventional historian's view.

---

[10]Ibid., 110.

[11]Theodore Koontz, "Christian Nonviolence," in *The Ethics of War and Peace*, ed. Terry Nardin (Princeton: Princeton University, 1995), 175.

[12]Iyer, *Essential Writings of Mahatma Gandhi*, 289.

[13]Koontz, "Christian Nonviolence," 179.

Realism and Apocalypticism

The modern system of nation-states can be well understood using the analytical tools of nonviolence history. That system emerged from early modern Europe's need to constitute a sense of identity on a non-religious basis. Nationalism encourages all individuals to identify their own selves with the "self" of the nation. Everyone's fear of loss of self is projected onto the imperiled state. In fact the modern state can be seen as a collective effort to articulate our shared fear in political terms, so that we can avoid facing the true nature of our individual fears. The state, so filled with fear, acknowledges no limits on its right to employ violence to protect itself. Gandhi understood the fundamental error of this approach and its tragic consequences. Every political state, he said, "while apparently doing good by minimizing exploitation, does the greatest harm to mankind by destroying individuality. . . . The state represents violence in a concentrated and organized form. The individual has a soul, but as the state is a soulless machine, it can never be weaned from the violence to which it owes its very existence."[14]

Realism is the political theory that justifies the nation-state system. Its tone is inherently defensive and conservative. It focuses on fear of what might be lost rather than hope for what might be gained. In this century, as the great Realist theorist Hans Morgenthau points out, the language of Realism has softened: "The 'maintenance of the status quo' yield[ed] to the 'maintenance of international peace and security.' "[15] But the goal—preventing any real change in the prevailing world order—remained much the same. So Realists speak of peace using images of order, balance, and stability, rather than images of innovation, growth, and change. Their policies focus on the need to prevent disorder or (to use their favorite term) "instability." This was the attitude that drove so many white conservatives and

---

[14]Mohandas Gandhi, *Sarvodaya* (Ahmedabad: Navajivan, 1951), 74.

[15]Hans Morgenthau, *Politics Among Nations: The Struggle for Power and Peace*, 5th ed. (New York: Alfred A. Knopf, 1973), 92-93.

even liberals to block the progress of the civil rights movement, leading King to write wryly: "I have almost reached the regrettable conclusion that the greatest stumbling block is . . . the white moderate who is more devoted to 'order' than to justice, who prefers a negative peace which is the absence of tension to a positive peace which is the presence of justice."[16]

On the level of individual psychology, it is easy enough to understand the link between fears of unpredictable disorder and the ultimate fear of losing oneself. In order to feel securely autonomous, we must feel a significant degree of control over our environment. Control implies a predictable correlation between our actions and the ensuing results. That predictability, in turn, requires an orderly environment in which cause-and-effect sequences can be reliably predicted. For a self that feels its own existence at risk, any disorder appears to be a threat. Realism transfers this psychological model to the state. On the level of the state, however, disorder is unavoidable. The state has a sense of separate identity only because it insists on its difference from other (often very similar) states. It must refuse to cooperate with the others in order to feel distinctive. So the state's existence seems to depend on being part of an anarchic international system—the very system that necessarily threatens its existence. Disorder is an ineradicable part of the system. So the system is bound to perpetuate a cycle of fear-driven violence that is its very lifeblood.[17]

Realism has long been the dominant vocabulary and viewpoint among policymakers in many nations. In the United States, however, we have traditionally been reluctant to accept it as dominant. Realism assumes that all nation-states are driven by the same forces and motivations. But public discourse in the United States has traditionally assumed that this nation is motivated by a quest for moral or religious values and that it has a special, perhaps sacred, mission to realize those values in its political life. Throughout U.S. history

---

[16]King, *Strength to Love*, 260.

[17]See David Campbell, *Writing Security* (Minneapolis: University of Minnesota, 1992), chapters 2, 3.

Americans have often said, either explicitly or implicitly, that only this nation could lead the world to its highest state of perfection—often called the millennium. This assumption first arose among the early English colonists, who used the Bible as a model to interpret their own experience. The Old Testament, as they understood it, said that the Israelites would have to go through much suffering and destruction in order to achieve their divinely promised greatness. The New Testament said that crucifixion must precede resurrection and that the world would have to go through ultimate suffering and destruction as the prelude to the millennium.

Many people in the U.S. have used this apocalyptic model to help them endure whatever difficulties came their way. So when they saw examples of international conflict and disorder, they did not accept the Realist view that this was just "politics as usual." Rather, following the biblical model, they took it as one chapter in a special, perhaps divine, plan for world history, which would eventually elevate the United States to its rightfully superior place. In this framework, any source of disorder and danger could easily seem to be evidence of the approaching consummation of history. Every feeling of political or social threat could easily be transformed into a feeling of cosmic threat—"the end of the world as we know it"—which the Bible seems to hold out as a necessary stage in God's plan for history. Images of global catastrophe were an intrinsic part of the language that people used to express their highest hopes for the world. Inasmuch as they carried a millennial hope, these images were, in a strange way, as comforting as they were frightening.

In the United States, during the late 1930s and 1940s, Realism met apocalypticism and the two combined to form a new way of talking and thinking about the world, first among U.S. policy makers and then among the American public. Realism made fear of disorder an inevitable foundation of all discourse and policy. Apocalypticism made every instance of perceived disorder a trigger for fear of "the end of the world as we know it." This new combination laid the foundation for U.S. public discourse throughout the Cold War, and indeed up to the present day.

From World War II to the Cold War

Fear has always been part of the discourse of U.S. foreign policy and policymakers. In the years just before and during World War II, however, fear became the central and driving force. And this fear was now fear for the very existence of the nation. This fear grew out of the continuing economic Depression, the rise of fascism, and new technologies that made the world seem much smaller and the United States much more vulnerable than ever before. But this fear also reflected the rising influence of the vocabulary and viewpoint of the new geopolitical Realism in U.S. foreign policy.

Well before the United States entered World War II, its leaders were already blending the fear-laden language of Realism with religiously-tinged apocalyptic warnings of the end of civilization. President Franklin Roosevelt, for example, said that "if civilization is to survive, the principles of the Prince of Peace must be restored. . . ."[18] "Never before since Jamestown and Plymouth Rock has our American civilization been in such danger as now."[19] Privately, Roosevelt expressed the real basis of his fear: the shifting world power alignment threatened U.S. economic and social stability. And he genuinely held this stability to be the substance of civilization. He wrote privately that he hoped the British, already fighting the Nazis, would be able and willing "to save civilization."[20] Similarly, when the Nazis conquered France, Roosevelt's Secretary of War, Henry L. Stimson, declared that "our civilization is hanging by a thread."[21] *Time-Life* publisher Henry Luce, in his famed 1941 editorial "The American Century," warned that America must become the "powerhouse" of the "ideals of civilization," or else "this nation cannot

---

[18]Franklin D. Roosevelt, "Quarantine Speech," in *Great Issues in American History*, ed. Richard Hofstadter (New York: Vintage, 1937), 391.

[19]Franklin D. Roosevelt, "Radio Address, December 29," in *Main Problems in American History*, ed. Howard Quint et al., 5th ed. (Chicago: Dorsey 1988), 263.

[20]David Reynolds, "Power and Superpower," in *America Unbound: World War II and the Making of a Superpower*, ed. Warren F. Kimball (New York: St. Martin's, 1992), 19.

[21]Godfrey Hodgson, *Colonel: The Life and Wars of Henry Stimson, 1867-1950* (New York: Alfred A. Knopf, 1990), 219.

truly endure."[22] A year and a half before Pearl Harbor, a group of top corporate executives wrote: "What interests us primarily is the longer-range question of whether the American capitalist system could continue to function if most of Europe and Asia should abolish free enterprise."[23] Ultimately, writes historian Thomas McCormick, these business elites feared "the unacceptable risks of Armageddon."[24]

Throughout World War II many elite leaders voiced similar warnings of the threat to "civilization." As historian Barry Karl puts it, the true war aim was not victory but survival.[25] Government planners took an "almost obsessive interest in the future, in stark contrast with the behaviors of nearly every other country, [which] testifies to an American predisposition for organizing [postwar] reality."[26] This obsession was driven in part by fear of the Soviet Union. If the defeat of Germany left the Soviets in control of most of Europe, the Joint Chiefs of Staff stated, "we would have to conclude that we had lost the war."[27] In a larger sense, however, it reflected more general fears of a postwar collapse or radical transformation of the American domestic system. Diplomat Averell Harriman voiced an especially widespread fear when he worried that "economic stagnation in the United States would drag the rest of the world down with us."[28] Vice-President Henry Wallace linked this directly with the growing fear of communism: "In the event of long-continued unemployment, the only question will be as to whether Prussian or Marxian doctrine will take us over first."[29] As World War II drew to an end, the joy and optimism of victory remained tempered by the legacy of fear that had

---

[22]Henry R Luce, "The American Century," *Life* (February 17, 1941): 62.

[23]Thomas J McCormick, *America's Half-Century* (Baltimore: Johns Hopkins University, 1989), 31.

[24]Ibid., 32.

[25]Barry Karl, *The Uneasy State* (Chicago: University of Chicago, 1983), 208.

[26]Carlo Maria Santoro, *Diffidence and Ambition: The Intellectual Sources of U.S. Foreign Policy* (Boulder, CO: Westview, 1992), 34.

[27]McCormick, *America's Half-Century*, 36.

[28]Thomas Paterson, *On Every Front* (New York: W. W. Norton, 1979), 72.

[29]Walter LaFeber, *America, Russia, and the Cold War, 1945-1990*, (New York: Alfred A. Knopf, 1991), 9.

driven the war effort and postwar planning. The question was whether "the world as we know it" would survive.

As these representative quotations suggest, "the world as we know it" meant a world organized and guided by U.S.-led capitalist interests. U.S. Realist elites fought primarily not out of moral opposition to fascism, but out of fear for American interests. What they feared most was the loss of U.S. power and wealth, as historians such as Howard Zinn and Gabriel Kolko have shown. They fought not to make the world better but to prevent it from changing too radically to the benefit of others.

Both before and during the war, nonviolent activists adamantly expressed their beliefs that the fear of a loss of power and control were actually the driving forces of U. S. foreign policy. Although they were among the first to condemn the evils of fascism, they saw the conflict as a product of a world economic and political crisis in which no major power was totally innocent, and none could claim to embody pure virtue or the goodness of "civilization." Dorothy Detzer of the Women's International League for Peace and Freedom pointed out that the war could not "permanently settle conflicts or heal the wounds that brought them into being."[30] John Haynes Holmes (one of the first to spread Gandhi's teachings in the United States) contended that the United States and its allies were as responsible as Hitler for these wounds and hence for the war.[31] It was clear to these activists that all of the great powers had contributed to the conflicts by using violence to pursue their own national wealth and power.

Watching the war unfold from afar, Gandhi urged the Czechs, the Jews, and other victims of Nazism to respond with disciplined nonviolence. However he recognized the great difficulty of this response, since it "was only possible for those who had no fear of

---

[30]Howard Zinn, A People's History of the United States (New York: Harper & Row, 1991), 416.

[31]Robert Cooney and Helen Michalowski, The Power of the People (Philadelphia: New Society, 1987), 80.

death."[32] When his advice went unheeded, he concluded that "the victors employed the same means as the vanquished. There was only a question of degree."[33] So there was no reason to think that after the war they would act differently. A. J. Muste had seen this before the United States entered the war: "The problem after a war is with the victor. He thinks he has just proved that war and violence pay. Who will now teach him a lesson?"[34]

Muste was right. The Realist view that had fueled United States policy dictated that the victorious nation would have to prepare for a dangerous postwar world. It would have to assume that other nations would challenge its power, and it would naturally arm itself against those further threats. This was indeed what happened. After the war, most U.S. leaders spoke quite openly of their fear that the postwar chaos held the seeds of another world war, another depression, or both. When Dean Acheson, who would become the chief architect of U.S. Cold War policy, surveyed the world scene he saw not triumph but "social disintegration, political disintegration, and a great deal of economic disintegration."[35] By 1947 virtually every influential voice in the United States assumed that the Soviet Union intended to exploit this chaos for its own aggressive purposes. If not strenuously contained, it would follow in Hitler's footsteps and spread its "Red fascism." The goal of all policy was now "containment."

Years afterward Martin Luther King Jr., succinctly summed up the roots of the Cold War: "The nations have believed that greater armaments will cast out fear. But alas! They have produced greater fear."[36] "Russia fears America. America fears Russia."[37] There were Americans who recognized this tragic pattern at the time and spoke out against it. The best known was Henry Wallace, Truman's

---

[32]Judith M. Brown, *Gandhi: Prisoner of Hope* (New Haven: Yale University, 1989), 321-323.

[33]Iyer, *Essential Writings of Mahatma Gandhi*, 281.

[34]Zinn, *People's History of the United States*, 416.

[35]Paterson, *On Every Front*, 13.

[36]King, Martin Luther Jr., *A Testament of Hope* ed. James M. Washington (San Francisco: Harper & Row, 1986), 513.

[37]King, *Strength to Love*, 112.

Secretary of Commerce. He pointed out that the Soviet Union had good reason to fear the United States. America was "trying to put Russia in an impossible position by ganging up with Britain against her." Specifically, the United States was challenging Russia by ringing it with military bases. It would naturally appear to the Russians that the United States was planning to dominate it by either intimidation or another war.[38] Stalin's intention to rebuild his military was simply "taking up the challenge."[39] " 'Getting tough' never brought anything real and lasting—whether for schoolyard bullies or businessmen or world powers," Wallace said in a well publicized speech. "The tougher we get, the tougher the Russians will get."[40] A week later Wallace was fired by President Truman.

This analysis does not in any way exculpate the Stalinist regime. Gandhi himself recognized that "a country like Russia, which stood by the rights of its people, has been caught up in establishing an imperialistic state." And he added: "How tragic it is!"[41] But the tragedy was compounded by the failure, on both sides of the Iron Curtain, to recognize how much the fears that drove policy on one side mirrored the fears that drove policy on the other. The Cold War mindset in the United States blended anti-Soviet attitudes with a more generalized sense of fear that had already seized Realist policy-makers during World War II. This combination created what Daniel Yergin calls "the gospel of national security." "We must remember that 'national security' is not a given, not a fact, but a perception, a state of mind," Yergin writes. He describes the mindset of early Cold Warriors in words that are hauntingly predictive of later events such as the 1991 Gulf War: "Virtually every development in the world is perceived to be potentially crucial. An adverse turn of events anywhere endangers the United States. Problems in foreign relations are viewed as urgent and immediate threats. Thus, desirable foreign

---

[38]Daniel Yergin, *Shattered Peace* (Boston: Houghton Mifflin Co. 1977), 249.
[39]Michael Sherry, *In the Shadow of War* (New Haven: Yale University 1995), 126.
[40]Paterson, *On Every Front*, 105.
[41]Iyer, *Essential Writings of Mahatma Gandhi*, 268.

policy goals are translated into issues of national survival, and the range of threats becomes limitless."[42]

"National security" meant, in effect, the permanent ability to prevent global disaster. U.S. leaders called the antidote to their fear "stability." This notion became virtually the definition of peace. And, since it took on that role before U.S. leaders committed themselves to rivalry with the Soviets, it had a life of its own. Peace meant containing not just the Soviet Union but all sources of "instability." If fear of the Soviet Union had not been so widespread, some other embodiment of fear would have arisen.

In a state dominated by national security discourse, the traditional language of millennial hope for a better future was still employed. But now it was so deeply intertwined with apocalyptic fear that one could not voice hope without evoking fears of global disaster. Since fear was the dominant tone, expressions of hope actually ended up promoting and reinforcing fear. All talk of peace now evoked and reinforced images of threat, insecurity, and the absence of peace. So the wall of containment, seen as the key to peace, had to be built ever higher to protect against the ever growing feelings of insecurity that the policy of containment created. The difference between creating new order and protecting the old was largely blurred, for whatever creation occurred was in the service of protection. Above all, the new was intended to protect the old. The United States waged Cold War, as it waged World War II, to stave off the manifold changes it feared, for every change seemed to portend catastrophe. As always in Realism, fear of loss was the mainspring of every action.

The ideal of national security created "a warless world that is also a peaceless world."[43] The difference between war and peace was now hard to find. In other words, there was no difference between winning the war and keeping the peace. Since we could never escape from apocalyptic fear, there was no escape from violence and no possibility

---

[42]Yergin, *Shattered Peace*, 196; cf. Melvyn Leffler, *A Preponderance of Power* (Stanford, CA: Stanford University, 1994), 83, 87.

[43]Karl, *The Uneasy State*, 235.

of peace as Gandhi and King meant it—a truly nonviolent world in which love, not fear, is the basis for our actions. This genuine peace was ruled out in principle.

The World Today

American public discourse in the 1990s is built upon the premises forged by the Cold War. Policymakers still form their policies by identifying threats to be controlled and developing plans to control them. The threats are still articulated in terms of the pervasive evil of "instability," and the plans are still legitimated as attempts to bring stability and order. One obvious example is the potent appeal of George Bush's "New World Order" slogan during the Persian Gulf War.

Fear of nuclear danger persists on our national agenda because it serves us especially well. Nothing else can summon up, in such an immediate and vivid way, a concrete image of "the end of the world." When the Bush administration stirred up a war to implement the "New World Order," its most persuasive "evidence" of Iraq's "instability" presented to the public was the Iraqi nuclear program. The nuclear threat, now relegated to "rogue" or "pariah" states such as Iraq, Libya, and North Korea, can always be counted on to stir public fears of "instability" on an apocalyptic scale. The threat posed by such states is construed literally in public discourse. But as nonviolence history shows, it is the discourse that creates the threat, not vice versa. We must have such a threat to fear and control, for we know no other way to talk or think about our role in the world.

The fears of "the end of civilization," which were once concretized almost exclusively in nuclear weapons, have now been extended to a host of other fears that play a similar role: drugs, terrorism, immigration, and the like. All have come to symbolize that pervasive fear of disorder so fundamental to the Realist/apocalyptic synthesis. Consider two widely read and widely praised articles that claim to offer a new paradigm for the post-Cold War world, but actually exemplify the continuing power of this very old paradigm.

Samuel Huntington tells us that the next global war, if there is one, will result from "The Clash of Civilizations", because "the paramount axis of world politics will be the relations between 'the West and the Rest.'" The "Rest" are all the non-Western civilizations where, Huntington claims, Western ideals such as human rights and the rule of law—the foundations of our social order—"are least important." The clash of civilizations will "require the West to maintain the economic and military power necessary to protect its interests," The greatest danger today, he argues, is the "burgeoning alliance between the Islamic and the Confucian civilizations—"a renegades' mutual support pact, run by the [nuclear] proliferators and their backers." This alliance is building its arsenal of modern weapons, including nuclear and chemical weapons, and NATO must do more to defend against the "[p]otential threats and instability it creates. Huntington, a well-known theorist of "realism," urges the West to increase its ability to impose order on an increasingly restless world. He also urges the West to acquire a greater understanding of non-Western cultures.[44]

Another article often cited in the same breath as Huntington's, Robert Kaplan's "The Coming Anarchy," suggests that such efforts at understanding are futile. Kaplan contends that "criminal anarchy" will engulf the whole "third world" in the twenty-first century, as the world map becomes "an ever-mutating representation of chaos." The affluent in the "first" world, and a few lucky folks elsewhere, will still be able to live in "a home—order, that is, bespeaking dignity." But the vast majority will live in *"nature unchecked,"* "a rundown, crowded planet of skinhead Cossacks and *juju* warriors, influenced by the worst refuse of Western pop culture and ancient tribal hatreds." This will breed "a new kind of war." War "will have more in common with the struggles of primitive tribes than with large-scale conventional war."[45]

---

[44]Samuel Huntington, "The Clash of Civilizations," *Foreign Affairs* (Summer 1993): 41, 47, 49.

[45]Robert Kaplan, "The Coming Anarchy," *The Atlantic Monthly* (February 1994), 62, 63, 72, 75.

Nonviolence history teaches us that fearful images such as these, purveyed by "experts" and accepted as objective reality, have in the past led to the very wars the "experts" feared. Nonviolence history teaches us, too, that these fears are interpretations, not simply responses to "objective" dangers or "objective" events. Yet these fear-laden images persist, for understandable reasons. The underlying fear, as always, is fear of loss, fear of change, and ultimately fear for one's own self. We can avoid dealing with, or even acknowledging, this fear by immersing it in a great national fear. Of course, any fear is easier to bear when it is shared with so many others.

The goal of nonviolence history is to demonstrate how public discourse and public policy perpetuate our underlying fears, barring the way to positive peace. Positively, nonviolence history shows that we can attain a genuine feeling of personal security only through a radically new understanding of national security, based not on fear but on hope and love, believing with King

> that one day mankind will bow before the altars of God and be crowned triumphant over war and bloodshed, and nonviolent redemptive goodwill will proclaim the rule of the land. "And the lion and the lamb shall lie down together and every man shall sit under his own vine and fig tree and none shall be afraid."[46]

---

[46]Coretta Scott King, *The Words of Martin Luther King Jr.* (New York: Newmarket Press, 1983), 91.

THE FUTURE

6

ENGAGED BUDDHISM: GANDHI'S *AHIMSA* IN PRACTICE[1]

Sallie B. King

This is a fascinating study because we know from MacQueen's chapter how deeply Gandhi was affected by the story of the founder of Buddhism. Now Sallie King reveals how a form of Buddhism is in turn influenced by Gandhi's active nonviolence. She accomplishes this wonderfully by taking us from country to country to meet one heroic Buddhist after another. Not until King pointed it out did we really notice how "much peace leadership [is] coming from the Buddhist world in the twentieth century."

S*cene:* A refugee camp in Cambodia, 1978. In three and a half years and as a direct result of Khmer Rouge policies and brutality, an estimated two to three million Cambodians, one-third of the country's population, have died of starvation, disease, overwork, torture, and execution. Almost all of Cambodia's 3,600 Buddhist temples have been destroyed. Only 3,000 of the former 50,000 Buddhist monks have survived.

A man with shaven head, wearing a plain saffron robe, arrives at the refugee camp. He is a Buddhist monk. As he enters the camp, he

---

[1]The ideas in this article overlap slightly with Sallie B. King, "Buddhism and Social Engagement," in Paul O. Ingram and Sallie B. King, eds., *The Sound of Liberating Truth: Buddhist-Christian Dialogues in Honor of Frederick J. Streng* (Richmond, Surrey, England: Curzon Press, 1999).

distributes copies of the *Metta Sutta*, the Buddha's teachings on love and kindness, to these survivors of the Cambodian Holocaust. All around him people prostrate themselves on the ground, wailing loudly at the mere sight of this embodiment of decency and compassion. Over and over again, the monk repeats a verse of the Buddha's teachings:

> Hatred is never overcome by hatred;
> It is overcome by love.
> This is the eternal law.

The monk's name is Maha Ghosananda. He himself has lost his entire family in the Cambodian Holocaust. He is called the "Cambodian Gandhi."[2]

In 1996 Maha Ghosananda was nominated for the Nobel Peace Prize. He stands there with considerable Buddhist company. In recent years, the Nobel Peace Prize has been awarded to two Buddhist leaders: His Holiness the Dalai Lama of Tibet (in 1989) and the Burmese pro-democracy leader, Aung San Suu Kyi (in 1991). Many other Buddhist leaders also have been nominated for the Nobel Peace Prize in the last several years, including the Vietnamese Thich Nhat Hanh (nominated for the prize during the Vietnam War by Martin Luther King, Jr.), Sulak Sivaraksa of Thailand, and Dr. A. T. Ariyaratne of Sri Lanka. These prizes and nominations are evidence of the dramatic peace leadership being given in the contemporary world by Buddhist leaders, a leadership that is far out of proportion with the small number of Buddhists in the world.

Why is there so much peace leadership coming from the Buddhist world in the twentieth century? What are its origins and nature? And what are the connections between these Buddhist peace leaders,

---

[2]This scene is recounted in the "Editor's Introduction," in *Step by Step* by Maha Ghosananda, edited by Jane Sharada Mahoney and Philip Edmonds (Berkeley, CA: Parallax Press, 1992), 3-23. The quotation is from *Dhammapada* 1.5. See Yeshua Moser-Puangsuwan for a chapter in this volume specifically devoted to the mission of Maha Ghosananda.

Mahatma Gandhi, and Martin Luther King Jr? This chapter will address these questions.

Engaged Buddhism

Buddhism in the twentieth century shows the world a dramatic new face of social and political engagement: Engaged Buddhism. Throughout Buddhist Asia, as well as in the West, Buddhists are actively responding to the problems, crises and disasters confronting their societies in creative, nonviolent ways. Little known in the West, and only partially understood even in Asia, these many instances of Engaged Buddhism are changing the face not only of Buddhism, but of Buddhist societies as well. Let us briefly survey Engaged Buddhism.[3]

In India, B. R. Ambedkar converted to Buddhism as a social-political-spiritual act repudiating the social-political-spiritual entity of Hinduism and its caste system. Millions of untouchables followed him and today continue to construct a Buddhism that can be a vehicle to relieve the oppression of some of the most oppressed people on earth.

In Sri Lanka, A. T. Ariyaratne heads the largest non-government organization in Asia: the Sarvodaya Shramadana, a grassroots "development" movement that to "develop" impoverished Sri Lankan villages according to Buddhist values, rather than either capitalist or socialist values. "Development" as Sarvodaya espouses it is a holistic process that includes spiritual, psychological, and moral development along with the more traditional economic development, while traditional culture and the environment are cherished and protected. Sarvodaya Shramadana has also played a major role trying to bring about a peaceful resolution of the violent conflict between the Tamil minority and Sinhalese majority in Sri Lanka.

On 2 October 1996, the birth anniversary of Mahatma Gandhi, the government of India announced that the 1996 Mahatma Gandhi

---

[3]For more information, see Christopher S. Queen and Sallie B. King, eds., *Engaged Buddhism: Buddhist Liberation Movements in Asia* (Albany, NY: State University of New York, 1996).

Peace Prize would go to Ariyaratne, the founder and President of the Sarvodaya Shramadana. The award letter reads, in part, as follows:

> On the occasion of the 125th Birth Anniversary of Mahatma Gandhi on 2 October 1994, the Government of India instituted the Gandhi Peace Prize for Social, Economic, and Political Transformation through Non-violence, with the intention of encouraging the promotion of Gandhian values around the world. . . . The Prize is intended to honour a person who has worked selflessly for peace, non-violence and amelioration of human suffering, particularly of the less privileged sections of society, thereby contributing towards social justice and harmony.[4]

In the Tibetan Liberation Movement, the Dalai Lama and thousands of monks, nuns, and laypersons struggle nonviolently for the liberation of Tibet from Chinese control; protection of the Tibetan religion, culture, and ecology are stressed along with political relief. The Dalai Lama, deeply revered and loved by millions of Buddhists, is also the best-known and most widely respected Buddhist leader among non-Buddhists.

In Burma, as thousands of monks demonstrated in the streets, Aung San Suu Kyi led the pro-democracy party to electoral victory against the tyrannical military government of Burma. As a result, she was kept in house arrest for many years. Recently released, she continues to speak and work for dialogue, reconciliation, democracy, and humane values.

In Thailand, the Buddhist layman Sulak Sivaraksa works tirelessly to challenge the Thai government to become more humane and democratic. He also has organized dozens of organizations dedicated to ecological protection, protection of the traditional Siamese culture against Western encroachment, interreligious cooperation, relief for

---

[4]The first award, the 1995 Gandhi Peace Award, was given to the Honorable Julius Nyerare, the former President of Tanzania.

the poor, and the like. Also in Thailand many individual monks work creatively to help villagers burdened by debt and poverty and to protect the environment, which is being devastated by deforestation.

In the wake of the Cambodian Holocaust, Maha Ghosananda, the "Cambodian Gandhi," works to heal the wounds of the Holocaust among Cambodians both at home and abroad. A separate chapter in this book is devoted to him.

During the war in Vietnam, the Buddhist "Struggle Movement" or "Third Way" led a popular anti-war movement that refused to side with North or South, but sided with the people, all people who were party to the war and the devastation it produced. Since the war, Thich Nhat Hanh, one of the leaders of the anti-war effort, has emerged as one of the most important leaders of Engaged Buddhism. He has worked creatively to develop its theory and practice with workshops for Vietnam veterans, psychologists, and other helping professionals, artists, and families. In addition, he has worked with relief efforts for Vietnamese boat people and the impoverished in Vietnam today.

In Korea, the reformist Won Buddhism movement has a broad program of social and economic support for the needy, has built new educational, medical, and financial institutions, and stands out among Buddhist groups for having brought women to positions of leadership and real equality. Also in Korea, the Zen monk and activist Pom-ryune Sunim lives among the poor and leads a group dedicated to protecting the environment by bringing about a personal transformation of individuals' relationships with nature. He also leads efforts to meet the needs of the poor, in both North and South Korea.

In Taiwan, the Fo Kuang Shan, much like Won Buddhism, has brought women to positions of leadership and has built and peopled new educational and medical institutions. Also, Master Cheng Yen, founder of the Tzu Chi Foundation, is called the "Mother Teresa" of Taiwan for her work bringing medical care and compassion to the poorest and most needy there.

In Japan, the large Nichirenite movements, Rissho Kosei-Kai and Soka Gakkai, bring millions of lay Buddhists into daily acts of generosity, compassion and socially oriented self-help. Soka Gakkai is unique among Engaged Buddhists for having its own political party, the Komeito, which has succeeded in having a number of its members elected to the Japanese Diet. Also based in Japan is the Nipponzan Myohoji, an energetic anti-war and anti-nuclear group that leads marches and vigils throughout the world. Throughout the Buddhist world, Buddhist nuns and quasi-nuns organize to urge improvements in education, training, living conditions, and opportunities.

Finally, Western Buddhists, who are almost all laypersons, engage as Buddhists in every kind of nonviolent social activism imaginable: anti-war work, environmental protection, animal protection work, work with AIDS patients, work with the homeless. They also engage in more traditional forms of social engagement in ways consciously inspired by their Buddhist values, as parents, social workers, teachers, and artists.

Although not exhaustive, this survey gives an idea of the nature and scope of socially and politically Engaged Buddhism. Engaged Buddhism is found throughout the Buddhist world. In some countries (e.g., Sarvodaya Shramadana in Sri Lanka) it may well be making the most important contribution to the humane development of its society today. In other cases, e.g. isolated monks working in Thailand or Korea, it is much more limited in what it has been able to accomplish far. In some instances, Engaged Buddhism is heart-stoppingly heroic: In Tibet and Vietnam, people have suffered terrorism, imprisonment, torture, and death in some of the most heroic and widespread nonviolent responses to the violent and devastating conditions of war, foreign invasion, and state tyranny that the world has ever seen. In other cases, it is much more humble, for example, in its expression in ordinary, daily acts of kindness and generosity.

Sources, Resources, and Sparks

What values do these disparate movements hold in common? What are they based upon in Buddhism and what do they draw upon from other traditions? Why did they emerge now, in the last half of the twentieth century?

Buddhist Sources

Engaged Buddhism is a modern manifestation of the oldest and most basic values and beliefs of Buddhism, as expressed in the Four Noble Truths, the principles of compassion, selflessness, interdependence, karma, and the five lay precepts.

The Four Noble Truths summarize the basic teachings of the Buddha. Briefly stated, these are: (1) suffering (the problem that Buddhism addresses); (2) the cause of suffering (the analysis to help us understand the cause of suffering in order to remove it; in Buddhism the deep cause of suffering is understood to be attachment to self); (3) the cessation of suffering (the goal of Buddhism and the hope it offers); and (4) the Noble Eightfold path (the practical way to achieve the goal).[5] Buddhism, thus, is quite practical. Its reason for existing is to cure the ills or suffering of all beings who suffer; the Buddha is called the "great physician," come to cure the ills of all sentient beings.

Traditionally Buddhism has emphasized a deep, spiritual cure for suffering, since it sees the root of suffering in a fundamental human illness: attachment to self. Nevertheless, it has always been normative Buddhist practice to help the suffering in whatever practical way one could. The practice of compassion—practical care for the suffering—has always been the single most important practice of the Buddhist layperson. It is understood as a practice that not only directly helps the other, but also contributes to one's own spiritual development by promoting a focus on others that helps one to focus less on oneself. Thus a spiritual cure for suffering includes by definition not only meditation practices designed to make a person more selfless, but also practical acts of compassion that themselves nurture and reinforce active concern with the welfare of others.

---

[5]See the description of the Eightfold Path at the end of the next chapter.

Interdependence is another fundamental Buddhist principle that plays a major role in underpinning social concern. Buddhism is unusual among world religions in its claim that there is no self or soul in a human being, no separate core that constitutes a person's identity. Without a self or soul, Buddhism says that a human being is the product of many things, constantly changing moment by moment. Thus "I" am the air I breathe in, the food I eat, the sensations I feel, the experiences of seeing, hearing, tasting, smelling, and touching that I perceive, the ideas I think, the emotions I feel. As a consequence, it is clear that "I" cannot be separated from my physical, social, and cultural environment. This is what Buddhists mean by "interdependence." As Thich Nhat Hanh, an Engaged Buddhist leader, puts it: the tree is made up of non-tree parts—the sun, the rain, the soil. Similarly, "I" am made up of "non-me" parts—the sun, the air, the food I have eaten, the books I have read, the places I have visited, my family, my friends, my society and government, and ultimately the world. If these things were not there, or were different, I would not be here, or would be different. I cannot be separated from them. Consequently, my natural and healthy concern for my own well-being cannot be separated from a natural and healthy concern for the well-being of others, who are part of me, and of whom I am a part. When others are threatened, I am threatened. When others are suffering, I am suffering. As Thich Nhat Hanh said during the war in Vietnam, the suffering caused the Vietnamese people by the bombing and the oppression "hurts us too much. We have to react."[6] Thus the monks and nuns had to come out of the monasteries and into the villages and cities to help prevent and heal the suffering that all shared.

The idea of karma, the law of cause and effect, also plays a major role in Buddhist social activism. According to Buddhism (and Hinduism), every action one performs in thought, word, or deed, sows a seed that must sometime in the future come to fruition. A hateful

[6]Thich Nhat Hanh in Daniel Berrigan and Thich Nhat Hanh, *The Raft is Not the Shore: Conversations Toward a Buddhist/Christian Awareness* (Boston: Beacon, 1975), 99.

act will bring a hateful consequence, a loving act, a loving conse-quence. This is a law of the universe to which there are no excep-tions; there is no escaping the consequences of one's acts once one has done them. The *Dhammapada*, a text attributed to the Buddha, gives a particularly pertinent instance of this law: "Hatred is never overcome by hatred; it is overcome by love. This is the eternal law."[7]

Think Middle East; think ex-Yugoslavia. Group A hits Group B; when opportunity presents itself, Group B hits back. This angers Group A, which retaliates by hitting Group B again. Group B then seeks revenge. Action causes reaction. The cycle never ends as long as it is played out on that level. The only way to break the cycle is to introduce a radically new factor, called here "love." Think of Mahatma Gandhi's controlled, nonviolent response to British tyranny; think of the handshake between Itzhak Rabin and Yasser Arafat. Of course, one act, however heroic, cannot undo the karmic weight of years of hatred and violence. It takes acts of equal magni-tude to cancel each other.

There is no doubt that this principle plays a role in Engaged Buddhism, sometimes in silent but crucial ways. A few years ago, Dith Pran, the subject of "The Killing Fields" (the film about the Cambo-dian Holocaust) visited my campus. He claimed that the Cambodian people do not want revenge upon the Khmer Rouge, the brutal oppressors, torturers, and killers of millions of Cambodians. I could scarcely believe this and pressed him on this point. He explained: 'The Cambodian people do not want revenge because they do not want to suffer anymore. They have suffered enough.'[8] That explained it. That Cambodia is a nation of saints was more than I could believe. But that Cambodians, raised on the *Dhammapada*, deeply understood that *for their own good* they had to restrain their anger. They under-stood that to stop the cycle of killing they had to refuse to kill those who had killed—this I could believe. They know that if they strike

---

[7]*Dhammapada*, 1.5.

[8]Dith Pran, inexact quote in a comment to the author, at James Madison University, Harrisonburg, Virginia, 1995.

back at the Khmer Rouge they are only making inevitable the day when the Khmer Rouge or their descendants will once again strike back. Of course, they want the Khmer Rouge to be disarmed and their power to be eliminated by an effective government. But they do not want to act on their anger; they do not want to seek revenge—so that they themselves will not suffer anymore.

Finally, the five lay precepts, going back to the earliest days of Buddhism, represent the fundamental Buddhist ethical posture, the ethical minimum for a Buddhist. The first precept is *ahimsa*: nonharmfulness to any being capable of experiencing suffering. This precept, in fact, is the substance of the other four precepts: no stealing, no lying, no sexual misconduct, no ingesting of intoxicants. These are all aspects of the fundamental concern to avoid causing suffering to any sentient being, oneself or others. The spirit of this ethic permeates contemporary Engaged Buddhism.

Engaged Buddhists: Gandhi and Martin Luther King Jr.

With one exception, which will be discussed shortly, Engaged Buddhists frequently cite Mahatma Gandhi as a major inspiration. The most direct link between Gandhi and Engaged Buddhists is found in Sarvodaya Shramadana and its founder, A. T. Ariyaratne. The name "Sarvodaya" itself is taken from the Gandhian movement, which Ariyaratne studied in person with Gandhi's successor, Vinoba Bhave.[9] George Bond cites three important influences on the formation of the Sri Lankan movement that Ariyaratne gleaned from his studies with Vinoba: the idea of "selfless service for humanity as the highest form of religious practice"; the goal of working for a new, nonviolent social order; and the "focus on the village as the heart of this new social-economic-religious order."[10] These have remained central principles in Sri Lankan Sarvodaya to this day.

---

[9] I take my information on the relationship between Ariyaratne and Gandhian thought from George D. Bond, "A. T. Ariyaratne and the Sarvodaya Shramadana Movement." In *Engaged Buddhism*, 121-146.

[10] Ibid., 122-123.

Ariyaratne's development of the Sri Lankan movement was by no means a simple copying of the Gandhi model, however. Clearly, Ariyaratne went to India already committed to the idea of selfless service for humanity through nonviolent means on the basis of his own Buddhist values. Having digested his experience in India, Ariyaratne reinterpreted the term "sarvodaya" itself. While Gandhi had explained it as the "welfare or uplift of all," Ariyaratne explains the term in his movement as meaning the "awakening of all."[11] (This "awakening" includes such modern social goals as the awakening of an impoverished village to its needs and its ability to meet them, as well as the traditional Buddhist goal of spiritual awakening.) Of course, the many years of experimentation and work in Sri Lanka have themselves shaped the movement in ways particularly suitable to the Sri Lankan culture. For example, Buddhist monks provide a very visible part of the labor and leadership of the movement, a factor that legitimizes it in the eyes of traditionally-minded people. In short, while the foundations of the Sarvodaya Shramadana movement of Sri Lanka rest securely in Ariyaratne's Buddhist principles, a key inspiration and a concrete direction was indicated by the Gandhian movement in India.

The Dalai Lama is another socially Engaged Buddhist who acknowledges the inspiration Gandhi represents on the basis of their shared values, in this case, nonviolence. The Dalai Lama is leading a nonviolent movement for Tibetan national sovereignty and religious freedom in a struggle with the Chinese, who overthrew the Dalai Lama's government in 1959. One of the most important values that the Dalai Lama and the Tibetan Liberation Movement represent is nonviolence, nonviolence even in the face of foreign invasion, loss of sovereignty, the death of perhaps one million Tibetans, the devastation of the Tibetan land, the suppression of native religion and culture, the loss of basic human rights, and a policy of cultural genocide. In this policy the Tibetan people are being made a minority

---

[11]George D. Bond, *The Buddhist Revival in Sri Lanka: Religious Tradition, Reinterpretation and Response* (Columbia: South Carolina), 243-244.

in their own country through the transfer of large numbers of Han Chinese into Tibet. Short of killing everyone, it is difficult to imagine what more the Chinese could do to wipe out the Tibetans as a people.

Most people think of nonviolence as something to be embraced "as much as possible"; one tries to find a nonviolent resolution, but if that effort fails, and the harm or injustice one faces is severe, then violence may be used as a last resort. The Dalai Lama and the movement he leads represent a radically different attitude towards nonviolence. Even in the face of the greatest ills one can imagine, he remains staunchly committed to nonviolence, while remaining equally committed to changing the situation. Clearly, with these shared basic values, Gandhi must be an inspiration for the Dalai Lama. This is not to say that he learned these values from Gandhi; the Dalai Lama is regarded by the faithful as the incarnation of Avalokitesvara, the *bodhisattva* of compassion: if he does not exemplify nonviolence, who ever will?

In his autobiography, the Dalai Lama speaks of his thoughts upon visiting Rajghat, the site of Gandhi's cremation:

> It was a calm and beautiful spot and I felt very grateful to be there, the guest of a people who, like mine, had endured foreign domination; grateful also to be in the country that had adopted *Ahimsa*, the Mahatma's doctrine of non-violence. As I stood praying, I experienced simultaneously great sadness at not being able to meet Gandhi in person and great joy at the magnificent example of his life. To me he was—and is—the consummate politician, a man who put his belief in altruism above any personal considerations. I was convinced too that his devotion to the cause of non-violence was the only way to conduct politics.[12]

---

[12]The Dalai Lama, *Freedom in Exile*. Cited by Jose Ignacio Cabezon, "Buddhist Principles in the Tibetan Liberation Movement," in *Engaged Buddhism*, 305. The analysis that follows is also guided by Cabezon's understanding.

The particular sources of the Dalai Lama's commitment to a politics of nonviolence are traditional Buddhist principles. Much like the Cambodians, he recognizes that for practical reasons, nonviolence is the best approach:

> Anger, jealousy, impatience and hatred are the real trouble-makers; with them problems cannot be solved. Though one may have temporary success, ultimately one's hatred or anger will create further difficulties. With anger all actions are swift. When we face problems with compassion, sincerely and with good motivation, it may take longer, but ultimately the solution is better, for there is far less chance of creating a new problem.[13]

For practical reasons, to ensure a long-lasting resolution a win-win outcome is best. Thus feelings of hostility towards the "enemy" and the desire for victory over the other are not helpful. In this context, the Dalai Lama urges us to overturn our ordinary way of regarding the enemy and look upon him or her as our friend.

> Only when someone criticizes and exposes our faults are we able to discover our problems and confront them. Thus is our enemy our greatest friend. He provides us with the needed test of inner strength, tolerance and respect for others. Instead of feeling anger toward this person one should respect him and be grateful.[14]

A final Engaged Buddhist whom we may mention as inspired by Gandhi is Thich Nhat Hanh, an ideological leader of the Buddhist anti-war movement during the war in Vietnam. Referring to some of the activist monks, he wrote:

---

[13]Ibid., 305.
[14]Ibid.

I believe with all my heart . . . that the monks . . . did not aim at the death of the oppressors but only at a change in their policy. Their enemies are not man, they are intolerance, dictatorship, cupidity, hatred, and discrimination which lie within the heart of man. . . . If we kill man, with whom shall we live?[15]

This last line became the refrain of a popular anti-war song in Vietnam during the war.

Note how much this perspective resembles Gandhi's principle "hate the deed, not the doer." This is particularly striking as the two views are based upon opposite views of human being: Gandhi's belief in the Atman within each individual person and Nhat Hanh's adherence to *anatman*, the very lack of such a thing. Both views remove the possibility of branding a person as "evil," which might justify making the person the target of anger or revenge, while they open the door to social activism (including educational efforts) by pointing at the social and attitudinal causes of violence and injustice as the appropriate target of our intervention.

Nhat Hanh, like the Dalai Lama, is a great admirer of Gandhi. He admits that at first he admired Gandhi for his success, which he feels is a superficial way to open to another's influence.[16] Later that admiration deepened into an admiration of the principled nonviolence itself.

Not only was Nhat Hanh inspired by Mahatma Gandhi, he was also strongly connected with Martin Luther King Jr. In 1966, the two met and had a long conversation about the war in Vietnam. Afterwards, they held a joint news conference in which King, for the first time, publicly repudiated the war, speaking of the similarity he saw between the Vietnamese Buddhist peace movement and the American civil rights movement. King, himself a Nobel Peace Prize laureate,

---

[15]Thich Nhat Hanh quoted in "Visit from a Buddhist Monk," *Fellowship: The Magazine of the Fellowship of Reconciliation* Vol. 32, No. 7 (1966), 3.

[16]Thich Nhat Hanh, quoted in Catherine Ingram, *In the Footsteps of Gandhi: Conversations with Spiritual Social Activists* (Berkeley: Parallax Press, 1990), 89.

nominated Nhat Hanh for the same award in 1967, saying, "I do not personally know of anyone more worthy of the Nobel Peace Prize than this gentle Buddhist monks from Vietnam."[17] Nhat Hanh has said of Martin Luther King: "I was . . . very influenced by his understanding of nonviolence, but it was not through words. His enthusiasm, his sincerity, his presence made me believe in the path of nonviolent action." He told him, "You know, Martin, in Vietnam they consider you a bodhisattva."[18] (A bodhisattva is an "enlightenment being," a kind of saint who incarnates wisdom and compassion.) Theirs was a strong relationship cut off in its infancy.

In contrast, there is one group of Engaged Buddhists who do not speak fondly of any inspiration given them by Gandhi: the ex-Untouchables. The first instance of Engaged Buddhism occurred in India, contemporaneously with the birth of the newly independent nation, and led by one of its founding fathers: B. R. Ambedkar. Ambedkar began life as a Hindu Untouchable, a person regarded as so low within the Hindu caste system and so impure that his mere touch could "pollute" the person touched. Many millions of other Untouchables were his peers. After receiving a British and American education, Ambedkar incredibly rose to the highest circles of influence in the newly forming nation as the principal author of the Indian Constitution and a cabinet minister in the new government. These were not his only great contributions.

Upon his return from abroad and until the end of his life, Ambedkar was a spokesman for the Untouchables and a fiery leader on their behalf. He was not satisfied with Gandhi's espousal of the Untouchable cause, his renaming of the Untouchables as the "Harijan," the children of God, nor the legal outlawing of Untouchability in the new nation. Ambedkar was convinced that only the elimination of the caste system as such would liberate the "low-born" of Hindu society and make India a just society. While they were

---

[17]Ibid., 78.
[18]Ibid., 87.

filled with compassion for the condition of the Untouchables, who lived in unspeakable poverty, ignorance and disease, Gandhi and his supporters were not in favor of bringing the entire caste system per se to an end.

Dissatisfied with the reforms espoused by Gandhi and the Congress and disappointed by the results of his own efforts to directly reform Hindu society, Hinduism itself finally became repulsive to Ambedkar, who vowed, "I will not die a Hindu." After decades spent researching the religions of the world, and just weeks before his death, Ambedkar converted to Buddhism in a public ceremony and was joined in the conversion by about a half million other "Untouchables." Many millions have followed since. To Ambedkar's followers, conversion is a social and political act: à renunciation of an utterly unjust and unreformable social system. They also see it as a claiming of human dignity and human rights. Despite his strenuous efforts to work on their behalf, these "new Buddhists" do not feel inspired or encouraged by Gandhi, whom they see as a powerful man who refused to take the action they needed and renounce the cause of their suffering: the caste system.

Tools

Some people think that Engaged Buddhism is not really Buddhism, or that it is just the product of an undue Western influence that has caused Buddhism to lose its own true nature in its activist engagement with social issues.

I have tried to show above that Engaged Buddhism is fundamentally a modern expression of traditional Buddhist values and principles. This, I believe, is its most important source. But there is no denying a certain amount of Western influence in Engaged Buddhism. As we have seen, Mahatma Gandhi had a substantial influence on Engaged Buddhism and he was deeply influenced by the West himself. Like Gandhi, several Engaged Buddhist leaders spent some years living in the West receiving a Western education (Ambedkar, Thich Nhat Hanh, Aung San Suu Kyi, Sulak Sivaraksa) and many others are well-educated in Western thought and have extensive personal contacts with Western leaders. In addition, one can see in the speeches and writings of these leaders the use of modern social, economic, psychological, and political analysis of largely Western liberal origin. For example, groups working with poverty (Sarvodaya Shramadana, Ambedkarite groups) are keenly aware of the psychology and sociology of poverty and design holistic programs to address these multi-faceted ills. Sulak Sivaraksa and Thich Nhat Hanh are keenly aware of institutional structures of violence, of ideological sources of violence, of economic colonialism and the like, and address these vast challenges in their efforts to bring into being a less violent and more humane world.

These forms of analysis are important elements in Engaged Buddhism. But they should be seen as tools consciously chosen by intelligent and well-educated people on the basis of their own, distinct, Buddhist values. The basic impulse of Engaged Buddhism—the urge to prevent and assuage suffering—is deeply rooted in traditional Buddhist spirituality and values. The use of Western forms of analysis as a tool should not be regarded as undue Western influence on Buddhism since the spirit and values of Engaged Buddhism—compassion—remain unchanged.

Historical Necessity

Throughout Buddhism's 2500-year history, it was by no means unusual for individual monks to serve as advisors to rulers and in other ways to be on close terms with them. Moreover, as we have seen, it has always been fundamental to Buddhism to be concerned about and to actively respond to suffering. What is new in Engaged Buddhism is thus not its concern with suffering or even its involvement in issues of governing. What is new is its ability to galvanize millions into mass movements capable of (1) healing suffering and building peace (in Cambodia and throughout East Asia); (2) seriously challenging the hold on power of the rulers (in Tibet and Burma) and even of determining who must fall and who might rise to rule (in

Vietnam); and (3) aspiring to fundamentally transform the social, economic, cultural, and psychological institutions of their societies as a whole (in India and Sri Lanka). Thus its newness is a matter of scale (vastly expanded) and power (tremendously strengthened).

While Engaged Buddhism may be understood as a natural manifestation of Buddhist spirituality and principles, it must be asked why, if it is so harmonious with ancient Buddhist principles, it has not emerged until the twentieth century. The answer is easy: for the most part, the crises of the twentieth century made it a necessity. The twentieth century has been hard on Buddhist Asia, which has suffered genocide (Cambodia), modern warfare (Japan, Vietnam, Southeast Asia), the aftermath of colonialism (Sri Lanka in particular), foreign invasion and cultural genocide (Tibet), repressive governments (Burma, Thailand), and the eco-crisis (throughout Asia). In addition, the chronic conditions of sexism and extreme classism (in India's caste system) have been seen in Asia, as well as the West, in a new light in the twentieth century. Given the compassion and feelings of interconnection that are hallmarks of Buddhist spirituality, suffering of this magnitude could not fail to produce a Buddhist response.

Conclusion

Gandhi's activist *ahimsa* and Engaged Buddhism are close spiritual cousins. Though the religions—Hinduism and *Buddhism—are* different, many of the principles seem to be the same. To be sure, there are some differences as well, differences that parallel the differences between Hinduism and Buddhism. While Gandhi lived an ascetic life, Engaged Buddhists espouse mindfulness and self-discipline. While Gandhi spoke frequently of God as Truth, Engaged Buddhists eschew theistic language and speak instead of the Dharma (Truth or Reality). The similarities, however, run deeper.

In both Gandhi and Engaged Buddhism, there is an uncompromising adherence to nonviolence as a sacred principle, a means already constitutive of the end. In both, the deepest motivation seems to be a fundamental urge to walk the holy path that can only manifest itself in compassionate action to relieve the suffering of all who suffer. In both, selflessness is seen as essential and is generated both by such personal practices as meditation and ethical self-discipline and by the life of action on behalf of others. Each challenges its own religious tradition to reconceive the spiritual life as one that does not require withdrawal from the world, but on the contrary, the highest goals of which may be realized by a life of selfless action. Each knows that love does not point to passivity, but on the contrary to a life of engagement that actively works to overcome those things in the world that cause misery, whether they be spiritual, psychological, political, economic, or social. Each combines love with fearlessness, sometimes to the point of death.

The name of Mahatma Gandhi is immortal as the great pioneer of this path of spiritual social activism. Today Engaged Buddhists, not only the leadership but also many who participate in quieter ways, have grasped the torch that he offered to humankind and are holding it high.

7

THE BUDDHA IN THE BATTLEFIELD: MAHA GHOSANANDA BHIKKHU AND THE DHAMMAYIETRA ARMY OF PEACE

Yeshua Moser-Puangsuwan

We have already discussed the power and significance of walking in nonviolence. In this essay Moser-Puangsuwan gives us an insider's look at a special walk, called a Dhammayietra, which embodies Cambodia's ongoing struggle for peace. In 1997, with Cambodia in the midst of a violent civil war, Maha Ghosananda and his followers still walked on Dhammayietra VI. The walk called for an end to domestic violence against women, revealing the fundamental association between hearing the voices of women and advancing the cause of nonviolence. First nominated for the Nobel Peace Prize in 1994, Maha Ghosananda was awarded the prestigious Niwano Peace Prize on May 9, 1998 in Tokyo. In the third millennium, he vows to continue the Dhammayietras "until we have peace."

> Hatred never ceases by hatred.
> Violence never ceases by violence.
> This is eternal law.
> —The Buddha[1]

---

[1] *The Dhammapada*. This is a collection of aphorisms (lt. Words of the Truth) from the long discourses of the Buddha, put together long after his death by the monastic order for simple and easy understanding of Buddhist Doctrine. This is the 5th of 423. Several verses are given throughout this article, from different translations.

T hree days before the fall of Saigon in 1975, a little known guerrilla force from the rural northeast of Cambodia swept into Phnom Penh from the jungles to claim a military victory over the central government. Called the Khmer Rouge, they had grown in strength in direct reaction to the US aerial bombing and land invasion of Cambodia from Vietnam, and the CIA-engineered overthrow of a neutral government. These victorious guerrilla fighters were greeted by the population of the capital who had hope that this was the final scene in their recent years of intense civil war, and that there would again be peace in their homeland. Instead a new and shadowy regime, known only as Angka (the organization) ordered the evacuation of all major cities in the opening step of its campaign to create a perfect proletarian state of rural workers. This vast social experiment, one of the most ambitious of its kind since the Cultural Revolution in China or the population displacements ordered by Stalin in the former USSR, resulted in the direct deaths through starvation or extra-judicial execution of between one to three million people, and a civil war that continues to today.[2]

As a result, an entire generation of men have been armed or sent into combat. Weapons are readily available throughout the country, and readily used. Weapons of war are often engaged to settle personal, marital, and business disputes. According to the Project on Domestic Violence in Phnom Penh, which has looked into the effects of the Khmer Rouge conditioning on Cambodian society today, "Violence became an integral part of the social order. Many were ordered to

---

[2]The political history of Cambodia is one of the richest in SE Asia and far beyond the scope of this manuscript to present. The Kingdom of Ankor was one of the first great civilizations in the lands south of China. It was saved from oblivion as a French colony in Indochina, although significantly smaller in size. For recent political history see: W. Shawcross: *Sideshow: Kissinger, Nixon and the Destruction of Cambodia* (London, UK: Deutsch, 1979) and W. Shawcross: *Quality of Mercy: Cambodia, Holocaust, and Modern Conscience* (London, UK: Deutsch, 1984) also N. Chanda: *Brother Enemy: The War After the War* (New York, NY: Collier Books, 1986) and D. Chandler: *Brother Number One: A Political Biography of Pol Pot* (Boulder, CO: Westview Press, 1992).

perpetrate violence while others volunteered. Violence was a learned and common response to a wrong or perceived wrong." This has created individuals who must be alert to enemies at all times and prepared to retaliate, even in the most trivial of circumstances.[3]

> Happiness follows a good action
> Like the wheel of a cart follows the Ox.
> – The Buddha[4]

Maha Ghosananda Bhikkhu is a humble and elderly Buddhist monk. He speaks little about himself and his early life. We know he was born in the early 1920s into a farming family in Takeo, a rural southern province of Cambodia. He entered a local monastery as a Samanera at the age of ten for several years of study and decided to take full ordination as a Buddhist monk on coming of age in 1943. Today, he is recognized as a living link to Khmer Buddhism from before the war years, and is revered throughout Cambodia as a voice of compassion and wisdom amidst the chaos that otherwise dominate the daily lives of the Cambodian people.

He will usually be found surrounded by a crowd of several hundred people who will come to hear his moral and spiritual teachings. Although all immediate members of Ghosananda's family "disappeared" under rule of the Khmer Rouge regime, today if asked how to respond to the Khmer Rouge, his being emanates compassion:

Noble minded or good people are embraced spontaneously by our love, but the unwholesome-minded must be included because they are the ones who need loving kindness the most. In many of them, the seed of goodness may have died because warmth was lacking for its growth. It perished from coldness in a world without compassion. Gandhi said "No one is

---

[3]*Plates in a Basket Will Rattle* (P.A.D.V., Phnom Penh) see particularly Part II, "Causes and Excuses."

[4]See note 1.

beyond redemption." I do not question that loving one's oppressors—Cambodians loving the Khmer Rouge—may be the most difficult attitude to achieve. But it is the law of the universe that retaliation, hatred, and revenge only continue the cycle and never stop it.[5]

Buddhism focuses on the study of the mind as a path to liberation from the causes of suffering. It teaches that our own suffering and the suffering of others is completely linked and interdependent. The center of Buddhist ethics is the Noble Eightfold Path, and the Five Precepts by which Buddhists live. The Eightfold Path includes Right Livelihood, namely a livelihood that does not cause suffering to ourselves and others. Over 2,500 years ago the Buddha listed as unskillful livelihoods the manufacture and sale of arms or any occupation, such as being a soldier or butcher, that involves taking the lives of sentient beings. The first of the Five Precepts is to avoid killing.

For his part, Maha Ghosananda has focused his teaching of peace and peacemaking directly on these basic Buddhist tenets. During a demonstration against the ongoing war he said:

All of us should observe the five precepts . . . but just keep one for now, that's enough. Just stop killing one another. If each one of us just stops killing, we will stop the war. It starts from one person . . . but it is not enough just to not kill, we have to tell everyone else around us so that it will spread. When you go home remind your family that everyone wants to live. Tell your husbands who are soldiers on this side in town, and your relatives who are soldiers on that side, in the forest, as well.[6]

---

[5]Maha Ghosananda, *Step by Step: Meditations on Wisdom and Compassion* (San Francisco, CA.: Parallax Press, 1991).

[6]Bernstein, Moser, "We Shall Cultivate Peace" *Seeds of Peace*, Sept. 1995.

As Ghosananda re-entered the world after a time of intensive meditation practice, his actions demonstrated the well known Buddhist Bodhisattva Vow: To Save All Beings from Suffering—in Cambodia and the Whole World. Just as Ghosananda left his quiet solitude, the first refugees from the darkness of the Khmer Rouge time began to spill into Thailand and create vast refugee camps. Maha Ghosananda visited them immediately, helping to found temples in the camps, regardless of which political faction controlled it. He also began to travel farther abroad, ministering to the spiritual needs of Cambodian refugees who had resettled in France, Australia and North America.

After his extensive service to Cambodian refugees, Ghosananda's understanding that only the practice of moral virtue can overcome dark politics in the world led him to co-found the Peace Council with other respected religious and social leaders such as the Dalai Lama, Bishop Desmond Tutu, and Oscar Arias in 1994.[7] Peace Councilors are not concerned with reconciling creed or theology, but instead concentrate their attentions on the world's agonies: war, violence, pollution, poverty, divisiveness, disregard for justice, aggression and hatred in the name of religion, social decay, environmental disasters, and despair. Although linking with religious peacemakers across the globe, Maha Ghosananda's most active work remains focused on his homeland, of which the most visible manifestation has been the mass walks for peace and reconciliation that have crossed Cambodia, step by step.

The Dhammayietras[8]

The collapse of the Cold War also meant a collapse of will for the political sponsors of war in Cambodia, and brought about the

---

[7]From the founding statement of the Peace Council: "[we] can work together to build bridges among all people, no matter how grave the differences may seem. With so much suffering on this Earth, the Peace council can help to bring our message of nonviolence, compassion and universal responsibility to people everywhere." —Maha Ghosananda

[8]Dhamma (truth) Yietra (pilgrimage or going on foot): The Pilgrimage of Truth.

conditions for talks on a "comprehensive political settlement." The superpowers now had need to demonstrate their concern for the suffering they had funded in Cambodia (and avoid any suit of war reparations). Within Cambodia, the primary combatants[9] were in a military stalemate and protracted conflict in a domestically unsustainable war lay on the horizon. After several pre-conferences that set conditions, all fighting factions in Cambodia and their political sponsors signed the Paris Peace Accords for a comprehensive political settlement in Cambodia. This laid the basis for the largest United Nations (U. N.) intervention in any country prior to that time. In fact, the U. N. was to become a government of a country by taking over key government ministries and disarming and reincorporating soldiers of various factions into civil society. The United Nations High Commission on Refugees (UNHCR) was to arrange the return of all refugees living in camps in neighboring countries (predominantly Thailand) to available lands within the country.[10]

Throughout the process of political negotiations and bargaining in the late 80s and early 90s, Maha Ghosananda acted to keep the focus on compassion for the suffering of the ordinary Cambodian. Then, as factional leaders met for the peace talks that led to the Peace Accords in Jakarta, Indonesia in 1988, Maha Ghosananda laid the groundwork for the events that have now become world famous, the Dhammayietra Walks for Peace and Reconciliation in Cambodia. He astonished the leaders of the four armed factions by announcing that he was launching a "fifth army—an Army of Peace." The simple monk asserted that it would be "an army absolutely without guns or

---

[9]The Four Factions involved in armed struggle in Cambodia were: The State of Cambodia (SOC), created under Vietnamese occupation in 1980; The Khmer Rouge (also DK or Democratic Kampuchea); The Royalist Sihanouk faction, known by their acronym in French-FUNCINPEC; and the KPNLF, a non-Communist group receiving US aid. The latter three were forced into an uneasy coalition called the Khmer Seri (Free Khmer) by international sponsors (led by China and the US) who were too embarrassed to be seen aiding only the Khmer Rouge. The DK however were the successful military force against the SOC.

[10]Yeshua Moser-Puangsuwan, "A UN Peacekeeping in Cambodia: Whose Needs Were Met?," *Pacifica Review* 7 (1995).

partisan politics, an army of reconciliation with so much courage that it turns away violence, an army dedicated wholly to peace and to the end of suffering." When asked by a reporter what the army of reconciliation might use for ammunition, Ghosananda replied, "Bullets of loving-kindness."

As the date for United Nations involvement in Cambodia, and the return of Cambodian refugees from Thailand drew near, fears about repatriation became widespread through the hundreds of thousands of refugees living on the Khmer/Thai border. Maha Ghosananda, with the help of the Coalition of Peace and Reconciliation,[11] mobilized his Fifth Army: the *Dhammayietra for Peace and Reconciliation in Cambodia,* intending to combat the peoples' fear by a peace walk through Cambodia to the capital city of Phnom Penh. The prevailing fear among Cambodians was of encountering the enemy, returning Cambodians). In response, the Dhamma- yietra proposed humanizing the opponent.

The Dhammayietra was opposed by political powers at all levels. First, Thailand refused to allow the refugee walkers to return to their camps and share their experience after the pilgrimage (an integral part of the process of the walk). Thai authorities only wanted them to go home and never return. Then the UNHCR did not want to surrender its authority over the refugees, even though joining the event was absolutely voluntary. So the UNHCR issued a threat that any refugee who joined the walk would lose all their privileges under the United Nations program. Finally the government in Phnom Penh, accustomed to absolute control over everything in the country, could not accept anything independently organized.

Maha Ghosananda nevertheless proclaimed that the walk would go on, and would advance over obstacles step by step. A small

---

[11]The Coalition for Peace and Reconciliation was founded in 1989 by the venerable Yos Hut and Brother Bob Maat S.J., both of whom had worked for the UN in the Cambodian refugee camps on the Thai border. They were disturbed to see how the UN was being manipulated by Security Council members and Thailand into supporting a civil war, and founded an organization to give a voice against the exploitation of the refugees by powers with other agendas than peace and reconciliation.

contingent of Buddhists from surrounding countries came to help, and sacred Bodhi trees from Sri Lanka were sent to be planted along the walk route. Two days before the walk was to begin two Japanese monks of the Nipponzan Myohoji Buddhist order began chanting in front of the regional Thai military command office, vowing not to leave until permission for the walk to proceed was granted. Within hours the Thai authorities granted permission to proceed. On the day the walk was to begin, nothing had yet been heard from the Cambodian capital. Thus the walk left on schedule with over a hundred refugees from several border camps who remained committed to the Dhammayietra regardless of the UNHCRs threat of loss of benefits. At the Thai-Cambodian border, the immigration authorities made no effort to hinder the group from crossing, and for many refugees, a journey home was about to begin.

From the very beginning this first walk by the Army of Peace began to have an effect. Unforeseen and unplanned for, walkers from the refugee camps began finding family members living in Cambodia whom they did not know were still living, from whom they had been separated for ten, fifteen, or twenty years. Walkers from the refugee camps in Thailand would briefly leave the walk for a house on the side of the road, or set out once the Dhammayietra arrived in a town, only to reappear hours later, beaming. An older woman returned to the Dhammayietra one morning in tears exclaiming, "I found my daughter! After twenty years! Now *she* has a daughter! And she told me my other daughter is alive! She lives near Phnom Penh and I can see her too when we get there." The following day another walker ran up and announced to the walk excitedly, "I just went to visit my uncle who I knew lived in this village, and there in his house was my father! I hadn't seen him in twelve years! Oh, how lucky I am!" That evening while some of the walkers were sitting under a tree where they would sleep another walker returned with two young boys. "Please meet my sons. They are twins. Thirteen years old! I last saw them when they were only twenty days old. Babies. We were forced apart by the war and now they don't know me." Deep reconciliation and re-connection were the result of the Army of Peace. This reconciliation became such a daily occurrence that walkers began renaming the walk Dhamma Teektong or True Contact.[12]

The Army of Peace had begun to heal the wounds of war. That healing also took symbolic form in the water blessing. The throwing of water is traditional during Khmer New Years festivities that were occurring at the beginning of the walk, and it is expected from the ordained clergy at times of auspicious rites such as weddings. However water blessing was sustained throughout the month of the walk, with people coming out along the roadside with buckets of water seeking the walkers' blessing by asking the walkers to throw it over them. Walkers would do so with their dippers or leafy branches and murmur "Songkriem jop howie" "The war is over!" As Maha Ghosananda explained to a walker from another country, "Mine are a simple people. To us water means cleansing. We are washing away the blood."

The Army of Peace also washed away psychic wounds as the walk unexpectedly began to attract hundreds of local participants as it passed through Cambodia. In Battambang, Cambodia's second largest city, several thousand people greeted the walk. One early morning a local woman came to the walk and said, "Last night I dreamt of my mother. I haven't seen her in a dream since she died during the Khmer Rouge period. She was making an offering to many monks. She looked happy. This morning I came to the market and saw the Dhammayietra with many monks walking in the front. It is a sign, and I know I must join you. I ran home to get some clothes and now I will walk with you relieved that my mother's spirit is now at peace." Some people joined only for a day, bringing rice and mangos, which were necessary for the sustenance of the walk. Others walked the entire way, and by the time the walk reached the capital thirty days later over a thousand walkers were at its core.

The Dhammayietra entered the capital on the day of the full moon in May, Buddhism highest holy day, Vesak. Tens of thousands

---

[12]Maat, Bernstein & Moser, "Washing Away The Blood," *Nonviolence Today* 29 (November-December 1992): 5-7.

of people looked on, or joined the Army of Peace, which now stretched for twelve kilometers along the main boulevard, walked in quiet dignity through the centre of Phnom Penh's war-weary population. As the "Army" decamped at a temple in the capital that night one of the eldest "soldiers," a grandmother, summed up the emotions of the walkers with words reminiscent of another Freedom Marcher in the American South, "My feet are sore, but my spirit is at rest."[13]

> If you make rice, you eat rice.
> – Cambodian Proverb

The Dhammayietra Movement

The Dhammayietra was originally planned as a one-time event. No one foresaw the results of deep reconciliation that the Walk had manifested. Many of those who had join from the refugee camps simply stayed in Cambodia after the walk, now settled with relatives with whom they had previously lost contact. Afterwards, the UNHCR that had so vehemently opposed the walk facilitated showing videos about the walk in the camps as a triumph in reconciliation. The Peace Walk now had wide publicity and wonderful success. And still there was need for peace, for more healing, for more reconciliation. Maha Ghosananda began forming a second Dhammayietra.

While the second Dhammayietra was assembling, potential disaster hit. The temple in which people had begun to gather for the pilgrimage became a battlefield as Khmer Rouge troops exchanged fire with Government soldiers and police. Combatants took positions on different sides of the temple and much of their ordinance went directly though it, wounding two people who had come to walk. During the fire fight, Maha Ghosananda appeared unshakable as he maintained a meditative posture throughout the attack at the base of the temples main altar. A rocket-propelled grenade that spun into the

---

[13]Ibid.

temple impacted a nearby wall but failed to explode, leaving only a full imprint in the fresco painted concrete wall. The following day was spent in introspection on the wisdom of pressing forward. Walkers reflected on a story from the time of the Buddha, in which he did not avoid walking into areas of conflict to settle a dispute. Maha Ghosananda counseled proceeding forward with compassion and conviction, "Indeed, this is why we must walk! Years of violence have brought great tragedy. More violence can only bring more harm. Now is the time for peace." Summoning their courage, the Army of Peace walked into northern war-torn Cambodia the next day.

In a later reflection on walking in northern Cambodia, one of the monks said, "Although it was not far from the capital, it was like a different country. People slept in bunkers at night for fear of rocket attacks. They came to share their suffering with us, baring their souls before we even asked how they were. Yet seeing us walking to visit them was healing. It was like visiting a sick person. Even if you don't have any medicine with you, the person feels better afterwards, just because of the visit. Echoing the monks observation in different words, a farmer who stood along the road cradling his son in his arms had said, "If this Dhammayietra brings us even a moment of peace, I offer my deepest gratitude, for then we can hope."[14]

The Army of Peace was able to win this reprieve for the villages through which it passed. As the Dhammayietra proceeded it became a moving zone of peace, for once again there was no military activity where the Walkers stayed for a meal or a night, or directly where they walked, even though acts of war could be heard on the horizon. As the walk progressed, many soldiers began to lay down their weapons and seek the blessing of the Dhammayietra. At one temple several heavily armed soldiers arrived to seek the blessing of protection from Maha Ghosananda, one of them saying, "We don't want anyone to be killed or hurt." One said, "Even though I am a soldier, I have no ill will in my heart. But I have to be a soldier so my family will eat. So

---

[14]Maat, Bernstein & Moser, "A Moment of Peace, A Glimmer of Hope," *Nonviolence Today* 34 (September/October 1993): 5-7.

please bless us in a way that our bullets don't hit anyone, and so that no one else's bullets hurt us."[15]

Before the second Dhammayietra reached Phnom Penh, the city was tense with the expectation of widespread violence in the coming election days. As the walk approached the capital, its number increased to over three thousand as many people spontaneously joined the walk. As the Dhammayietra traversed the capital, many businesses shut down with the swell of people joining the walk. One person who joined said "People were so afraid of the elections. They had started stockpiling rice in their homes. The walk has relieved us of our fear and given us new hope."

For the following two days the Dhammayietra focused on calming the capital. Despite rain, mud, and heat, thousands joined in walks around the capital, stopping for a time to hold public meditation at key points in the city. Normally busy intersections became quiet as thousands of people sat in them and softly chanted in Pali, "*Natthi santi param sukham*" "There is no happiness higher than peace."

News media from around the world had flown into Phnom Penh to record the predicted collapse of the world's largest peacekeeping effort in the forecast bloody elections. Most flew out the following week, disappointed by the elections in which over ninety percent of those registered took part in peaceful elections, bitterly claiming that there was no news to report. How typical: violence and war was considered "news"; the astonishing courage and success of peacemakers was not.

Since the 1993 elections, the Dhammayietras have grown into an annual event. They bring the message that peace is possible to a different part of Cambodia each year. While the Dhammayietra continues to call for an end to the civil war, it has added new issues on which it campaigns as well. The Dhammayietras call attention to the accelerated deforestation and drawing the link between logging and the ongoing civil war. There is also public education along the walk route of the dangers of land mines and unexploded ordnance

---

[15]Maat, Bernstein & Moser, "A Moment of Peace, 5-7.

(including how to avoid being injured, and information on where rehabilitation help is available). The Dhammayietra has begun a nonviolence training program that now holds sessions in over half the provinces of the country.

No longer just an annual event, The Dhammayietras have become a movement. The most remarkable aspects of this social movement is its specific focus on the development of Compassion. As a component of a mass movement, the focus on the development of compassion is certainly unique to Asia. The Dhammayietra movement believes that no other skill is as important as the development of compassion, a key virtue in Buddhism—both a method and a result—on the path of personal and social liberation. This dual focus that links personal and social change is perhaps one of the most unique aspects of the Dhammayietra as a mass movement.

The Walk itself is a tool for cultivation of compassion since, under Maha Ghosananda's spiritual leadership, it is mindful walking mediation. Mindfulness creates an active rather than a reactive mind. With enough time and effort, the serious practitioner of these methods of mental cultivation can confront extremely difficult situations. They can then respond quickly, with great clarity of mind, or with patience according to the situation. Without clarity of mind, people are prone to be reactionary, they are still controlled by the event that precipitated the reaction. The cultivation of non-reactivity does not mean inactivity. It means breaking the chain of being controlled by the event, and an ability to truly act creatively. Only the mind free of reactivity is truly capable of peace in action.

Each year the Dhammayietra movement is attracting more people, as they begin to understand the Dhammayietra path to peace. This path is expressed most eloquently in a series of banners now carried by the walk that proclaim the Dhammayietra prayer.

> Cambodia has suffered deeply.
> From deep suffering comes deep compassion.
> From deep compassion comes a peaceful heart.
> From a peaceful heart comes a peaceful person.

From a peaceful person comes a peaceful family and
community.
From peaceful communities come a peaceful nation.
From peaceful nations come a peaceful world.[16]

When asked how they can continue walking and organizing year
after year when they still have not yet attained their goal, veteran
walk organizer Kim Leng answered, "We know that the road to peace
is a long one. But it is the only road. What is the alternative in the
midst of all this violence? Do nothing? Then it's as if we're just lying
around waiting to die.[17] When asked how long the Dhammayietras
will continue, Maha Ghosananda smiles radiantly and says, "Until we
have peace!"

Maha Ghosananda on Peacemaking

Peacemaking requires compassion. It requires the skill of
listening. To listen, we have to give up ourselves, even our
own words. We listen until we can hear our peaceful nature.

As we learn to listen to ourselves, we learn to listen to
others as well, and new ideas grow. There is an openness, a
harmony. As we come to trust one another, we discover new
possibilities for resolving conflicts. When we listen well, we
will hear peace growing.

Peacemaking requires selflessness. There is no peace with
jealousy, self-righteousness or meaningless criticism. We must
decide that making peace is more important than making war.
Peacemaking is selflessness taking root. To make peace, the
skills of teamwork and cooperation are essential. There is little
we can do for peace as long as we feel that we are the only
ones who know the way. The road to peace is called the

---

[16]Yeshua Moser-Puangsuwan, "A Million Kilometres For Peace," paper delivered at the
International Peace Research Association in Brisbane, Australia in July 1996.

[17]"On the March Again for Nonviolence," *Phnom Penh Post*, May 31, 1996, 14.

middle path. It is beyond all duality and all opposites. Peace comes only when we stop struggling with opposites. The middle path has no beginning and no end, so we do not need to travel far on the middle path to find peace.

The middle path is not only the road to peace, it is also the road of peace. It is very safe, and very pleasant to travel.

Peacemaking requires wisdom. Peace is a path that is chosen consciously. It is not an aimless wandering, but a step-by-step journey.[18]

Noble Eightfold Path

An active path to be followed through this life as it avoids the extreme of self-mortification, which leads to a weakened intellect, and the extreme of self-indulgence that retards one's moral progress.

Right Understanding: Understanding of oneself as one really is.

Right Thoughts: Thoughts of selflessness, goodwill and harmlessness.

Right Speech: Refraining from falsehood, slandering, harsh words and frivolous talk.

Right Action: Not killing, stealing or committing sexual misconduct.

Right Livelihood: Not working in the five forbidden trades: Trading in arms, human beings, animal slaughter, intoxicants or poisons.

Right Effort: Applying oneself to practice of the teachings instead of simply making offerings or prayers.

Right Mindfulness: Maintaining a meditative attention to body, feelings, thoughts and mind objects whenever possible.

Right Concentration: The culmination of a life dedicated to the perfection of the prior seven factors bring this one into

---

[18]Maha Ghosananda, *Step by Step*, 51-53.

existence, which leads to penetrative insight into the nature of reality.

Five Precepts

The basic precepts of a Buddhist. Others are added on certain holy days which come four times per month in accordance with the phases of the moon:

Now I will teach the precepts of conduct for a householder:

(1) Let him or her not destroy life nor cause others to destroy life and also, not approve of others killing. Let him or her refrain from oppressing all living beings in the world, whether weak or strong.
(2) Knowing what belongs to others let him or her not steal anything from any place, nor cause to steal, nor approve of others stealing.
(3) Let him or her not transgress on another's spouse.
(4) Avoid telling lies, and do not cause others to tell lies, nor approve of others' telling lies.
(5) He or she should not indulge in taking intoxicants, nor should he or she cause or approve of others doing so.

The householder observing these duties with diligence is reborn in the sphere of self-luminant beings.[19]

---

[19]The Buddha, *Sutta Nipata*.

8

Martin Luther King Jr. and Nonviolent Justice Seekers in Latin America and the Caribbean

Paul Dekar

In Latin America and the Caribbean, with Paul Dekar as our guide, we will meet many peacemakers, such as Raul Suarez Ramos, Reverend Clara Rodes, and Virgilio and Margarita Mendez, All of these share Martin Luther King's vision "to promote genuine fraternity amongst the races; to work for economic justice; to render Christian faith concrete; to resist evil with the force of love." What impresses me most is the ordinariness of these extraordinary people. I doubt any of them will ever be internationally recognized. Yet it is the life and work of such people that the future of nonviolence depends. I hope their stories will inspire the rest of us ordinary people to struggle even more for the coming of the reign of justice and peace.

One day, Martin Luther King Jr. believed, youngsters will learn words they will not understand. Children from India will ask, "What is hunger?" Children from Alabama will ask, "What is racism?" Children from Hiroshima and Nagasaki will ask, "What is the atomic bomb?" Children from

Vietnam will ask, "What is war?" Dictionaries will cite these words as archaic, like stagecoach, galley, or slavery.[1]

King voiced his dream for humanity by expressions such as "the beloved community" or "the restoration of broken communities." While King never articulated systematically the content of these phrases, he called consistently for a frontal assault on poverty, disease, and ignorance. In the "I Have a Dream" speech, King communicated a vision of a world without hunger, inferior schools, racism, second-class citizenship, slums, and war.[2]

When King died, the dream did not die with him. Around the world, nonviolent justice seekers identify King's dream as a source of inspiration. Rosa Parks, the seamstress who in 1955 sparked the Montgomery bus boycott by civil disobedience, put it this way: "King made us believe in ourselves. He dreamed the beloved community. We are part of it. There is no pretending that we don't have problems. We have work to do." In response to King's vision, some have adopted a "Living the Dream" oath which reads, "In honor of Martin Luther King's life and work, I pledge to do everything that I can to make America and the world a place where equality and justice, freedom and peace will grow and flourish. I commit myself to living the dream by loving, not hating, showing understanding, not anger, making peace, not war."[3]

The legacy of King extends beyond the borders of the United States. Lewis V. Baldwin of Vanderbilt University has recently explored King's role in the struggle against apartheid in South Africa.[4] In this chapter, I want to do the same for another region, Latin America and the Caribbean. In three situations, ones of prolonged

---

[1]This is a paraphrase of a quote from Dr. King in *Reconciliation International* 6 (Spring 1991): 2.

[2]"I Have a Dream," the speech for which King is most remembered, can be found in *A Testament of Hope: The Essential Writings of Martin Luther King, Jr.*, edited by James M. Washington (San Francisco: Harper and Row, 1986).

[3]Interview with Rosa Parks, January 22, 1989. The "Living the Dream" oath originated on January 20, 1986, the first United States federal King holiday.

[4]Lewis V. Baldwin, *Toward the Beloved Community: Martin Luther King, Jr. and South Africa* (Cleveland: Pilgrim Press, 1995).

conflict (Cuba), of war termination (El Salvador and Nicaragua), and of trauma (El Salvador and Nicaragua), King's concern for the marginalized, for economic justice, and for a new social order, and his advocacy of reconciliation with and love for enemies, have inspired nonviolent justice seekers. Those in the Americas who have turned to King for guidance and who have adapted his methods to their particular situations may teach us all about what King's practice of nonviolence will look like into the third millennium.

Recalling the Life of Martin Luther King Jr.

Between December 1, 1955 and April 4, 1968, from the time when the Montgomery bus boycott catapulted him to prominence until his assassination in Memphis, Tennessee, Martin Luther King Jr. was at the center of a maelstrom. Claiming the right to protest for right, King led a broad movement for economic, political, and social change that sought nonviolently to eliminate structural violence in such forms as segregation, poverty, and war. By passage of civil rights and voting rights legislation, he advanced racial equality. In planning the Poor People's Campaign, he envisioned a movement seeking to liberate the poor, dispossessed, and exploited of the whole world. By criticizing United States military involvement in Vietnam, he confirmed the relationship between military and social expenditures and helped hasten an end to the conflict. While King did not produce these advances single-handedly, he aided a generation, African-Americans in particular, to believe they could overcome obstacles to the establishment of the beloved community.

As we turn to King's influence in the Americas, it is natural to ask, why King in Latin America and the Caribbean? Did King focus on problems there? During the 382-day Montgomery bus boycott, King appropriated nonviolence as a way not simply to correct a particular civil rights abuse, but also to move toward wider goals. He called for genuine intergroup and interpersonal living. He came to regard nonviolence alone as the means by which this goal could be attained. He understood the aftermath of nonviolence as reconciliation and the creation of the beloved community. In one address, King stated:

> Peace is not merely absence of some negative force—war, tension, confusion, but it is the presence of some positive force—justice, goodwill and the power of the kingdom of God. . . . [P]eace is not merely the absence of tension [in race relations] but is the presence of justice. . . . And even if we did not have this tension, we still wouldn't have positive peace. Yes, if the Negro accepts his place, accepts exploitation, accepts injustice, there will be peace. But it would be a peace boiled down to stagnant complacency, deadening passivity, and if peace means this, I don't want peace. If peace means accepting second-class citizenship, I don't want it. If peace means keeping my mouth shut in the midst of injustice and evil, I don't want it.[5]

In another address, King urged resisting systemic evil everywhere because, as he put it:

> Those of us who live in the twentieth century are privileged to live in one of the most momentous periods of human history. It is an exciting age filled with hope . . . in which a new social order is being born. We stand today between two worlds—the dying old and the emerging new.[6]

King often referred to events in the Caribbean and Latin America. For example, in 1963, he noted that the Cuban missile crisis had dwarfed other issues. A year later, when King was in Oslo, Norway to receive the Nobel Peace Prize, King acknowledged that he had met

---

[5]"When Peace Becomes Obnoxious," *Louisville Defender*. Sermon preached on March 29, 1956, copy in the *Martin Luther King, Jr. Manuscript Collection* at Memphis Theological Seminary file 8 (hereafter cited by MTS file number).

[6]"The Birth of a New Age," talk given November 7, 1956 upon receiving the Alpha Phi Alpha fraternity award. MTS, 18.

in London, England with people of color engaged in freedom struggles everywhere, including the West Indies. He urged them to deal nonviolently with problems faced in the region.[7]

These comments reflected King's growing attention to global affairs. In many speeches, he expounded three basic themes: the inter-related structure of reality, the need to eradicate racism in all its manifestations, and the call to peace-building. King wove these together in a speech in Jamaica. "All life is inter-related. Somehow we are all caught in an inescapable network of mutuality tied in a single garment of destiny . . . whatever affects one directly will affect all indirectly." He went on to challenge students "to work passionately and unrelentingly to get rid of the last vestiges of racial injustice. I need not remind you that racial injustice is still a reality in our world, and all men of good will must work to make racial justice a reality." He saw the need for an alternative to war and bloodshed, whether in Vietnam or the Dominican Republic. "The nations of the world must come to see that another design for understanding must be created, the grand design for peace and brotherhood." Finally, he condemned the failure of the richest nation in the world to share its bounty with the world. King proposed sending food to alleviate hunger "in the wrinkled stomachs of the millions of God's children in Asia, Africa and South America and in our own country who go to bed hungry at night. We spend far too much of our national budget establishing military bases around the world rather than bases of genuine concern and understanding."[8]

We have seen that from the Montgomery campaign on, King associated the particular struggles of people in the southern United States within a framework of wider movements for social change. He understood the nonviolent uprisings of oppressed peoples around the world as a sign of the old order passing away and a new order being born. By the end of his life, he was advocating a complete reordering

---

[7]"Bold Design for a New South," in *Testament of Hope*, 112; interview regarding Nobel Peace Prize, Oslo, Norway, December 9, 1964, MTS file 328.

[8]"Facing the Challenge of a New Age," Address at Valedictory Service, University of the West Indies, Mona, Jamaica, June 20, 1965, MTS file 400.

of United States society and the building of a better world. In "Where Do We Go from Here?" his last presidential address to the Southern Christian Leadership Conference, King appealed for justice, not charity. King said, "We are called upon to help the discouraged beggars in life's marketplace. But one day we must come to see that an edifice that produces beggars needs restructuring."[9]

King's Legacy in the Americas[10]

To further my own understanding of how and why King has become an important figure in the Americas, I visited four centers named after King: the Dr. Martin Luther King, Jr. Memorial Center (Centro Memorial Dr. Martin Luther King, Jr.) in Havana, Cuba; the Martin Luther King, Jr. High School in San Salvador, El Salvador being developed under sponsorship of Emmanuel Baptist Church; the Martin Luther King Institute for Study and Social Action (Instituto de Investigaciones y Accion Social Martin Luther King) at Upoli Polytechnic University in Managua, Nicaragua, sponsored by the Baptist Convention of Nicaragua; and the Martin Luther King Evangelical Nicaraguan University, also in Managua.

Picture with me approaching the King Center in Havana. The city shows signs of material decay because of the thirty-five year-old United States blockade. Physically, the center is next to Ebenezer Baptist Church, the name of the church in Atlanta pastored by Daddy King and his son. The King Center and church building are located in the Mariana *barrio*, a largely poor, Afro-Caribbean neighborhood. A receptionist greets those entering and directs visitors to the proper activity or office. There are announcements of various programs. Literature is available, including *Caminos* [Roads], a new periodical intended to provide the poor a voice as they reflect on appropriate paths to follow in such areas as community development

---

[9]*A Testament of Hope*, 250.

[10]This section draws from interviews conducted during 1996. I want to express thanks to Memphis Theological Seminary and a Lilly Foundation grant (No. 90375) for support of the research for this chapter.

or struggle against the blockade. My copy includes words from King's last sermon, delivered April 3, 1968 on the eve of his assassination in Memphis and the lines, "I hear the call, 'Go Down Moses,' . . . the call of the Savior. . . ."

Inside the courtyard is a mural entitled The Little Yellow Bus. The artist Mario Torero depicts a bus, King, and another nonviolent activist Cesar Chavez, whose words grace the mural: "We have something the rich do not own. We have bodies and spirits and the justice of our cause as our weapons." One is reminded of an incident in July 1994, when United States officials at the Mexican border held up a shipment of humanitarian aid destined for Cuba. Unwilling to abandon the supplies, several caravanistas, including the Reverend Lucius Walker, Jr., Executive Director of Pastors for Peace, initiated a hunger strike. A yellow school bus became a symbol of solidarity between citizens of the United States and Cuba. After twenty-three days, the White House gave in to enormous grassroots pressure and allowed the bus to be taken to Cuba.

Raul Suarez Ramos is the center's director as well as pastor of Ebenezer Baptist Church and a member of Cuba's parliament. In an interview, Suarez explained that he founded the center nearly ten years ago in order to enable a largely white congregation to minister in its surrounding community in the light of specific needs of people. The name King was chosen because Suarez identified his own pastoral vocation closely with King's: to promote genuine fraternity amongst the races; to work for economic justice; to render Christian faith concrete; to resist evil with the force of love. When the King Center first opened, it emphasized social programs: repairing deteriorating neighborhoods, building homes, experimenting with solar heating in a limited way, providing medical services, offering the aged help in areas such as physical and psychological therapy. As financial support for its work has increased, the King Center has expanded work in all these areas, with increased attention to the needs of women, children, and youth. A new focus is ministry with a small number who are HIV positive. In addition, the Center has embarked on programs of popular education modeled on ideas of Paolo Freire and the base communities characteristic of liberation theology. Objectives include empowerment of people, capacity-building and reflection on the Cuban reality.

Like many Evangelical Christians, Raul Suarez has paid a great price for his witness. He has worked the sugar cane fields. He has been expelled from a Southern Baptist-dominated denomination. His wife and co-pastor, the Reverend Clara Rodes, died November 4, 1994 due to complications following a kidney transplant operation. She lost her struggle to live after having a heart attack in hospital. Chances for the success of the operation were exceptionally good had needed medicines been available.

Raul Suarez recognizes that his faithful persistence has borne considerable fruit. His 1991 Christmas sermon was the first message by an Evangelical Christian heard on Cuban radio in 28 years. Today, the King Center receives financial and other resources from around the world, both governments [except the United States] and non-government agencies [including some in the United States]. In November 1992, Fidel Castro was present at the Center when Lucius Walker accompanied first shipment of Pastors for Peace supplies. Clara Rodes has become a symbol throughout the Americas of the place of women in the search for justice and human dignity.

In San Salvador, El Salvador, Emmanuel Baptist Church has sponsored the new Martin Luther King, Jr. High School. Around 1958, the congregation's founders, Virgilio and Margarita Mendez Gomez began evangelizing in the San Jacinto barrio, near the country's presidential mansion. They went to neighborhood homes and created ministries to deal with concrete needs: educational opportunities and medical services for children, youth and adults in the city and countryside. Serving the poor and the marginalized, they found God.

As war engulfed the country, many of the congregation's leaders, including co-pastors Miguel Tomas Castro, son-in-law of Virgilio and Margarita, and Raul Pacheco found themselves in exile in Canada. There, they studied King's writings and found in him a model for the work they envisioned once they could return to their country. They came to regard Emmanuel Baptist Church as a seed of the future beloved community. They encouraged the congregation to strengthen its work in conflict zones, especially amongst orphans and other *desplazados*, or displaced people. Among them were Sara Noemi Brizuela Quijada and Ana Maria Paiz, whose *quinceaños* or Afiesta rosa" [fifteenth birthday party] I attended in May 1996, lives symbolized on a poster in the church foyer: in the face of every child, we see God with us.

In 1988, after three years in exile, Miguel Tomas Castro and his family returned to El Salvador to participate in rebuilding the country after the war. In 1996, Raul Pacheco returned as well, accompanied by other displaced members of the congregation. Inspired by King's emphasis on love of enemy and forgiveness, they helped the congregation to understand the potential of King's ideas to El Salvador's future reconciliation. They adopted strategies to reconstruct communities through educational, medical and agricultural programs. One ecumenical land distribution program was called, "To Be with My Brothers and Sisters" (SERCON). In an interview, Castro explained that, "We are living here together, sharing the good that we have. Food is for the people who need it, not only church members, nor those who have accepted Jesus Christ. Food is given as a testimony to the love of God." Envisioning a future day of peace with justice, he continued, "Baptists in El Salvador don't dance, but when peace comes, we will dance."

At present, Emmanuel Baptist serves twenty-eight communities helping ex-combatants from both sides of the conflict, caring for the basic needs of children and developing the capacity of women to deal with an enormous range of problems. They support reforestation and sustainable agriculture. Here are two examples: Zacamiles, near Suchitoto in Cuscatlan Province, was greatly affected by the war. When I first visited the area in 1992, Emmanuel Baptist was contemplating resettling refugees returning there from Honduras. Now seventy families have homes, land, clean water, a school attended by 169 students and a health clinic. Last year villagers had excess corn and beans to sell, giving them a measure of economic security they have not experienced for years.

In Codeusemi, near San Rafael in Morazan Province, I met with a community of ex-combatants. They face numerous frustrations resulting from the slow pace of implementing the peace accords. If they have land, typically they have no money for seed, fertilizer or staples. Quickly they go in debt. Ultimately they lose their land. On the wall of the community center, a graffito reads "Seremos un pueblo libre con trabajo, justicia, pan y libertad." "We will be a free people with work, justice, bread and liberty."

Raul Pacheco, who lost twenty-two relatives during the war and has resumed his role on the pastoral team of Emmanuel Baptist Church, insists that it was a sermon by King on forgiveness that inspired him to return to the country from exile and begin work in the area of community development in rural settings as part of the process of implementing the peace accords signed in 1992. Another witness to the impact of King is Salvador Amaya, widower of Maria Christina Gomez, one of over eighty thousand killed in El Salvador as they lived out their Christian calling. "We, her brothers and sisters are suffering for our Savior in the land which bears His name. Our days have been filled not only with anguish, but also joy, for we know that, by our suffering, we are making a way for the establishment of a society founded on peace and justice."

King's vision of the beloved community has inspired creation in San Salvador of a high school named after King. An expansion of the primary school, which occupies the facilities of Emmanuel Baptist Church during the week, the high school will offer students opportunities to study King. In terms of the appropriation of King as a model, creation of an educational institution named after him is a notable development.

Another example is the Martin Luther King Institute for Study and Social Action (Instituto de Investigaciones y Accion Social Martin Luther King) at Upoli Polytechnic University in Managua, Nicaragua. Founded in 1967 by the Baptist Convention of Nicaragua, the university launched the King Institute in 1994. Housed in the university and supported in part by UNESCO funding, the institute offers courses, sponsors conferences, and publishes an extraordinary periodical *Cultura de Paz* [Culture of Peace]. Each issue features a profile of advocates of nonviolent action such as King, Tolstoy, Albert Schweitzer, and Thomas Merton. The relevance of their nonviolent teaching to aspects of the Nicaraguan reality is the focus of these articles.

Denis Alberto Torres and his brother Jose Miguel Torres Reyes, respectively director and researcher with a principal focus on theological reflection concerning the economic, political, and social situation in the country, are two of the staff of the King Institute. Denis and Miguel grew up in a household committed to the construction of a society based on principles of justice and peace. Their father, the Reverend Jose Miguel Torres Reyes (b. 1914) led a reform movement and founded a community, *Luz en la selva* ("Light in the forest") as a way to build civil society and realize God's will that humanity should experience *shalom* on earth. In the 1970s, Denis and Miguel followed their father into Christian service. They supported the revolutionary fight against Somoza and, after the Sandinistas came to power, became involved in agrarian reform. They sought a new way to express this pastoral vocation when, in 1990, Violeta Barrios de Chamorro became President of Nicaragua. With other Baptist leaders, they envisioned a new role for the chief educational institution of the Baptist denomination, Upoli. As a way of projecting students into society, they sought to link teaching, research, and action. In this way, they believed the institution would contribute to national reconciliation, support gains of the revolutionary era in such areas as health and literacy, and empower people to survive in the face of harsh economic forces in the 1990s, including the rise of individualism, materialism, and structural adjustment.

Miguel Torres deems Upoli, a college supported by Baptists, a logical place to house a research institute named after King. He regards King, more than any other Baptist in history, as a model for having inveighed against all the dehumanizing forces that threatened Nicaraguans: poverty, discrimination, and violence. For Miguel

Torres, to remember King is to take up his work, mobilizing people in the struggle to build a society on the foundations of love, justice, equality, human rights, peace, and nonviolence.

Similar reasons led to the opening in early 1996 of the Martin Luther King Evangelical Nicaraguan University, also in Managua. According to the university's rector, Wolfgang Bautz, King combined the roles of scholar, preacher, theologian, and leader of social movements for change. For Nicaraguans, King's testimony articulated in his August 1963 "I Have a Dream" speech in Washington offers the greatest hope of promoting a society of human dignity, justice, and love. To underscore the weight King attributed to nonviolence as the way to build such a society through nonviolence, the university invited Arun Gandhi, grandson of Gandhi and founder of the M. K. Gandhi Institute for Nonviolence in Memphis, Tennessee, to speak during ceremonies marking the university's inauguration.

Many Nicaraguans have learned from King. In Managua, Hugo Silva, businessman and member of Beersheva Baptist Church, shared having lost his parents over fifty years ago due to intervention in Nicaragua by the United States. In his youth, he came to believe only violent means could bring justice to the nation. Christian conversion and reading King's writings led him to reject armed force as a way to effect change. Through his church, he attempts to live out King's ideals through specific projects, a health clinic and a primary school. Another individual influenced by King is Gustavo Parajon, pastor and medical doctor. During the 1960s, when Parajon was a medical student in the United States, King inspired him to use health in the service of peace. After a devastating earthquake in 1972, Parajon founded the Comite Evangelico Pro-Ayuda y Desarrollo (CEPAD; Evangelical Committee for Aid and Development) and a parallel organization, PROVADENIC, among Baptists. Realizing the need for work with the poor, Parajon encouraged CEPAD to do housing, medical and agricultural projects throughout the land, for which reason he came to be discredited by Contra supporters. During the 1980s, Parajon helped negotiate an accord between the Indians of the Atlantic Coast and the Sandinista government. Subsequently, he shared, with Catholic Cardinal Obando y Bravo, leadership in the reconciliation process that continues in the country.

In the Americas, people do not generally make a distinction between nonviolence and armed struggle. They see them as two aspects in their resistance against repression. While people may engage in a range of nonviolent activities such as strikes or symbolic public acts of noncooperation, the goals of those who have used nonviolent means, whether to defend their rights or to transform a system of organized exploitation, are the same as those engaged in armed conflict. There are notable cases in the Americas when nonviolent civilian insurrections have brought down governments, for example, those of Jorge Ubico and Maximiliano Hernandez Martinez who ruled Guatemala and El Salvador respectively between 1931 and 1944. The failure of successor regimes to achieve larger objectives, however, set in motion events by which structural violence would be challenged violently.

In fact, many Latin Americans deem certain forms of nonviolence as inappropriate, ineffective, or imported. Even those who may use nonviolent methods as part of their struggle tend not to condemn those who take up arms. Many reflect on the difficulty of adapting King's methods to Latin American contexts. From these witnesses to situations of structural violence in the Americas, one discerns that individuals approach choices as to whether violent or nonviolent action is needed from a pragmatic or utilitarian perspective. Commitment to strive actively for change and a sense of duty so strong that one is prepared to die for it are the motivations that energize people, not devotion to an ideology. When people in the Americas mention King, neither his advocacy of nonviolence nor his awarding of the Nobel Peace Prize are as important as his vision, the integrity by which he lived it out, and his martyrdom. Dom Helder Camara, Brazilian archbishop and one of Latin America's best known proponents of active nonviolence, sums up:

> I respect those who have felt obliged in conscience to opt for violence, not the facile violence of armchair guerrillas, but

that of the men who have proved their sincerity by the sacrifice of their lives. It seems to me the memory of Camilo Torres and Che Guevara deserves as much respect as that of Dr. Martin Luther King. I accuse the real abettors of violence, all those on the right or on the left who wrong justice and prevent peace.[11]

There is no easy way to delineate the process by which nonviolent justice seekers in the Americas may have come to appropriate King's thought and forms of action. In contexts of intense personal and structural violence such as Cuba, El Salvador, and Nicaragua, where justice seekers have lived with the tension of deciding how to promote change, active resistance to evil has included myriad forms of unarmed struggle—economic, ideological, political, spiritual—anything short of cooperation with the system. Nonviolence has never been the only option. When Arlen, a young woman and a member of a Baptist church in Nicaragua, left for the mountains to join the Sandinistas, she took a Spanish translation of *Strength to Love*, *La Fuerza de Amar*, with her. She was killed brutally by the National Guard, so we cannot know what impression King's book made on her.

Despite the ambiguity of this illustration, and the force of the arguments of critics of nonviolence, many in the Americas draw on the judgments and resources of King as well as their analysis of their concrete reality and resources of their own culture. *La Biblia Latinoamerica*, a widely distributed version of the Bible, features prominently a photo of King. His writings circulate in Spanish translations. Workers with organizations like the International Fellowship of Reconciliation, Mennonite Central Committee, Peace Brigades

---

[11]*Reconciliation Quarterly* 10 (June 1980): 22. Camara made the same point in an address in Toronto, Ontario, Canada, February 1977. In an interview May 25, 1996, Dean Brackley, professor at the Central American university of San Salvador associated King and Archbishop Oscar Romero, murdered on March 24, 1980, who anticipated that his blood would be "like a seed of liberty and a sign that our hopes will soon become a reality." Placido Erdozain, *Archbishop Romero: Martyr of Salvador*, trans. John McFadden and Ruth Warner (Maryknoll: Orbis, 1981), 75.

International, and Witness for Peace use nonviolent methods and offer training in nonviolence.

Frequently, members of these organizations and Latin Americans more generally do refer to King. The following are but three examples. At a meeting on "Nonviolence: A Power for Liberation" held November 28-December 3, 1977, Latin American Catholic bishops invoked King's name. Citing King as a martyr in the struggle against racial prejudice, the bishops declared:

> We feel the moment has come to shatter the vicious circle of violence and oppose these systems by means of a determined, persevering action without violence—forthright and clearly defined, on the order of active noncooperation—with a view to totally transforming the structures of political and economic violence prevailing in our countries.[12]

In June 1989, Julio Quan, formerly Director of the School of Political Science at the National University of Guatemala, acknowledged the importance of King for social movements in his country.[13] On May 18, 1992, Father Miguel D'Escoto, formerly Nicaragua's Minister of Foreign Affairs, evoked King's memory and the death of Jesus when he characterized nonviolence as being able to say every minute of his life:

> This is my body and this is my blood which I make available for the cause of brotherhood and sisterhood. And I am willing, and I am not only willing, I risk it every minute, to be taken at any time, as we continue to struggle so that no one is

---

[12]Adolfo Perez Esquivel, *Christ in a Poncho: Testimonials of the Nonviolent Struggles in Latin America*, trans. Robert R. Barr (Maryknoll, NY: Orbis Books, 1984), 132.

[13]Julio Quan interview in *Unarmed Forces: Nonviolent Action in Central America and the Middle East*, ed. Graeme Macqueen (Toronto: Science for Peace, 1992), 26.

excluded from the one family that we are meant to be under God.[14]

To summarize, we discern that King has become a model in the Americas not simply as a theorist of nonviolent action or as a Baptist. Many identify King as a Christian silenced for his pursuit of justice, a goal they pursue in their struggle against structural violence. In each case, they have undertaken health initiatives as crucial to transforming violent cultures to more just ones.

Health Initiatives as Peace Initiatives[15]

A crucial direction for nonviolence in the third millennium arising from the case studies we have examined is the linkage between health and peace. We may understand the health and peace connection when nonviolent efforts in a particular situation serve simultaneously to improve the health of a group of people and to heighten peace, whether this peace be internal to the group or between two or more groups. In the three contexts we have just considered, situations of prolonged conflict (Cuba), ending war (El Salvador and Nicaragua), and trauma reduction (El Salvador and Nicaragua), we find an important connection between health initiatives as peace initiatives. Indeed, health workers provide a bridge to peace.

An obvious way in which health care workers serve as a bridge to peace is that, as a group, they have some commitment to human welfare and access to people suffering in zones of conflict. Even in situations of extreme conflict, there is space to build peace, space that is often dangerous, tenuous, and shifting, but space nonetheless. In 1984, the Pan American Health Organization launched a forum for dialogue, cooperation and understanding that is seen to have helped

---

[14]Esquivel, Ibid; Julio Quan interview; Miguel d'Escoto, "The Third Day of Creation," *SHAIR*, Summer 1992, 16.

[15]See an essay by Graeme MacQueen, Richard McCutcheon, and Joanna Santa Barbara, "The Use of Health Initiatives as Peace Initiatives," *Peace and Change* 22 (April 1997): 175-197.

build momentum for the signing of the Central American Peace Accords. Similarly, during the civil war in El Salvador, the Duarte government and Farabundo Marti Front for National Liberation (FMLN) agreed to annual "days of peace," humanitarian cease-fires that contributed to establishing a framework of dialogue that led to the signing of the peace accords in 1992. The explicit aim of the cease-fire was to save the lives of children dying of easily preventable diseases, but an additional outcome was to foster a climate where the parties could negotiate. Finally, UNICEF has developed a "measurement for peace" initiative as a model of how health workers can remain active in the peace process once armed conflict has ended. The model includes trauma healing workshops, truth commissions and the construction of superordinate goals as a way to transform conditions that led to conflict in the first place. The goal is to make reconciliation possible in situations of extreme conflict through the sharing of resources needed for the health and well-being of the whole population.

Conclusion

In this chapter, we have sought to add to the understanding of the legacy Martin Luther King, Jr. In Latin America, King is widely recognized as an important symbol. Inspired by King, practitioners of nonviolence struggle for basic rights, justice, and peace. They seek to transform conflict, end war, care for victims, effect real change, and eliminate structural causes that generate violence.

Nonviolence advocates who invoke the name of Martin Luther King, Jr. often meet with the reply that an armed response to violence is legitimate and just. Yet, though subjected to the same violence as those who engage in armed struggle, many resist injustice nonviolently. Generally, the goals of those who opt for nonviolent means are the same as those engaged in armed resistance, namely, to overcome discrimination, to defend their rights, to change conditions of structural violence or to end a system of organized exploitation. In situations permeated by violence, the crucial question is rarely a matter of ends. Armed versus unarmed force are varying dimensions of process to eliminate evil. For those confronting the direct brutality of war, economic or political injustice and human rights violations, the crucial question is to care for the means of working for a better world. To the end of mending the world there is no ready-made path. For those who walk the way of nonviolence, the road is made by walking.[16]

In the mid-1980s, at the height of the conflict between the *contras* and Sandinistas, ordinary people manifested steadfast resistance to discrimination, injustice and war through non-violent means such as fasting, prayer, and walking. In 1986, for example, Miguel d'Escoto organized a non-traditional "via crucis," or way of the cross. For fifteen days, pilgrims walked 326 kilometers along the rugged hill country along the northern border between Nicaragua and Honduras, to Managua, Nicaragua's capital city. He mentioned King's dream of the beloved community as having energized the walk. One pilgrim who walked the route in sandals was a seventy-two-year old peasant woman named Eulalia Hernandez. When I asked in an interview what she hoped to accomplish, she said, "peace." "How would the walk achieve peace?" "Through our sacrifice," she responded. With thousands of others, she is one of the steadfast resisters to domination who are helping to bring the beloved community closer to reality.

---

[16]Much quoted are words of Antonio Machado y Ruiz, "For you who walk there is no road. The road is made by walking." ("Caminante, no hay camino. Se hace el camino al anda."). Machado (1875-1939) was the Spanish existentialist poet who fled Spain in 1939 because of his support of the Spanish Republic. The author has seen the quote on posters and walls throughout Latin America.

9

A LIFE OF INTEGRITY

Shelley M. Douglass

As we come to the United States, we meet Shelley Douglass—another such "ordinary/extraordinary" person. Her own journey in the struggle is a microcosm of the U.S. peace movement. In "A Life of Integrity" Douglass gives us her view of "the legacy and the future" of nonviolence in America and clearly articulates a realization that has been glimmering throughout all our studies so far: ". . . that the quest for nonviolence is first a spiritual one conducted within our own hearts and then carried into the world beyond. . . . that nonviolence, if we are committed to it at every level, will challenge us as deeply as it challenges those whom we confront. . . ."

My son Tom and I spent an inspiring afternoon at the Birmingham Civil Rights Institute[1] a year ago. We wandered through the exhibits that show the history of racism in the city: separate and unequal schools, labeled water fountains and lunch counters, the dogs and guns and fire hoses that greeted efforts to make change.

We visited a display featuring the actual door of Dr. King's jail cell[2] in Birmingham's city jail, and we heard his speeches piped into

---

[1] The Birmingham Civil Rights Institute and Museum is an adventure into history that the reader may want to take: along with riveting displays on civil rights history, it includes an extensive archive of written materials and oral history interviews. Birmingham Civil Rights Institute, 520 16th St. N, Birmingham, AL.

[2] This door is so important because it was in his cell at the city jail that King wrote his "Letter from the Birmingham Jail," calling white leaders to account for their refusal to support the struggle. See *A Testament of Hope: The Essential Writing of Martin Luther King*,

the big rotunda. Walking through the Institute is a harrowing experience, recalling as it does the suffering and sacrifice that achieved what measure of justice we have today; it is also an inspiring and challenging way to spend an afternoon.

At the end of our visit Tom said to me, You were so lucky to be born then! You weren't alone, you were part of a Movement.

Is there still a movement? What is the future of nonviolence in the United States? What can we learn from the past? What are our tasks and our methods? What are the signs of the times, and how are they directing us?

Tom was right: it was a blessing to be born when I was born, and to be active in the movements of the Sixties and later. There was a sense of unity and purpose and possibility that now seems to be lacking.

I became aware of justice issues in time to enter into the struggle for civil rights while the commitment to nonviolence was still clear, while the goals were still obvious and seemed achievable. Voting rights, equal rights to education, to public services, access to simple things like a lunch counter hamburger or a job at the supermarket—it was clear where the injustice lay, clear that the laws were wrong. It seemed equally clear that we could change the laws, correct the injustice, and make sure that the American dream was shared by all American citizens. We could do that—were doing it—through nonviolence, love, self-sacrifice.

We were simultaneously naïve and wise: wise in knowing that our souls and our country depended upon the eradication of these blatant evils in ourselves and in our country. Our naïveté showed in our disillusionment at the failure of "the system" to change gracefully; in our shock and dismay at the faults of racism and sexism in our own ranks; in our failure to realize that racism and the growing brutality

---

Jr. ed. James M. Washington (San Francisco: Harper & Row, 1986).

of the Vietnam War[3] were not aberrations but natural outgrowths of an exploitative system.

We know more now. We know that the quest for nonviolence is first a spiritual one conducted within our own hearts and then carried into the world beyond. We know that no system of thought or government is going to be perfect, and that the same struggles will be waged repeatedly in each village, city, and country. We know that nonviolence, if we are committed to it at every level, will challenge us as deeply as it challenges those whom we confront; we know that we will continue to deepen and reach out, to suffer and rejoice as we seek a new way of life.

We know that there is never a last word or a final battle. The fall of socialism opens doors to different evils, the "kinder" capitalism is more secretive in its exploitation. The arms race is ended, but the remaining superpower continues to stockpile nuclear weapons. The future of nonviolence in the United States is a continuing, a building upon the past, a refusal to be silent when fashion has bypassed our concerns.

We have a strong and continuing tradition on which to build. We can reach back into the story of this place and find examples, analysis, and a developing methodology. The First Peoples, here before anyone else, had vibrant nonviolent traditions. The invaders themselves brought with them some voices that called for justice, for peace. William Penn and the Quakers in Pennsylvania are one obvious example, but there are others.

The abolitionist movement, the Underground Railroad, movements against various wars, the suffragist movement, the Catholic

---

[3]To understand the history, the idealism, and the disillusion of those days, read Tom Wells, *The War Within* (New York: Henry Holt, 1994).

Worker,[4] the Fellowship of Reconciliation,[5] the War Resisters' League[6]—all of these currents and many more have contributed to a river of alternative possibilities.

As I write the river is flowing underground, out of public sight and media awareness, but still it flows deep, strong, and turbulent. Sea-going rivers respond to the tide, and movements are like those rivers. At times they rise up, visible and vocal, to counter an injustice or call for change. The "movement years" of the '60s and '70s were high tide years. At other times the tide is low, and it seems that the river is about to dry up and disappear. Instead it continues to flow in its bed, digging ever deeper at the rock, until high tide comes again.

During these low tide periods the memory of marches and demonstrations has been enshrined, as though such things will never happen again. Behind the public shrines small communities, dedicated individuals work and wait, building the base for the next high tide. Perhaps when it appears it will indeed take a totally new form—who knows? The animating spirit, however, is that Wind of God that has blown down through the centuries. It blows gently now; later it will again become a gale.

Low tide periods incorporate the insights gained during the high tides. Lessons we have learned in the past are now being built into our ways of living and working, and because these ways of living and working are the channel for the nonviolence of the future, we can say something about the direction we are taking.

---

[4]Founded in the 1930s by radical activist-turned Catholic Dorothy Day, and French peasant-visionary Peter Maurin, this movement has been the cradle for many an activist, Catholic and otherwise. There are over 100 Catholic Worker houses in this country today, each with its own newsletter. Two of the most important are *The Catholic Worker*, 36 E. St. New York, NY 10003, and *The Catholic Agitator*, 632 N. Brittania St., Los Angeles, CA 90033.

[5]The Fellowship of Reconciliation is an international movement of religiously based pacifists active for peace and justice since the First World War. They can be reached at FOR, Box 271, Nyack, NY 10960.

[6]The War Resister's League, which often cooperates with both the Catholic Worker and the FOR, is also an international association of pacifists with less emphasis on religious affiliation.

Nonviolence will become more and more rooted in spirituality. We have learned that only to our detriment can faith traditions be left behind if we are to be firm in our stance and able to weather our own failures as well as systemic evil and others' betrayal. A good friend of ours, a traditional Native American elder, used to tell us, "Go back to your own tradition. You cannot grow from my roots, you have to find your own." She was right, I think. Not that our own traditions are without fault—far from it—and not that we cannot learn from hers, but that our history is our own, our traditions have shaped us. That is where we must dig, face our own failures and sins, and find the nourishment that can sustain us.

If we simply deny our history and traditions, we deny ourselves and our ancestors. Love of neighbor grows from self-acceptance, not self-denial. As a white middle-class woman, for example, I must come to terms with my own race and class privilege—I cannot renounce them and become black or destitute. As a Roman rite Catholic I must mine the riches of my tradition, knowing full well the failures and injustices of my Church.

Each of us faces a similar task in the world: winnowing our history, repenting, claiming. One of the processes quietly being lived these days is that sorting and claiming, moving from denial to acceptance and to peace. We are learning to stand in our own place, each with unique strengths and weaknesses, good and evil.

In my own Christian tradition there is creative, hopeful work being done by people like Megan McKenna,[7] Walter Wink[8] and Ched

---

[7]Megan McKenna, teacher and storyteller, mediates upon Biblical passages and characters with an eye to justice. A place to begin: Megan McKenna, *Parables: The Arrows of God* (Maryknoll, NY: Orbis, 1994).

[8]Walter Wink's powerful series on the role of power and the Powers in the New Testament is formative for many who try address worldly forces: Walter Wink, *Naming the Powers* (Philadelphia: Fortress Press, 1984), *Unmasking the Powers* (Philadelphia: Fortress Press, 1986), and *Engaging the Powers*, (Philadelphia: Fortress Press, 1992).

Myers,[9] who are seeking out the radical roots of the scriptures, and in so doing finding new depths of nonviolent tradition for us to draw on.

Dialogue continues between people of different traditions, each enriching and respecting the other. Thich Nhat Han,[10] leader of the Buddhist School of Youth for Social Service during Vietnam war days, has become a spiritual leader among Buddhists and Christians in the United States, doing important work for reconciliation among veterans of that war. Seeds of hope for future nonviolence are sown by each trip of reconciliation, each healing retreat.

We have learned that the future of nonviolence requires respect for our own traditions and a willingness to learn from others. This attitude of respect and the willingness to learn will facilitate our efforts to link globally. It has become clear over the last ten years (if not before) that nonviolence has a universal quality about it, and can be used within any culture, to address any injustice. We in the United States have an imperialistic tendency to see ourselves as the center of the world, its problems and its solutions, but we are beginning to learn that we are only part of a global structure, much of which is more advanced than we are.

As we move from being a creditor nation to being one of great debtors,[11] as our own population is increasingly divided between the super-rich and the poverty-stricken, we realize that the problems and injustices we face are part of an interwoven network of government and finance, which uses violence to enforce its economic will. We are learning the workings of international banking and finance, and

---

[9]Ched Myers has developed ways of reading the Gospel that allow us to read it alongside the newspaper and better comprehend each one. Ched Myers, *Binding the Strong Man* (Maryknoll, NY: Orbis, 1988); *Who Will Roll Away the Stone*, (Maryknoll, NY: Orbis, 1994).

[10]Thich Nhat Han, leader of the Buddhist Third Way movement in Vietnam during the war and much hated by both sides for his advocacy of nonviolence, now lives in exile in France and works tirelessly for peace and reconciliation. See his audiotapes "Teachings On Love," available through Credence Cassettes, P.O. Box 419491, Kansas City, MO 64141-6491.

[11]Two very important books to understand this crucial reality: Paul Valley, *Bad Samaritans* (Maryknoll, NY: Orbis, 1990), and Jack Nelson-Pallmeyer, *Brave New World Order* (Maryknoll, NY: Orbis, 1992).

finding it increasingly necessary to become involved in networks that address questions of economic exploitation and injustice across national boundaries but from common understandings and strategies.

What was once a nice sentiment or a religious slogan has become a hard truth: injustice anywhere leads to injustice everywhere. When one suffers we are all at risk. Translate that: $5 or $10 an hour jobs are not safe in this country when workers elsewhere are literally dying to do the same work for 5¢ or 10¢ a day.

Corporations whose goal is to make a profit think in global terms, sending work and materials to those places where costs are lowest and regulations fewest. Nonviolent movements will have to adopt the same attitude if we are truly to care for each other and the earth: we Americans too will have to learn to work cooperatively with diverse peoples and cultures, and have the humility to listen to other voices, adopt other ways.

We come again full circle to the need for spirituality. Gandhi used to say that nonviolence was not a discipline for the weak, but for the strong. The spirituality of nonviolence is not a pink-and-pretty greeting card sentiment, but a strong and uncompromising commitment to limiting and transforming the self so that we may all thrive equally together. What we seek from our traditions includes not only an affirmation of our unity and our call to love, but ways of growing beyond selfishness to full and free self-giving, the unthinking placing of the whole before our own interests that is still to be found in a few elder cultures.

The nonviolence of the future will be more and more anticipatory and proactive. As we learn about each other and communicate more we will begin to strengthen those networks that help us work together—networks like International Fellowship of Reconciliation,

Pax Christi,[12] Christian Peacemaker Teams,[13] Global Peace Teams,[14] and other such initiatives will grow and develop. More frequently, potentially violent situations will be identified and help solicited to defuse conflict before it reaches a flash point. Reconciliation teams will be sent into regions like Bosnia before the slaughter to create justice and offer conciliation.

In the same way teams will go to areas of hostility after violence occurs to help heal and rebuild. They may well incorporate into their work Gandhi's advice to a Hindu who had seen his only son murdered by Muslims: go and adopt a child and raise him as a Muslim. True nonviolence will sometimes require virtue that will seem superhuman until we find that we are able to attain it, with prayer, with support, with commitment.

Deeply spiritual, rooted in tradition, aware of the world, linked across miles and borders, thoughtful and anticipatory, the nonviolence of the future will still be home-based, tried and developed in local communities by those how live and work there.

Nonviolence begins at home, with the little things. It has been forcefully brought home to us that we cannot change the world for children while we neglect our own; we cannot nurture justice and benefit from exploitation. Nonviolence will continue to mean a firm place in our own neighborhoods, experimenting in whatever way is given to us to bring about better lives for our neighbors and ourselves.

As I write and as you read these words there are un-numbered unknown people in every part of this country praying, working, hoping for a better world. Some of them are trying to renew the

---

[12]Pax Christi, international Catholic peace organization can be reached at, 348 East Tenth St., Erie, PA 16503-1110.

[13]Christian Peacemaker Teams, an ecumenical group from Anabaptist roots, sends teams of observers into areas of conflict including Israel, Washington DC, and Eastern Europe: Christian Peacemaker Teams, PO Box 25, North Manchester, Indiana 46962.

[14]Global Peace Teams, a new venture seeking UN support for peacemaking teams, can be reached through Sr. Mary Evelyn Jegen, SND, Mt. Notre Dame, 701 E. Columbia Ave., Cincinnati, OH, 45215.

political process,[15] some of them quietly serve the poor or carefully organize pressure groups for change; some work to end abortion, some oppose the death penalty. Each little step taken makes a forward motion that ultimately moves us all together.

Nonviolence begins at home, with the little things. It begins with you, reading this book. It begins in your concern for people who are starving, people who are shot to death, for the earth and its preservation. Our work for justice can begin anywhere: with our own lives, with the city council, with peace in Bosnia or an end to sanctions on Iraq, with concern for global warming or nuclear proliferation.

What we discover as we address our concern is that it is connected to other concerns, like a spider-web or a piece of woven fabric. Pull one thread, you're linked to the whole. Change one stitch, you change the pattern. We are in fact all one, all linked together.

For many years my main focus was opposition to the nuclear arms race, to Trident submarines and missiles in particular. Now my main focus is living and working with homeless families here in Birmingham. When I spoke against the Trident system I would point out that we in the United States are only six percent of the world's population, but we consume twenty-five to thirty percent of the world's goods. In order to disarm, I would say, we need a more equitable distribution of the world's resources.

Now my life is centered on a related fact: one percent of the United States public earns forty percent of the nation's wealth; about thirty-eight million people, over fourteen million of them children, live in poverty in this country. When I talk about violence in our streets, about children sleeping overnight in the woods or dying in a hail of bullets, I always say that in order to solve these problems, we need a more equitable distribution of the nations goods.

I remember one courageously honest Trident worker who said to me at a public talk, "If you're asking me if I want to blow up the

---

[15]For example, an initiative from church roots and facilitated through the Sojourners community in Washington DC, "Call to Renewal," which seeks to infuse American politics with a sense of compassion and the value of all human life. Call to Renewal and Sojourners Community, 2401 15th St. NW, Washington, DC 20009.

world, the answer is no! But if you're telling me that to keep from blowing up the world I have to give up my TV, my VCR, my boat, and extra car, forget it!"

Most of us feel that way at some level. The issues we address, whether we deal with neighborhood violence or poverty or nuclear proliferation and the starvation of whole populations, all boil down to this very personal question. Is it more important for me to have my luxuries, or for all of us to survive?

The future of nonviolence (the future of the world) depends upon our answers to that question. Those of us who are rooted for the long haul bear a responsibility for sharing the joy and excitement of nonviolent living, so that people in love with their televisions and VCRs can see an alternative life, one where excitement grows from creativity and friendship, where risk is taken in person and bodies are birthed to be nurtured.

This sense of joy and adventure is known to us who have experimented in nonviolence,[16] but it is foreign and even frightening to those who have not. There is a zest that comes with living on the edge, living out one's beliefs, that is not duplicated in any other way. Regardless of the issue we address or the manner in which we address it—whether we're sitting in a jail cell for civil disobedience or fashioning a political campaign to change the balance of power, acting on our deepest beliefs is exhilarating.

Those of us who have tasted that feeling are not likely to settle any longer for television or movies: we want the real thing! Hunger and thirst for justice, for nonviolence, cannot be fulfilled by substitutes. In the end, the nonviolence of the future will be propelled by our own deep desires to be real, to be authentic, to be persons of integrity. We do not sacrifice our comfort or risk our lives for less than that—to live, to be fully human beings. In that commitment to a life of integrity we will find the impetus to take whatever steps need to be

---

[16]One of the most moving evocations of the joy and hope to be found through nonviolent action—and a good example of the interplay between scripture and a nonviolent life is in my husband's book, Jim Douglass, *The Nonviolent Coming of God* (Maryknoll, NY: Orbis, 1991).

taken, just as those who have gone before us have done. Another chapter waits to be written in our ongoing story of human love and transformation.

10

VOICES IN THE WILDERNESS: NONVIOLENCE AND THE ONGOING WAR AGAINST IRAQ[1]

Kathy Kelly

One of the most courageous peacemakers I have ever met is Kathy Kelly. Her article is the enactment of so much that we have been learning in our walk. Here is an ordinary person, challenged to be nonviolent, reaching out, despite fearful opposition, to her Iraqi brothers and sisters. With Kelly, we can journey to Iraq and back again, growing with her in nonviolence as we go. More importantly, we can be invited to join Kelly and the members of "Voices in the Wilderness," as they struggle against this injustice. In his January 1, 1996 letter to the UN, former U.S. Attorney-General Ramsey Clark wrote that the sanctions against Iraq are the "one crime against humanity in this last decade of the millennium that exceeds all others in magnitude, cruelty and portent." If we accept Kelly's invitation, then we need not merely reminisce about Gandhi's and King's liberation movements years ago, remembering the courage it took to face down powerful evils. We can engage in such a struggle right now.

It is January 16, 1997 and with wind chill temperatures at minus fifty degrees, Chicagoans are braced for frigid weather. I arrive breathless but on time for a Religious Studies Class at De Paul University, where my Kenyan friend, Dr.

---

[1]An earlier version of this chapter appeared as "The Children of Iraq" in *The Link* 10 (January-March 1997), published by Americans for Middle East Understanding.

Teresia Hinga, teaches a class on conscience and moral choice-making. I feel awkward, pulling off boots, scarves, and several sweaters as the class members, bemused, listen to her introduction. Teresia warmly welcomes me as a woman who went to Iraq during the Gulf War and was part of a peace camp on the border between Saudi Arabia and Iraq. She tells them that I have returned to Iraq several times since then, at great personal risk, and she urges them to listen to what I have to say.

I don't want to disappoint Teresia. I know that she focuses on ethical systems and tries to clarify the complexities of Catholic moral theology. But I am about to be stubbornly simplistic. "The most important ethical question we face, right now, is this: how can we learn to live together without killing one another. I don't believe in killing and I claim my religious right not to kill."

I quote Rabbi Abraham Heschel on pacifism: "There are no absolute pacifists, only biographical ones." I tell them that now, at age forty-four, I can at least say that I passionately want to be a pacifist. Learning to be a pacifist has caused me to refuse to pay taxes (when fifty per cent of them go to the military) and taken me to several war zones. I mention that I spent a year in prison for planting corn on a nuclear missile silo site, and would like, some day, to tell them more about that. But this day marked the sixth year since the Gulf War began, and I feel drawn toward talking with them primarily about moral choices in relation to that war.

I was in Iraq during the first fifteen days of the Gulf War, one of seventy-three volunteers from eighteen countries who joined a "peace camp" called the Gulf Peace Team. We intended to sit in the middle of a likely battlefield and call for an end to hostilities. I feel a glimmer of pride recalling that we succeeded in setting up an encampment in the desert almost exactly on the border between Iraq and Saudi Arabia and not far from a U.S. military camp.

Then the U.S. started the bombing. "Weren't you scared?" blurts a woman sitting in front of me. I shake my head. "No, honestly, what I felt was the deepest dismay I've ever known. I remember that every dog in the region began barking when the U.S. and allied war planes began to fly overhead. Those dogs barked themselves hoarse. I felt that was the most appropriate response to the war. The bombers flew overhead every night, sometimes departing once every five minutes. And each one carried a devastating payload of bombs. I imagined there would be nothing left of Iraq."

On January 27, 1991, anticipating that the ground war would begin, the Iraqi government decided to evacuate us by bus to Baghdad. They sent in a team of civilians to persuade us to pack and accompany them to Baghdad. We were divided about whether to stay or to go. A hard argument ensued, followed by a brief but moving demonstration by those who chose to stay but were forcibly removed.

By late afternoon, we were aboard buses traveling a road that was under constant bombardment. The buses swerved around huge bomb craters, and we saw the charred, smoking remains not only of oil tankers, but also of an ambulance, a passenger bus, and several civilian cars. Later I learned that even the Station Chief for CBS News had been attacked from the air while driving a tiny Toyota.

You see, one hundred percent of all bombing shown to us on TV was so-called "smart bombing," but after the war, the Air Force announced that only 7 percent of the bombing was "smart bombing"—and a quarter of *those* missed their targets, falling sometimes on civilian dwellings, schools, churches, mosques, or empty fields. The other ninety-three percent of the 88,500 *tons* of bombs dropped from jets alone (not counting bombing and missiles from ships), fell on neighborhoods, houses, and people. The smart bombs that *were* accurate, together with the rest kilotonnage, wiped out electrical generating plants and sewage treatment networks for every city and every village in Iraq—including those of the Kurds in the North. We systematically destroyed Iraq's infrastructure—bridges, roads, and highways, canals, hydroelectric dams, communication centers. We destroyed eighty-five percent of the farms and ninety percent of the fisheries.

On February 12, 1991, the Allied assault on Iraq was at full throttle. As Christians throughout the world observed Ash Wednesday, Muslims marked the special 'Id al-Fitr feast. Families in a prosperous Baghdad neighborhood, families had decided to celebrate the 'Id despite of the relentless bombing. They were to make use of the Ameriyah bomb shelter, the best Baghdad had to offer except for the shelter under the Al-Rashid hotel.

As evening fell, the whole neighborhood gathered for a common meal, not unlike middle America's potluck suppers. After eating, the men left to make room in the shelter for as many women and children as possible, including refugees from other areas. Mothers, grandmothers, infants, children, and teens hoped to sleep in safety during the blistering explosions. That night, two U.S. "smart bombs" found the ventilation shafts of the Ameriyah shelter. The exit doors were sealed and the temperature inside rose to 500 degrees Fahrenheit. Of the estimated 500 to 1300 people in the shelter, all but seventeen perished.

In March, 1991, a Red Crescent vehicle delivered four of us study team members to the Ameriyah neighborhood. Stepping out of the van, pen and notebook in hand, I think we must have been like Germans who first went to the death camps after World War II. Stretched across the brick facades of each house surrounding the cavernous remains of the shelter were black banners, bearing in graceful white Arabic writing, the names of the people from each home who had died in the massacre.

I had begun to cry, staring at the scene, when I felt a tiny arm encircling my waist. A beautiful Iraqi child was smiling at me. "Wel-kom," she said. Then I saw two women dressed in black cross the street. I thought surely they were coming to withdraw the children who now surrounded us. As they drew closer, I spoke the few Arabic words I knew: "Ana Amerikyyah, ana asifa"—I'm American and I'm sorry.

But they said, "La, la, la –" "No, no, no –" and they explained, "We know that you are not your government and that your people would never do this to us." Both the women had lost family members to the American bombs. Never again in my lifetime do I expect to experience such forgiveness.

I remember their words, and then was told that back in the U. S., college students hoisted beers to cheer the war on, shouting "Rock Iraq! Slam Saddam!" Soldiers sang out "Say hello to Allah!" when they blasted Iraqi targets. And the unforgettable words of General Colin Powell, when asked about the number of Iraqis who died in the war: "Frankly, that number doesn't interest me."

The students shake their heads and feel troubled.

I hold up a poster bearing photos from my visit to the Ameriyah neighborhood and point to the little girl who welcomed me. I wonder, is she a teenager now? Did she survive the ongoing economic war? Is she lucky enough to get clean water and adequate food in spite of the merciless embargo that has created a veritable state of siege in Iraq?

I am pleading with the students now, even though they show no opposition whatsoever. I want to immunize them from the contagions of residual war hysteria, from the temptation to consolidate all of Iraq into one demonized figure, Iraq's President Saddam Hussein. I want them to wonder whether or not the U.S. in fact wants to keep Saddam Hussein in power until they have carefully chosen a replacement who can control Iraq's military and its resources in ways that serve U.S. national interests.

Another misconception the students might encounter is that Iraq was an enormous, threatening power in the region. I launch into another story, in hopes of correcting the media cultivated fear of an Iraqi menace.

When Gulf Peace Team members settled into Baghdad's Al Rashid hotel on January 27, 1991, we discovered that all but a handful of international journalists had left Iraq. One press crew had abandoned an old manual typewriter. We quickly appropriated it and began typing by candlelight, thinking we ought to produce a press release just in case Peter Arnett ever took notice of us. While I was pounding away on the typewriter, one of our Iraqi "minders" shyly asked whether we would type something for them. We said we'd like to read it first. He handed me a letter addressed to then-Secretary-General of the United Nations, Javier Perez de Cuellar; to the International Committee of the Red Cross, and to various nongovernmental organizations (NGOs). The letter, signed by a cabinet-level official, begged the recipients to try to halt the indiscriminate bombing of civilians in Iraq and of the Baghdad–Amman road, the only escape route for refugees and the only passage for humanitarian relief entering Iraq. We quickly agreed to type the letter. The man handed me dog-eared stationery and carbon paper which had been used at least twenty times.

I thought to myself, "I'm from the country that is pounding these people back to the stone age. I'm typing official government correspondence, by candlelight, on an abandoned, antiquated typewriter, using wrinkled stationery and used carbon paper." And I thought of the Pentagon and the State Department, with their high-tech machinery, sophisticated software and hordes of well-equipped workers, all in support of the war. Yet Americans had been persuaded to fear the Iraqi menace.

How I wish that these stories of six years ago could be followed by post-war tales of reconstruction and reconciliation. Not so. Forty five days of bombardment came to an end, but a more lethal means of warfare against Iraqi civilians has never stopped. Six years of economic sanctions have cost the lives of over half a million children under age five. I show the class a poster made from photos our delegation took in August, 1996—haunting pictures of emaciated children, infants who look like old men, hairless and skeletal. I remember cradling the fragile body of one of the children and wondering if I was interrupting the final hours, together, for the mother and her child.

I feel that I'm more responsible for Iraq's government than any one of these children whom I met last summer. I come from the country whose oil-consumptive lifestyles helped bring about an oil-rich government. (And I don't even have a driver's license.) How can we impose collective punishment on children for the actions of a government that western diplomacy and weapons cannot control?

Democracy is based on information. Yet the U.S. military-industrial-congressional-press complex strangles the flow of information about suffering and death caused by U.S. reliance on weapons and military strategies to enforce so-called U.S. national interests. When *Voices* takes dramatic nonviolent actions that risk our health and/or liberty, we hope to bring attention to truths which we think, if understood, would deeply disturb masses of people. We think most people don't want to pay for wasteful, destructive policies that cause innocent people to suffer and die.

One student offers a thoughtful question. "What can you tell us about what Iraqi people think? I mean, they must want things to change. Why aren't they taking some steps?"

There is an Iraqi professor in the room, Dr. Almaney. I feel a surge of admiration for him as he turns to the student and proceeds to give a perfectly honest, direct answer. He asks students to understand that while Iraqis are very unhappy over their present conditions, it is not so easy for them to make a change. First of all, freedom of speech is not so readily enjoyed in Iraq as it might be in other countries. You can imagine further how sadly diminished free speech becomes when education and communication structures have been gravely weakened. When families are worried about where their next meal will come from, they are not so likely to involve themselves in organizing political movements. What's more, because of sanctions, almost every family in Iraq directly depends on government rationing to get whatever meager food supplies they have. Dr. Almaney said that many people in Iraq have good reason to fear that if Saddam Hussein's government went out of power the country could sink into a bloody civil war, one which could be exacerbated by hostile neighbors. I interject that the U.S. has heavily equipped neighboring states with huge arsenals of weapons, that among the top ten consumers of U.S. weapons are Egypt, Saudi Arabia, Israel and Turkey.

Dr. Almaney is kindly and professorial as he earnestly presents each point. In contrast, I feel angry and cynical. "Keep your eye on the ball when you analyze U.S. policy in the Middle East," I urge. "But remember, the 'ball' is oil. As long as Saddam Hussein rules Iraq, the U.S. has an excuse to keep Iraq out of the oil market. That means that other OPEC members can charge higher prices for their oil. We don't get our oil from Iraq. Ours comes primarily from Nigeria and Venezuela. Japan and Germany get their oil from Iraq and they are two of our top economic competitors. Watch how the mark and the yen have fallen against the dollar in the past years. Japan just announced that it is cutting its foreign aid—not its military—in half because of budgetary constraints. The U.S. wants to control the regions where our competitors get their oil. What's more, as long as the Saudis and Kuwaitis can charge higher prices for oil, they'll have higher revenues and can spend more money consuming our top export—weapons. The sanctions keep U.S. weapon companies happy, they keep oil producers happy—and if over half a million children pay the price, dying rapidly from diarrhea and other water-borne diseases, or enduring slow, strangulating death from starvation—well, U.S. policy makers have said that is an acceptable price to pay. So the war continues, but the victims are primarily children."

"Thank you so very much for listening," I say, and mean it, then hurriedly distribute *Voices in the Wilderness* literature, while inviting students to involve themselves in our work. As students file out, several say they never knew this was happening, others ask me to please call on them when we need help, almost all of them murmur a word of appreciation. Teresia embraces Dr. Almaney and me before we leave. "So you see," she says, her voice rich and warm, "the wilderness can be penetrated."

The Silent War

It's August 10, 1996, a sweltering day in southern Iraq, during one of the hottest summers on record. I sink onto my bed at the Basra Towers Hotel, grateful for the overhead ceiling fan and the promise of slightly less intense heat as evening falls. I don't feel particularly tired, but my companions insisted I take a break because I fainted after visiting the Basra Pediatrics and Gynecology hospital.

Dr. Tarik Hasim, the brilliant young director of residents, took us on a heartbreakingly thorough tour of several children's wards. "This is gruesome," my friend Brad Lyttle declared, after seeing so many skeletal infants, writhing in pain on blood-stained, rotted foam mats, with no anesthetics, no antibiotics, and barely any medicine at all to help them. We saw children with severe malnutrition, respiratory diseases, leukemia, kidney disease, and other serious ailments. Many faced imminent death because they lacked access to medicine. In one room, fourteen unusable incubators were stacked against the wall because parts were unavailable to repair them. The blood bank consisted of one miniature refrigerator and an ancient centrifuge. On one wing of the hospital there was only one operating bathroom. It was crowded with women and children trying not to slip on a puddle of dirty water that covered most of the floor.

Mothers stay with their children day and night. Dr. Hasim explains that the hospital is very short-staffed. Doctors cannot earn enough to feed their families, so some leave to work instead as taxi drivers, street vendors, or waiters. Nurses likewise find it impossible to continue practicing their skills. This means mothers must remain at the bedsides of their afflicted children, hopeful finding someone else to care for their households and their other children.

The temperature in Basra today is 140 degrees. Under these conditions, one should drink at least a gallon of water a day. Yet even the bottled water, for the few who can afford it, is contaminated. The sanctions prevent Iraqis from importing chlorine to purify their water. At the water ministry, officials showed us rusted, corroded pipe sections with large holes that allow contaminants to leak into Basra's drinking water. The eight-year Iran–Iraq war interrupted construction of the water filtration system and the project was never completed.

I reach for the bottled water that Archbishop Kassab gave us. "Drink this," he said, "and mark your bottles. We call this sweet water, water from Baghdad—I can tell you that if you drink the bottled water here it will make you very sick." I think of the desperately ill children I met earlier today, and put the bottle aside. Suddenly the lights go out and the ceiling fan stops. "Not again," I mutter, annoyed at myself for not thinking to bring candles on this trip. I grope my way downstairs to the hotel lobby. Already the staff has mustered up their spare candles, eager to help foreigners like me.

Saad leans on the counter. "You know, Ms. Kelly," he says, "another thing we say is this: forty-five days of bombardment were better than these sanctions. You bomb us, and, O.K., after forty-five days we can rebuild. But the sanctions destroy us and after six years we have nothing left to rebuild with."

When the Hysteria Subsides

I sit in my living room surrounded by some of the finest people in the world. It is January 18, 1997, six years since the Gulf War began and one year since a handful of us initiated "Voices in the Wilderness," a campaign to end the U.S./U.N. sanctions against Iraq. I again recall George Rumens's assurance that when the war hysteria subsided the more lasting response to the war would be deepest regret and remorse for the suffering we have caused. Often his words have been borne out. In the absence of warmongering media barrages that obscured and ignored Iraqi suffering, we have been heard, in classrooms, community rooms, and small town papers and radio stations. Consistently, a more sober response grows. "We didn't know. We didn't realize. . . ."

Now we must harvest the results of our first year of campaign work and carefully strategize next steps. We have spent most of the day together, informally evaluating, brainstorming and reminiscing.

Brad Simpson, a graduate student at Northwestern University, and I compared notes about a delightful and unusual experience we shared in common. Each of us, on separate occasions, traveled alone, on public transportation, into Iraq. Unable to speak Arabic, but wanting to give some indication of why we were going to Iraq, we handed fellow passengers the Arabic translation of a statement describing our campaign. They would invariably nod in approval as they read our intent. Midway through the document, they would reach a description of the U.S. government's punitive response to our efforts to bring medical relief supplies to Iraq. We have been threatened with twelve years in prison, a one million dollar fine, and a

$250,000 administrative fine. Those lines prompted enthused responses. "Yes, you are most welcome. Thank you. God bless you."

Brad chuckled, noting: "After the passengers finished the statement I immediately became the bus mascot. At the first rest stop, people ran to get me tea. They offered me cigarettes and biscuits. It was really cold and I was shivering in a light jacket. When I went back on the bus, there was a huge, thick blanket on my seat."

I tell the story of my own visit. We all share pictures and slides as well as stories. The pictures are crucial for our outreach and education. Most of the photos come from two hospitals, the main hospital in Basra, and the Qadissiya Hospital, on the outskirts of Baghdad, in a very poor area called Saddam City. During an August 1996 visit to the Qadissiya hospital, I was determined to carefully identify some of the women and children we met, and to note details about their plight. What a grim necessity. Rick McDowell, a carpenter from Akron, Ohio, is an excellent photographer as well. We teamed up to snap photos of mothers and children and then, with a translator, question the weary mothers. How old are you? And your child? From what does your child suffer, and how long? Do you have other children? Who cares for them now?

Thus the stories emerge. Ana Anba is twenty-seven years old. She looks glassy-eyed, exhausted, and on the verge of tears. For eleven days she has been at the bedside of her nine-year-old son, Ali Anba. He is listless, barely conscious. Ali's illness began months ago with a respiratory infection. Ana has since purchased thousands of dinars of medicine, but Ali's condition has not improved. She wonders now if the medicine she bought on the black market was expired. Or perhaps it was not what he really needed. Also, knowing there is not enough food, she is anxious for her other children. We tell her that we hope her story will help awaken parents and families in the U.S. "When?!" she asks. The interpreter tries to gloss over her obvious anger. "She is frustrated and tired from six years of sanctions." Ana interrupts sharply. "In America, would women want this for their children?" Then she turns to her son Ali and whispers softly, "It is for the children that we ask an end to this suffering, not for us."

Yusuf Asad, seven months old, suffers from septicemia. A doctor tells us that the pale, gasping infant is very near death. Before coming to the hospital, his parents sold their television and other pieces of furniture to buy high priced medicines. "Nothing works," sighs his mother. "Since ten day he has been here." Yusuf's father makes a fist and points to his arm, telling us he's already donated all the blood he can for transfusions.

Along with notes and photos, we also pool the personal requests we received—notes slipped into our hands, begging for particular medicines. Even government workers in cabinet level ministry offices asked us for aspirins, eye drops and other over-the-counter items easily acquired in this country.

Our agenda is long and the tasks ahead seem daunting. Primarily, we need to find ways to dramatize our confrontation with the U.S./U.N. sanctions. The best way forward seems to be that of continuing our present effort: bring medical relief supplies to people in Iraq, in open and public violation of the sanctions.

"The biggest problem we face, as I see it, is Resolution 986," says Bob Bossie, a Catholic priest from Chicago, who traveled to Iraq twice this year and was part of the Gulf Peace Team. The "oil for food" deal passed under Resolution 986 is an excuse not to lift the sanctions, but it gives the impression to many people, even some of our supporters, that it will eliminate human suffering in Iraq. Really it is just a slower form of death.

Chuck Quilty, a social worker from Rock Island, reliably supplies us with primary source material. He notes:

> This article says Resolution 986 will make more food available, but Iraqis still won't get meat, eggs, milk, and other necessary ingredients of their diet. What's more, after funds earmarked for reparations, U.N. surveillance and maintenance of programs to assist people in the Kurdish north of Iraq are subtracted from the total, the Iraqis will receive less than $0.25 per person per day, and the continuing embargo on

other commerce prevents the repair and restoration of vital water, sanitation and medical infrastructures.

As Chuck speaks, I remember the uncollected garbage we saw in Saddam city, piled along the streets with no functioning trucks to carry it away. I remember the nightmare of fetid, backed up sewage in Basra. It is crazy to think that allowing limited purchase of food and medicine alone, apart from all these infrastructure needs, could address the health and sanitation needs of the whole society. It is not only crazy, it is criminal. How, we wonder together, can we find actions commensurate to the crimes being committed.

We might also raise concern about rises in congenital disease and fetal deformities that are prevalent in children under five in Iraq and in the children of Gulf War Veterans. The common denominator could be depleted uranium, chemical agents which were released by allied bombing or other environmental exposure. Nearly a million depleted uranium-tipped shells were used during the Gulf War spreading tons of highly toxic uranium oxide particles into the air. Researchers in this country say that those who inhaled DU during the war are now in the ingestion phase—i.e., it will travel through the blood stream and be deposited in organs, especially the kidneys. Kidney and liver dysfunction are now the fourth and fifth leading causes of death in Iraqi children under five. We are now selling DU to Kuwait and Saudi Arabia, among others. The truth needs to be made known for the benefit of all concerned.

Voices in the Wilderness

I am in a car driving from Baltimore to Washington, D.C. at 6:15 a.m. With me are Simon Harak, a Jesuit priest, and two women religious, Ardeth Platte, and Carol Gilbert. We four will later meet Art Laffin, a Catholic lay worker, at the Senate Hart Building. Our plan is to enter the Senate confirmation hearings for Madeline Albright's designation as Secretary of State.

On May 12, 1996, as U.N. Ambassador, she had been questioned by Leslie Stahl of 60 Minutes about the vast number of children dying in Iraq and those that Leslie Stahl had seen herself in traveling there for CBS News. At that time, Albright responded "It's a hard decision, Leslie, but we think the price, the price is worth it."

We arrive two hours before the hearing. Already thirty people are in line. Tucked inside our coats are folded enlargements of pictures that Rick took of Iraqi children whom we visited in August, children whose dark eyes plead for relief from starvation and disease.

Albright stresses her commitment to human rights, but as regards Iraq she only affirms readiness to maintain tough policy. As the applause subsides, I stand up. "Ms Albright," I call out, "over half million Iraqi children have died because of U.S./UN sanctions. In May, 1996, you told 60 Minutes that this was an acceptable price to pay in order to maintain U.S. interests in the region. Are you prepared to withdraw that dangerous statement?" A security guard, Officer Goodine, is at my elbow. Senator Jesse Helms motions to him to remove me, but the young officer raises his hand politely as if to indicate "Just a moment, let her finish," and he gently taps my arm. "These children are helpless victims," I call out again, moving into the aisle. "Ms. Albright, please, you could do so much good." The officer leads me out as though he were ushering at the opera. Simon Harak is already on his feet, asking Albright if she would impose the same punishment on any other country that fails to comply with U.S. demands—or is this treatment reserved for the Arab people only?

Ardeth, Carole, and Art rise, in turn, to speak. After we are all escorted out, Albright speaks to the Committee, saying, "I am as concerned about the children of Iraq as any person in this room. . . . Saddam Hussein is the one who has the fate of his country in his hands, and he is the one who is responsible for starving children, not the United States of America."[2]

Iraqi children are totally innocent of oil power politics. All those who prevent the lifting of sanctions, including Madeline Albright, are

---

[2]*Chicago Tribune,* January 9, 1997.

not. One-line disclaimers of responsibility may appear suavely diplomatic, but the children are dead and we have seen them dying. According to the U.N. itself, they died as a direct result of the embargo on commerce with Iraq. Many United Nations members favored significantly easing these sanctions. The U.S. government and Madeline Albright as its spokesperson prevented that from happening. This economic embargo continues warfare against Iraq, a silent war in which only the weakest, most vulnerable and innocent noncombatant civilians—women, children and families—continue to suffer.

Four delegations from *Voices in the Wilderness* traveled to Iraq in 1996, more in 1997, and still more will in 1998. Each group openly defies the sanctions by bringing medical relief supplies directly to Iraqi children and families. Our trips create a drama that we hope will gain attention for the plight of Iraqi people, especially the children. Upon return, we "hit the ground running," with presentations in classrooms and community groups. We contact our legislators, create displays, send out mailings, and try very hard to push the issue into the mainstream media.

Our fifteen minute confrontation at the seat of the world's sole superpower government garnered more public attention from the mass media mouthpieces of American culture than all of our trips to Iraq and our urgent pleadings put together in the preceding year. But I am afraid that the name of our campaign, Voices in the Wilderness, is all too apt.

Mohandas Gandhi, Martin Luther King, and the philosophers of nonviolence repeatedly discuss the relationship of means and ends. They uphold unyielding faith that truthful, just, and good means will ultimately lead to good ends. We must not be tempted to use dishonest and cruel means, even when it may seem an expedient calculation that such methods will hasten revolutionary changes, ending in good results for all of society. They argue that ultimately the means we use will determine the end we get. We want Americans to realize that we must be careful in using methods that only appear to be nonviolent, such as boycotts and embargoes. Though they seem to be nonviolent, they can in many actual cases bring about results that are brutally violent and destructive.

Shortly before the Gulf War began the opposition peace movement in the United States and Europe mobilized quickly, visibly, and vocally. After the end of the bombing war this movement evaporated rapidly, in the belief that the war was over. In fact, it had just begun. Today it continues in a quiet but devastating form, largely invisible to most people in the United States, Europe, and other distant countries.

After World War II, Milton Mayer went to Germany to interview the so-called "good Germans." He came back to write a book descriptively summarized in its title, *They Thought They Were Free*. Recently a book has come out by Daniel Johan Goldhagen, entitled *Hitler's Willing Executioners*, about the role of ordinary Germans in the genocidal policies of the Third Reich.[3] These books analyze propaganda in the guise of news and explain what people believed about their culture. There are many such books to be written about Americans in the twentieth century (the so-called "American Century"). Most Americans remain woefully ill-informed and misinformed about the purposes and effects of U.S. policies throughout the world.

Like voices in the wilderness, we are crying out to them: Look face to face into the dark eyes of the children of Iraq, as we have done, and do unto these little ones. . . .

Unto these little ones. . . .

---

[3]Milton Sanford Mayer, *They Thought They Were Free: The Germans, 1933-1945* (Chicago: University of Chicago Press, 1955; Daniel Jonah Goldhagen, *Hitler's Willing Executioners : Ordinary Germans and the Holocaust* (New York : Random House, 1996).

11

NONVIOLENCE IN THE SCHOOLS: PROGRAMS IN CONFLICT RESOLUTION

Philip J. Harak

These last two chapters explore various aspects of peacebuilding. Philip Harak begins with an all-too-real conflict between high schoolers Tom and Jamal. "If violence erupts [in this conflict]," Harak tells us, "it will become one of the 16,000 crimes that occur daily in schools. . . . The National Education Association reported in 1993 that each day, 160,000 students skip class because they fear physical harm." If there is to be peace for Tom and Jamal, and for our schools, where will it come from? Through his involvement with conflict resolution programs, Harak gives us hope that the dire difficulty of violence among our students may well yield rich human resources for nonviolence in the third millennium.

It is a Thursday afternoon and Tom, a senior wrestler on his high school team, has just decided to start the usual weekend party a day early. It has been a rough week after all. He has just learned from his guidance counselor that he was definitely not in the top half of his class. So that probably meant that he would, after all, have to join "the few, the proud, the Marines." As he walked from the guidance office, the bell signaled the end of third period. English class next. "Damn," he muttered. Now he had to deal with all the continuous arguing and carryover of the attitudes outside of class. Can't wait to get hammered tonight, he thought.

Just then, two friends of his meet him, and tell him that they saw his girl Ellen being really friendly with Jamal, a junior who plays on the football team.

"You just gonna let that happen, Tom?" they ask.

Adrenaline surges in him. Tom figures that Jamal would be at his locker now, and he marches down the hall, his friends behind him. Tom sees Jamal in a group, and pushes his way towards him.

"Hey nigger! You been talking to my girl after school, huh? I told you before to stay away from her." Friends of both begin to cluster around. Others stop and surround the two.

"Back up, genius. She had a question about math. Sure as hell can't ask you—you're too damn stupid! Can't tell time, you dumb whiteboy!" And the crowd begins chanting, "Fight! Fight!"

Let's pause a moment in this too-familiar high school scene. If violence erupts, it will become one of the 16,000 crimes that occur daily in schools, totaling nearly three million annually.[1] Since 1950, violent law breaking by juveniles has come close to tripling every twenty years.[2] From 1983-1992, there has been a 128 percent increase in murder and manslaughter by youths under eighteen, a ninety-five percent increase in aggravated assault, a twenty-five percent increase in forcible rape, and a twenty-two percent increase in robbery. We are all familiar by now with the tragedies of Columbine, Jonesboro, Jacksonville, Gainesville, Pearl, and Heath High Schools. The experience and threat of violence dramatically alters a young person's life, often inhibiting academic learning. The National Institute for Dispute Resolution (NIDR) cites data compiled by the U.S. Department of Justice showing teens twice as likely to become victims as adults; one-half of all violence against teens occurs in school build-

---

[1] Steven Edwards, Kenneth Guordz, Walli Islam, "Violence in Our Schools" (East Hartford, CT: H.S. In-House Publication, 1994), 2.

[2] National Institute for Dispute Resolution (NIDR): 1726 M Street, NW, Suite 500, Washington, DC 20036-4502. According to information faxed to me November 26, 1996. They cite here research conducted by Susan Lee Carter on the Mediation in the Schools Program, 1994.

ings, on school property or near school.[3] The National Education Association reported in 1993 that each day, 160,000 students skip class because they fear physical harm. Nationwide, between September 1986 and June 1990, at least seventy-five people were killed by guns at school, over 200 were severely wounded by guns, and at least 242 were held hostage at school by gun-wielding assailants.[4]

High school students like Tom, Jamal, Ellen and their friends are the leaders of the next millennium. If we wish to carry the legacy of Gandhi and King into the future, we must begin now to consider how we might train our high school students in the virtues of *ahimsa*—of nonviolence. In addition, we must create an atmosphere more conducive to peaceful conflict resolution, thereby more closely imitating a "beloved community."

Of course our scenario should have never been allowed to get to this point. Once racial epithets have been thrown, manhood has been challenged, and inadequacy ridiculed, it is nearly impossible to stop the violence. Even so, the friends of Jamal and Tom could have stepped in and defused the situation, instead of encouraging a fight. We will talk about that later. Right now, let us "rewind" the scene and see what new programs are being offered in our schools for nonviolent conflict resolution.

As a high school teacher and coach, I have been involved in conflict resolution studies and programs for several years. I have learned that conflict resolution programs in schools grew out of the social justice concerns of the 1960s and 1970s, when, in part motivated by the success of some religious groups' successful training, teachers began incorporating dispute resolution in instruction. Though only ten percent of schools presently have them, more and more schools are asking for them.[5] When I last checked the Web, I found over 100,000 hits for the title, "Conflict Resolution in Schools."

---

[3] Ibid.
[4] Edwards, et al., 2.
[5] Information taken from NIDR's document, *The History of Conflict Resolution*.

How can these programs help students like Tom and Jamal? What do they offer these leaders of the third millennium?

First of all, they offer an understanding of conflict. Contrary to popular belief, we are essentially peaceful animals, and learning to manage conflict is part of learning to be who we really are.[6] Conflict is a state of disharmony between incompatible persons or ideas or interests. It occurs all the time, both inside of us and outside. We can be in conflict with boyfriends and girlfriends, when hearing rumors and gossip, over turf issues, and within ourselves when we do not "measure up" to expectations. Look at Tom. He went into an internal conflict as soon as he heard from his counselor that he was not in the top half of his class. How did he respond? Maybe he wanted to hit the counselor. Maybe he was blaming his teachers or the school or his wrestling demands. He became angry. Maybe he was angry with his parents for their expectations of him. Maybe he was frustrated at his unmet goals, and angry at the quiet voice inside of him that kept telling him that if he had really applied himself, not drunk so much, that he would have succeeded.

Tom and Jamal have choices, of course, of how they are going to deal with their conflicts with each other. Besides violence, Tom could have pretended that no conflict existed with Jamal or with Ellen. Jamal could have given in to Tom's taunts, and backed off. One or both could have lightened the issue by joking, or employed a host of other avoidance behaviors. Several consequences can result from behavioral responses to conflicts. Those include escalation or de-escalation of stress, better or worse relationships, higher or lower self-esteem. Consequences tend to reinforce our beliefs about conflict, more firmly entrenching the person in a cycle of attitude about conflict/behavior in response to conflict/consequence/reinforcement

---

[6]See "The Seville Statement on Violence," *American* 45(October 1990): 1167-1168. Twenty international scholars dispelled five myths about violence and human genetics, showing for example that humans are not genetically predisposed to violence and war.

of initial attitude. Unless new understandings and alternative skills are learned, this cycle will be repeated.[7]

One apparently effective way to resolve conflict, as we have said, is to turn to violence. Violence is a power, and like all powers, has the ability to bring about change. Derived the Latin roots *vis* (force) and *latus* (to carry), "violence" literally means "to bear force against." Violence shares its etymology with "violate," and that is the sense victims of it often feel. More broadly, violence seeks to impose one's will on another in a way that violates that person's inherent right, and uses coercion and greater force so that one's power will prevail.[8] Violence is treating or responding to a person as a thing for the purpose of self-gratification.[9]

Some authors propose that people choose violence for self protection, serving a self interest, or for some social obligation, or combinations of the three.[10] Others suggest that violence is an unconsciously chosen action, motivated by a broad range of influences such as a behavior learned from parents, to an addictive response.[11]

David Johnson and Roger Johnson are researchers and educators who have been prominently involved for the past thirty years training teachers how to teach students to manage conflicts within the tenets of cooperative learning. They have established a national and

---

[7]"The Conflict Cycle," in the training manual, *Drugs Don't Work Training Manual: Peer Mediation, Training of Trainers* (Hartford, CT: Governor's Partnership for Connecticut's Workforce, n.d.). See this manual for a good discussion of sources and responses to conflicts.

[8]Elizabeth McCallister, Smith College, Northampton, MA, March 2, 1994 Lecture. McCallister is an activist and the wife of longtime peace and justice advocate Philip Berrigan.

[9]Fr. Immanuel Charles McCarthy, Amherst MA workshop, October 21, 1994. McCarthy, a Nobel Peace Prize nominee, is a brilliant apologist for Christic nonviolent love, and vigorous opponent of the Church's position on justified violence. He added that within a Christian context, apathy and silence in the face of relievable human suffering or injustice is also violence. Also, refusal to love as Christ loved can be a form of violence.

[10]Fr. I. C. McCarthy, "Boldly Like God, Go Against the Swords," from The Center for the Christian Response of Nonviolence, 3835 Independence Hwy, Independence, OR 97351. Taken from his fifteen-cassette taped presentation on Christian Nonviolence.

[11]For a good discussion of the latter, see G. Simon Harak, S. J., "After the Gulf War: A New Paradigm for the Peace Movement," *Journal of Humanistic Psychology* 32 (Fall 1992): 11-40.

international network of school districts in which their Peacemaker Program and cooperative learning principles are implemented. They conducted seven studies of peer mediation, mainly among elementary age school children. They found that before training, most students were involved in conflicts daily. The conflicts reported, in terms of frequency, were put-downs and teasing, playground conflicts, access or possession conflicts, physical aggression and fights, academic work conflicts, and turn taking.[12]

Johnson and Johnson report that within the U.S., there are two basic types of peer mediation programs within schools: cadre, and total student body programs (TSB). The former emphasizes training a small number of students to serve as peer mediators; the latter trains each student in school how to manage conflicts constructively.[13]

Let's return to Tom and Jamal, only this time add that there is a cadre of trained student mediators in their school. When we "replay" the scene, an adult will intervene and direct them to the mediation process. After an interview with a screening adult (sometimes an assistant principal; but it can also be the assigned coordinator), if they choose to, Tom and Jamal will sit with two peer mediators and begin resolving their dispute. Mediators are taught that there are specific techniques that help create agreements between our disputants, and in every mediation. The six steps are: (1) the voluntary, agreed upon establishment of the ground rules; (2) the telling of the stories and identifying and defining the problem; (3) identifying underlying issues and feelings; (4) generating options for solutions; (5) writing out and signing the formal agreement; (6) closure, with follow-up by coordina-

---

[12]David W. Johnson, Roger T. Johnson, "Teaching Students To Be Peacemakers: Results of Five Years Of Research," *Peace and Conflict: Journal of Peace Psychology* 1 (1995): 417-438. I have a reprint of the article, paginated from 1 to 31. Subsequent page references will be from my reprint. Above taken from p.8.

[13]The Community Boards of San Francisco Conflict Managers Program and The School Mediators' Alternative Resolution Team (SMART) are examples of a cadre; programs produced by the Chicago "Conflict Resolution Program" and the University of Minnesota Cooperative Learning Center, "Teaching Students To Be Peacemakers" are examples of total student body programs. Information taken from Johnson and Johnson, 6 & 7.

tor and disputants' agreement to return if mediation is unsuccessful in practice.[14]

While having a cadre is certainly preferable to having no program in school, some problems remain. In our replay, Tom and Jamal responded to an adult. That is not always possible, nor is it going far enough to teach individual responsibility in conflict management. Students in the cadre must also be leaders from within the student community, otherwise a student mediator will not have the perceived status to interrupt a brewing conflict. Even so, it is unclear how having a cadre will reduce the frequency or severity of violent outbreaks.

A TSB approach aims to change the atmosphere of the school, at least somewhat. TSB emphasizes training each student to constructively manage conflicts. A guiding principle here is that all students have the responsibility and the power to regulate their own behavior and that conflicts in others present an opportunity to help.

Johnson and Johnson tell us that a TSB program needs to have the following: (a) all students in the school know how to negotiate integrative agreements to their conflicts and how to mediate schoolmates' conflicts, (b) all students have the skills to use the negotiation and mediation procedures effectively, (c) the norms, values, and culture of the school promotes and supports the use of the negotiation and mediation procedures, (d) peer mediators are available to support and enhance students' efforts to negotiate, and (e) the responsibility for peer mediation is rotated throughout the entire student body so that every student gains experience as and expects to be a mediator.[15]

Within the TSB approach, Johnson and Johnson have created a Peacemaker Program which is closely based on the theoretical literature on conflicts of interest, integrative bargaining, perspective reversal, and third-party intervention. Students are taught to be peacemakers in four steps. First, they learn what is and is not a

---

[14]For a detailed discussion of these steps, see the *Drugs Don't Work: Training of Trainers Manual.*

[15]Johnson and Johnson, 6.

conflict. Second, they are taught how to negotiate integrative agreements to conflicts of interests. Third, they are taught how to mediate their classmates' conflicts. This step follows most of the above 6 steps in peer mediation. Here, if peer mediation fails, teachers and administrators mediate and arbitrate until the conflict is resolved. Fourth, the teacher implements the peacemaker program, where students receive thirty minutes of training per day for thirty days and then receive thirty minutes of training twice a week for the rest of the school year.[16] So if we replay our scene in a school with a TSB approach, let's look at some key changes in atmosphere and behavior. Tom has had a bad day—or a bad week. As I had alluded to earlier, here his friends would not be inciting a fight. I doubt that they would have told him about Ellen and Jamal, at least in that provocative way. There might not be the possessiveness of boy over girl. And if there were an exchange between Tom and Jamal, it would have been without the racial epithets. Though Jamal would have reacted angrily, their reactions would not have been as insulting. Finally, those crowding around would not be chanting "Fight!" Rather, having each been trained in conflict resolution, they would be using their energy to find ways to defuse the conflict, and to assist in resolving it.

The research is clear about this important finding: no student untrained in mediation principles applied conflict resolution skills to school or to real life conflicts.[17] And it seems that training all students begins to create an atmosphere quite different from that of the violent cultural norm. Where else have we heard of communities of nonviolence?

Bringing Gandhi and King to School

We know that both Gandhi and King stood for nonviolence. So in a sense, their thoughts are already being enacted in these resolution programs. And they believed that nonviolent conflict resolution must

---

[16]Ibid., 7.
[17]Ibid., 11-13.

be taught. However, I want to examine what further contribution they would make if we paid more conscious attention to their insights into the practice of *ahimsa*.

For both men, nonviolence was more than just a technique. It was an attitude of the heart and a way of life. Even more, it went beyond thinking about strategies in individual cases, and toward the creation of a whole new "politics" or system of relating to each other. Gandhi's ashram and King's "beloved community" offered profound challenges to families, neighborhoods, and countries that were deeply in the habit of treating each other violently. How might such challenges affect our understanding of nonviolent conflict resolution programs in the schools? Let us go back to the story of Tom, Jamal, and Ellen to find out.

First of all, Gandhi and King would remind us of the value of self-examination. Both emphasized the primacy of self-examination in nonviolence. King told an interviewer that he subjected himself to "self purification and to endless self analysis; [he] question[ed] and soul-search[ed] constantly. . . ."[18] Gandhi stated simply, "Nonviolence is impossible without self-purification."[19]

We would have to extend our self-examination to our families to uncover patterns of violence. Jamal and Tom's personal histories exposed them to family violence. Since Tom was a young child, his parents have struck him when he misbehaved. Among the many effects on him, Tom has learned what it means to use greater power in a relationship where conflict exists. The greater physical force is right, and necessary in underscoring important lessons. Jamal too was regularly slapped, beaten, and shoved by his parents when he acted against his parents' directions.[20]

---

[18]Martin Luther King, Jr., A *Testament of Hope: The Essential Writings and Speeches of Martin Luther King, Jr.*, ed, James M. Washington (New York, NY: HarperCollins, 1986), 376.

[19]Mahatma Gandhi, *Gandhi on Non-Violence*, ed., Thomas Merton (New York, NY: New Directions, 1964, 1965), 44.

[20]Fr. I. C. McCarthy's taped series on Christian Nonviolence, tape #11. Listen to that tape for a poignant illustration of the effects of parent's violence to his child. Philip Greven, *Spare the Child: The Religious Roots of Punishment and Psychological Impact of Physical Abuse*

Terry Kellogg, noted psychotherapist and specialist on family relationships, reports that eighty percent of learning by children is through nonverbal communications.[21] Parents are the agents of what children can understand about love. Violence is an agent for creating fear to get something done. Gandhi and King would point out, then, that a parent who uses violence fuses and confuses love and violence for the child. Love would use discipline, persuasion, conversion. Violence uses coercion, which seeks to alter behavior through fear of consequences, fear of greater physical force, and threats to survival.[22]

Their self-examination yields further destructive tendencies in their families. Both have had parents and grandparents who abuse alcohol. The young men, in turn, have begun drinking heavily almost every weekend. Addictions of their nature forbid honest self-appraisal. The challenge for both practitioners of nonviolence and recovering addicts is to embrace a lifestyle that demands a daily, searching moral inventory.[23] An unnamed sin, it has been observed, will repeat itself indefinitely and with zeal, until named, repented, and acted against.

(New York, NY: Alfred A. Knopf, 1991) is a powerful book on the effects of beatings under the auspices of religion.

[21]Terry Kellogg, with Marvel Harrison, *Broken Toys, Broken Dreams: Understanding and Healing Codependence, Compulsion and Family Relationships* (Amherst, MA: BRAT, 1990). Kellogg gives thorough accounts of the boundary violations, with a list of violating behaviors.

[22]McCarthy Lecture, Amherst, MA, October 21, 1994. McCarthy notes the New Testament's struggle between fear and love. Whereas love creates love, using fear sets up a mechanism to fear the user in the future, or to get a superior power of fear. Christians must use Christ as the ultimate norm of Christian conduct, and must "magnify" God through acts of mercy and love. Such actions directly contrast with threat and use of dominative physical force.

[23]Various Anonymous Authors, *Alcoholics Anonymous: The Story of How Many Thousands of Men and Women Have Recovered from Alcoholism* (New York, NY: Alcoholics Anonymous World Services, Inc., 1939, Third Edition), 58-71. Note especially steps 4 and 10 for purposes of daily self-examination. On how alcoholism affects family and friends of the alcoholic, and an adaptation of the "12 Step" AA program, see: Various Anonymous Authors, *Al-Anon's Twelve Steps and Twelve Traditions* (New York, NY: Al-Anon Family Group Headquarters, 1990); David L. Fleming, S. J., *The Spiritual Exercises of Saint Ignatius: A Literal Translation and a Contemporary Reading* (St. Louis, MO: The Institute of Jesuit Sources, 1978). Ignatius Loyola emphasized a twice-daily conscience examination (he himself examined his conscience *hourly* by the end of his life). For 500 years Ignatius' Spiritual Exercises have provided a brilliant path toward wholeness and discernment.

Teachers also must practice self-examination. We must habitually reflect on our motivations, behaviors, and thinking and especially monitor our interactions with students. When appropriate, a teacher must initiate amends in conflictual relationships with colleagues and students. The challenge to parents and educators is to take the necessary first step and to teach the ideas of conflict resolution—with its important tenets such as honoring your enemy's position—because people cannot act on or choose ideas they have not heard. Yet how can teachers teach what they do not know or model what they do not practice? Teachers cannot direct a student to be an agent for that which the teacher cannot do. A Hindu proverb says, "Reform yourself, and you reform thousands."[24]

If things like alcohol make self-examination impossible in the family, then the very structure of how and what we teach makes self-examination frightening for us teachers. And it is precisely those unexamined structures that we "take for granted" that the nonviolence of Gandhi and King would challenge. Take, for example, our paradigm of teaching. Schools are places of injustice when they systemically treat children as objects or recipients of adults' intentions.[25] Once children are objectified, even in the deceptively good rubric of their benefitting from what the expert adults pour into them "for their own good"—this creates an unjust and violent system.

---

[24]Jim Ballard, *When Teachers Change* (Winter Park, Florida: Continuing Education Institute, 1987). This excellent booklet offers concise and healthy ways for teachers to keep the focus on one's self, to stop victimizing students, and to allow them to be the doers in the education process.

As a teacher faced with the problem of school violence, I answer the question, What is the biggest challenge to bringing peace, by saying, "I am"—to borrow from Chesterton's rhetoric. I am also reminded of St. Augustine's adage that one should never fight against evil as though it were entirely outside one's self.

[25]*Drugs Don't Work: Peer Mediation Training of Trainers.* For a good analysis and inventory of adult attitudes and behavior toward children, see "The Spectrum of Adult Attitudes Toward Young People (47-49) and the accompanying inventory by Lofquist and Miller. This illuminative style delineator explains the variations within the continuum of seeing children within one extreme as adult "property," and subsequently justification for abusive treatment, to young people as resources, taking part in management decisions and sharing leadership and discipline roles within organizations.

Violence is used to enforce this paradigm and violence is used as a response by students. Violence has its own perverse law of continuity, and greater violence is sought to combat that which was perpetrated. Another potential response to injustice is apathy, which McCallister believes is the most prevalent response to injustice, and the worst, because it leads to a hardness of heart, to a life without passion, and a sinful destruction of the soul.

Self-examination often uncovers one's paradoxical, contradictory statements and actions, and makes it easier to see contradictions within systems. If we extend our Gandhi/King critique to the system of education, we might find more systemic underwriting of violence—unexamined and contradictory teachings on violence. Most school curricula teach U.S. history, for example, from the basis of war and other violent conflict actions. This excludes a rich history of many who sought justice through nonviolent means, or acted in opposition to war.

Let us suppose that the school does want to teach nonviolent conflict resolutions to students like Jamal and Tom. In 1991, however, they sent an entirely different message. In September of that year, Jamal and the entire student body were required to attend a celebration for Mr. Jackson, teacher from the school who fought in the Gulf War, upon his return to work. As part of the high school music course, his older sister played in the band that musically saluted Jackson. At the celebration, the principal lauded Mr. Jackson, and the entire school body honored his deeds. Perhaps because the military institution is so intricately woven into the fabric of our government and culture, one may miss the obvious contradiction of support of violent conflict resolution by a school nominally committed to student nonviolent conflict resolution.[26] Within recent history, the

---

[26]The Gulf War was a particularly atrocious war, but by definition as war it was the legalized homicide and destruction of people and property—the use of violence in conflict resolution. If we examine this particular war more than we were encouraged to by the media, we would find that Iraq, prior to the war, was a country of sixteen million people, half of whom were sixteen years old or younger. The U.S. and its allies unleashed weaponry stockpiled for massive war against another first world nation. Nearly completely defenseless

U.S. has invaded both Grenada and Panama, both tiny countries. What was the message told to U.S. citizens, to students, about conflict resolution? From what consistent moral ground, therefore, can adults condemn violence committed by young adults? Three weeks after Mr. Jackson returned from his deadly activities in the Gulf, the same principal and teachers were talking in the faculty room, saying how shocked they were at what they had seen the students doing earlier that day. A gang member returned to school after having served a ten-day suspension for beating a rival gang member into a coma over a turf issue. As he strutted triumphantly into the building, a mob of students were "high-fiving" him, clapping him on the back, shaking his hand.

Suppose we invite Gandhi and King to a deeper nonviolent critique of our school system. They would point out that school systems that espouse nonviolent conflict resolution must come to terms with their uncritical endorsement of military careers as viable options for their newly peace-trained youth. Adults in schools must examine themselves and ask if they truly believe in nonviolence as a way of life worthy for their students to live outside of school. Career centers regularly display numerous brochures, book covers, pencils, and other material from the military. We may not decide to remove military recruiting altogether, but at least have as an obligation as educators to present a balance of ideas about the military. We need to equally promote nonviolent career options, and bring in veterans from wars who have a different perspective on the realities behind killing and destroying.[27]

---

and with negotiation and even surrender disallowed, tens of thousands of Iraqis were slaughtered, and over one million have died since the end of the hot war. For an excellent overview of things we were not told or shown about the war, see G. Simon Harak, S. J., "Hypertexting the Gulf War," *Cross Currents* 41 (Winter 1991-92): 506-520, and Alan Geyer and Barbara Green, *Lines in the Sand: Justice and the Gulf War* (Louisville, KY: Westminster/John Knox Press, 1992).

[27]Organizations such as Vets for Peace will go to high schools, when invited, to speak to students about the realities behind the glittering appeal to warfare. I am reminded of that final powerful scene when the Jon Voigt character addressed students in the movie, *Coming Home*.

Teachers provide an invaluable resource for modeling conflict resolution skills. Tom was concerned that his English class had numerous unresolved disagreements and conflicts. Academic conflicts provide a rich field for hearing, tolerating, and integrating various ideas. Teachers can instruct students to incorporate within class discussions the skills mediators employ in the steps of negotiation. Teachers can also help students to find meaning within texts by teaching students to become reflective learners who need to examine their own beliefs, values, assumptions as part of interpreting new information. Within a cooperative or collaborative learning environment, differences are respected as valuable means by which new, more critical thinking can occur. This practice can expand to allow for greater spiritual and emotional exploration, as well.

Gandhi and King would also challenge us to use prayer as a central component to living a nonviolent life. Where does that find our disputants? Jamal's parents wanted him to find his own religion, so never exposed him to organized religion, or talked much about their sense of spirituality. Tom's parents enrolled him in Christian education classes, but he never learned about violence as a theological issue, nor was it ever made an issue for Christians in sermons during Sunday service. If Tom and Jamal felt connected to a community that made nonviolence a value, they could both help others and be helped by others who struggle to live that virtue.

In his book, *The Stride Toward Freedom*, King relates a time in his life that he reached a "saturation point" in fear and exhaustion, and was ready to quit his public Montgomery bus protest. He had just received another late-night threat, and in his desperation, "took [his] problem to God." He reported feeling in that moment an experience of the Divine that was unlike any previously. He felt assurance, and although the "outer situation remained the same, God had given [him] inner calm." That calmness was not shaken, he wrote, when three days later his house was bombed. He met that horrible violence with an acceptance and strength that was a direct outcome of his complete reliance on God.[28]

Gandhi wrote that the "root of *satyagraha* [a term he coined meaning "holding on to truth" and by extension, resistance by nonviolent means] is in prayer. A *satyagrahi* relies upon God for protection against the tyranny of brute force."[29] He believed that his "greatest weapon was mute prayer," and "properly understood and applied, is the most potent instrument of action."[30] The person praying is at once given a sense of immensity, which broadens perspective. This practice reverses the narrowing effects of conflict and violence. And for the recovering addict, prayer is recognized as an integral step in gaining a free life.

Our self-examination shows that public schools do not permit institutionalized prayer. King himself agreed with this distinction, asking that within our pluralistic society, "who is to determine what prayer shall be spoken, and by whom?"[31] A person giving up the protection of violence needs to be aware of the protection of a Higher Power in its stead. That is why Gandhi wrote that prayer certainly required a "living faith in God." But he did not pray to a Christian God. He thought that "[s]uccessful *satyagraha* is inconceivable without that faith. God may be called by any other name as long as it connotes the living Law of Life—in other words, the Law and the Lawgiver rolled into one."[32] In the future, schools can allow for students to pray to a God of their understanding as part of the entire process of understanding and resolving conflicts nonviolently. Without endorsing any one religion, allowance for a faith and communication with God is a way to honor and recognize the importance that many of its practitioners—and our principle proponents of nonviolence—have discovered.

---

[28] *A Testament of Hope*, 509.
[29] *Gandhi On Nonviolence*, 30.
[30] Ibid., 45, 70.
[31] *A Testament of Hope*, 363.
[32] *Gandhi on Nonviolence*, 31.

Gandhi's words still serve as strong motivation: the future will depend on what we do in the present.[33] Schools should teach skills in nonviolent conflict resolution, through teachers' words and actions. Self-examination, personal responsibility, and reliance on personal connection to a Higher Power will be central in this new community. That is what Gandhi and King said and did, after all.

In this new school community—one more closely mirroring King's "Beloved Community"—teachers will remind students what we have known but our culture keeps hidden: that when we act violently, we act contrary to our true nature and pay a great personal cost.[34] We teachers must be willing to risk treating students as partners in the education process and to construct classrooms that promote interdependence, healthy conflict management, and by extension a just school culture. When we stop treating students as objects, a veil will be lifted. We will be able to see and to help young people see that people are intrinsically valuable and sacred and not anyone else's property. Treating a human as a thing will be recognized as an early form of violence. Such a community would have quickly caught Tom's implication that Ellen was his property and used their learned skills to help him see it.

The leaders in the third millennium will have learned and experienced the truth Gandhi spoke when he said that love or nonviolence was at the nature of our being.[35] Tom and Jamal will have learned to act harmoniously with their nature—and from a place that Gandhi thought had crucial importance: our schools. For he said that "the alphabet for *ahimsa* is best learned in the domestic school . . . [I]f we secure success there we are sure to do so everywhere else.

---

[33]Ibid., 74.

[34]I have discovered this both empirically, through interviews with students who were violent, in my ministry with prisoners and with others, and through literature, such as Dostoevsky's brilliant portrayal of Raskolnikov's disintegration in *Crime and Punishment*. An excellent new study of this disintegration is Dave Grossman, *On Killing: The Psychological Cost of Learning to Kill in War and Society* (New York, NY: Little, Brown & Co., 1995).

[35]*Gandhi on Nonviolence*, 25.

For the nonviolent person, the whole world is one family. He will thus fear none, nor will others fear him."[36]

---

[36] Ibid., 67.

12

REVISITING "SELF-SUFFERING": FROM GANDHI AND KING TO CONTEMPORARY NONVIOLENCE

Joseph W. Groves

Like all the U.S. writers in this collection, Joseph Groves is concerned more with action than with theory. Like Kelly and Douglass, he gives us an insider's look and powerful insights into local and international nonviolent campaigns. Like Kelly and Harak, he takes us into a classroom to provide an environment for reflection and appropriation. Groves goes on, however, to examine a facet of nonviolent peacemaking that many of us in the peace movement are familiar with, but too often leave unaddressed: the problem of post-traumatic stress syndrome (PTSS) for peacemakers. Is it not traumatizing to confront such danger and threats from those who espouse violence? Is it not traumatizing to be criminalized in the course of our nonviolent resistance? In this important chapter, Groves uses the reflections of both Gandhi and King, together with the experiences of himself and other peacemakers, to confront those questions.

*R*eflections and Memories: December, 1995, Shiloh Baptist Church, Greensboro, North Carolina. I am listening to ministers from the Greensboro Pulpit Forum, an organization of African-American pastors, explain the need for civil disobedience in support of the workers at the K-Mart Distribution Center. They speak

202 NONVIOLENCE FOR THE THIRD MILLENNIUM

eloquently of the need to engage in "redemptive suffering" on the model of Jesus and Martin Luther King Jr. They explain their duty to Jesus to lead their churches in support of the workers and to "bear suffering on behalf of the poor and downtrodden, no matter what the cost." I look around at an audience that is over fifty percent White K-Mart workers and local activists, some of whom are Jewish and most of whom are secular. I feel a disconnection between the strongly Christocentric language and this part of the audience. I am surprised by the language of suffering applied so strongly to a demonstration planned in cooperation with the police and for which the maximum charge was misdemeanor trespassing. Most of us in the room join the protest and are arrested in subsequent weeks.

June, 1990, A Trip to the West Bank. I am near the end of a month's stay on the West Bank helping establish a program of nonviolent presence and witness in the midst of the *intifada.* Finally I catch up with Abbas, a street organizer committed to the "unarmed resistance" of the *intifada* whom I know from a visit in 1989. As we talk about the situation, I ask Abbas about a Palestinian armed raid on Israeli beaches the week before. I expect him to dismiss it as counterproductive, perhaps even joke about it, as most other Palestinians do. But Abbas is silent, then fixes me with his eyes, and says, "I've spent eight months in administrative detention since you saw me last year." Over the next three hours he gives me a day-by-day description of his forty-seven days of physical and psychological torture by the Israelis as they attempt to extract a confession about his *intifada* activities. By the end of the three hours, Abbas's eyes are glazed and there is a film of foam around his mouth. He concludes by saying: "That's why we raid beaches and hijack airliners. If that makes me a terrorist, I'm glad to be called a terrorist. I will not accept that kind of humiliation any more." He then invites me home to see his family and have dinner. I decline because the last taxi to Jerusalem leaves in thirty minutes and I have to catch a plane the next day.

Fall, 1988, Teaching a Course in Nonviolence. This group of students is notably engaged and exciting. There are a number of activists in the class, mostly women, who respond enthusiastically to

Gandhi and King. But when we reach the section on self-suffering in Joan Bondurant's *Conquest of Violence*, the discussion turns skeptical and distanced, and the class ends even more unresolved than usual. About once a week after that, the students turn back to self-suffering, with a discussion that is usually oblique and unsatisfying. Near the end of the semester, during yet another discussion on the same topic, one of the women blurts out, "I've spent most of my life trying to *find* a self. Damned if I'm going to start *losing* it by submitting to suffering! "Students nod in agreement. By the end of the semester, I still haven't figured out how to deal with the question adequately.

Questions

These three reflections/memories illustrate some of my questioning of the role of self-suffering in nonviolence resistance. To frame these questions I will first look at some basic formulations in the thought of Gandhi and King, whose activism and extemporaneous theorizing has given shape to much nonviolent resistance in this century. Then I will interweave their more detailed thinking about self-suffering with two examples of nonviolent resistance: the struggle for Palestinian independence, focusing on the nonviolent engagement of Middle East Witness (MEW) and the Christian Peacemaker Teams (CPT),[1] a local, community-led boycott of the K-Mart corporation in Greensboro, NC.[2] Undergirding these explorations are the questions

---

[1]Middle East Witness was an organization modeled on Witness for Peace that tried to bring together Christian, Jewish, and Palestinian activists to establish as ongoing nonviolent presence of U.S. activists in Palestinian villages. It began work in 1988 and ceased operations in 1992, a casualty of post-Gulf War indifference to Palestinians. I was a member of the Steering Committee and coordinated the training program for delegations and volunteers. Christian Peacemaker Teams is a Mennonite-based organization that operates peace teams in several locations, including a team based in Hebron on the West Bank that started work in 1995. My discussion of CPT is based on a one-day visit with them in Hebron in 1995 and ongoing contact with the team through their email dispatches.

[2]In September 1993, the workers at a new K-Mart Distribution Center in Greensboro, NC, began an effort to unionize because of racial and economic discrimination. In November, 1995, in response to the workers request for community support, local activist groups, led by the Greensboro Pulpit Forum, began a boycott of K-Mart and local

and issues raised by my students as they grapple with and engage in nonviolent resistance. Finally, I will turn to a reconsideration of the role of self-suffering in nonviolent resistance to see where these explorations have led me.

Basics

Gandhi

Just what was it about Bondurant's discussion of self-suffering that caused students who were committed to nonviolent social change to pull back and rethink? This statement from Gandhi in part kindled their dis-ease:

> Just as one must learn the art of killing in the training for violence, so one must learn the art of dying in the training for nonviolence. . . . The votary of nonviolence has to cultivate the capacity for sacrifice of the highest type in order to be free from fear. . . . He who has not overcome all fear cannot practice *ahimsa* to perfection.[3]

It captures in brief four themes about self-suffering that run through Gandhi's writings. Self-suffering includes a willingness to die. It is predicated on freedom from fear. It is tied to a religious understanding of the role of sacrifice. It is a necessary condition for being a *satyagrahi*.

---

demonstrations including civil disobedience that resulted in some 200 arrests. K-Mart felt enough pressure to offer the workers an acceptable contract in August, 1996. The struggle for fair treatment and better wages still continues. I followed the workers' actions from the beginning and participated in the planning and execution of the civil disobedience. Details of the Greensboro protests are available in "The Story of the Greensboro K-Mart Workers: Moving Toward Authentic Community" (unpublished, but available from Joe Groves), and Barry Yeoman, "No Ways Tired," *Southern Exposure* 24 (1995): 15-20.

[3]Joan Bondurant, *Conquest of Violence: The Gandhian Philosophy of Conflict* (Berkeley: University of California, 1965), 29.

The massacre of some 400 unarmed Indian protesters in the Jalianwala Bagh in 1919 precipitated a major debate in the independence movement over whether or not the protesters should have fought back rather than running. For Gandhi neither option was the response of nonviolent resistance:

> The pledge of nonviolence does not require us to co-operate in our humiliation. . . . It was, therefore, for instance, no part of the duty of the Jalianwala Bagh people to run away or even turn their backs when they were fired upon. If the message of nonviolence had reached them they would have been expected when fire was opened on them to march toward it with bare breasts and die rejoicing in the belief that it meant the freedom of the country.[4]

Gandhi counseled accepting death joyfully, inviting it by standing, exposing oneself, and walking toward the guns. He regarded this extreme stance as necessary to break the cycle of fear that makes subjugation of a nation possible.

> [General Dyer, the British commander] wanted us to run away from his fire, he wanted us to crawl on our bellies and to draw lines with our noses. That was part of the game of "frightfulness." When we face it with eyes front, it vanishes like an apparition. . . . The might of the tyrant recoils upon himself when it meets with no response, even as an arm violently waved in the air suffers dislocation[5]

If resisters are willing to accept death, they have affected part of the cycle of fear; they now have the courage to die themselves. But that is no more than soldiers are willing to do in battle. Fully to break

---

[4]M. K. Gandhi, *Young India*, October 20, 1921, in Raghavan Iyer, ed., *The Moral and Political Writings of Mahatma Gandhi* (Oxford: Clarendon Press, 1986); *Non-violent Resistance*, ed. Bharatan Kumarappa (New York: Schocken, 1965), 57.

[5]Gandhi, *Young India*, October 20, 1921; *Non-violent Resistance* 57.

the cycle of fear, unarmed resisters must walk openly toward possible death. This breaks two additional elements of the cycle. It shows the enemy that fear is no longer an effective deterrent and that the enemy has nothing to fear from the resisters.

These elements of self-suffering are rooted in the practical, political, psychological (though visionary) realities of the Indian struggle against occupation. But Gandhi's understanding of self-suffering also stems from his religious convictions and is rooted in an ascetic ethos of sacrifice, self-purification, and mortification of the flesh.[6] Usually such ascetic activities are reserved for individual religious purification. Gandhi alters (or broadens) their purpose to include a focus on *social resistance*.

> Sages of old mortified the flesh so that the spirit within might be set free, so that their trained bodies might be proof against any injury that might be inflicted on them by tyrants seeking to impose their will on them.[7]

In fact, Gandhi makes the readiness for extreme self-suffering a condition for all *satyagrahi*:

> The third lesson [of *satyagraha*] is that of suffering. He who has not the capacity of suffering cannot non-cooperate. He who has not learnt to sacrifice his property and even his family when necessary cannot non-cooperate. It is possible that a prince enraged by non-cooperation will inflict all manner of punishments. There lies the test of love, patience, and strength. He who is not ready to undergo the fiery ordeal

---

[6]"Mortification of the flesh has been held all the world over as a condition for spiritual progress. There is no prayer without fasting in its widest sense. A complete fast is a complete and literal denial of self. It is the truest prayer. 'Take my life, and let it be consecrated, Lord, to Thee,' is not, should not be, a mere lip or figurative expression. It has to be a reckless and joyous giving without the least reservation. Abstention from food and even water is but the mere beginning, the least part of surrender." Gandhi, *Harijan*, April 15, 1933; *Non-violent Resistance*, 318.

[7]Gandhi, *Young India*, June 16, 1920; *Non-violent Resistance*, 114.

cannot non-cooperate. A whole people cannot be considered fit or ready for non-cooperation when only an individual or two have mastered these three lessons. A large number of the people must be thus prepared before they can non-cooperate.[8]

This is a major source of conflict for us in Gandhi's teaching: he claims that *satyagraha* can be practiced by all, yet he requires of all the spiritual development usually reserved for "saints." This is one of the problems with which my students struggled. We must remember, however, that his insistence on self-suffering sprang from years of intense struggle for national liberation. That does not mean, however, that self-suffering is necessary and central in *all* cases of nonviolent resistance.

King

Martin Luther King Jr. gave the most detailed description of his philosophy of nonviolence shortly after the Montgomery boycott. In "An Experiment in Love" (1958) he articulated six characteristics of nonviolence.[9] Self-suffering is treated as one of the defining characteristics of nonviolence:

A fourth point that characterizes nonviolent resistance is a willingness to accept suffering without retaliation, to accept blows from the opponent without striking back. "Rivers of blood may have to flow before we gain our freedom, but it must be our blood," Gandhi said to his countrymen. The nonviolent resister is willing to accept violence if necessary, but never to inflict it. He does not seek to dodge jail. If going

---

[8]Gandhi, *Young India*, January 8, 1925; *Non-violent Resistance*, 67.

[9]The article continues to be the basic statement of his philosophy today. Our literature for civil disobedience accompanying the K-Mart boycott used a summary from this article; the Martin Luther King Jr. Center for Nonviolence in Atlanta states his philosophy in the same six steps.

to jail is necessary, he enters it "as a bridegroom enters the bride's chamber."

One may well ask: "What is the nonviolent resister's justification for this ordeal to which he invites men, for this massive political application of the ancient doctrine of turning the other cheek?" The answer is to be found in the realization that unearned suffering is redemptive. Suffering, the nonviolent resister realizes, has tremendous educational and transforming possibilities. "Things of fundamental importance to people are not secured by reason alone, but have to be purchased with their suffering," said Gandhi. He continues, "Suffering is infinitely more powerful than the law of the jungle for converting the opponent and opening his ears which are otherwise shut to the voice of reason."[10]

Unlike Gandhi, King did not see self-suffering as good or attractive in and of itself. Instead, it is a virtue made out of necessity. In his most personal elaboration on self-suffering, he stated:

Recognizing the necessity for suffering, I have tried to make of it a virtue. If only to save myself from bitterness, I have attempted to see my personal ordeals as an opportunity to transfigure myself and heal the people involved in the tragic situation which now obtains.[11]

He expresses the value of suffering in the oft-repeated phrase, "Unearned [or unmerited] suffering is redemptive." This redemptive nature is twofold. One aspect is converting the opponent by reaching beyond the level of reason and touching the heart. King gives two different grounds for this redemptive element. In his sermons, he links the redemption of the oppressor to Christ's suffering on the cross. In

---

[10]Martin Luther King Jr., "An Experiment in Love," *A Testament of Hope*, ed. James M. Washington (San Francisco: HarperCollins, 1991), 18-19.

[11]Martin Luther King Jr., "Pilgrimage to Nonviolence," *Strength to Love* (Philadelphia, PA: Fortress Press, 1963), 154.

his essays, he treats the redemption of the oppressor in more detail and in psychological terms of shame, guilt, and paralysis-producing confusion.[12] In both cases this aspect of redemption is a matter of faith and hope for King rather than a reality. He only glimpses its possibilities rather than seeing it take place on a widespread basis.

King sees the other aspect of redemption, self-transformation, as a reality in people's lives. Nonviolent resistance produces a "new Negro" who has self-respect, courage, and inner strength, who can look the white oppressor in the eye.[13] He usually avoids parallels to Christ's suffering and biblical language in talking about self-transformation. Instead, he describes the psychological reality. While King's Christianity echoes in the phrase "unearned suffering is redemptive," like Gandhi, he develops its significance with both religious and secular language. If anything, King's focus on the psychology of nonviolence is stronger than his emphasis on its Christian bases.

The power of King's vision—and the reality of personal transformation that it produced—have become central to the theory and practice of nonviolent resistance. But contemporary nonviolence must also work in the shadow of the real and perceived failure of the civil rights movement to produce the social transformation that it sought. King's legacy is not unproblematic.

Explorations

Both Gandhi and King develop much more complex attitudes towards self-suffering than this brief examination indicates. But contemporary writings on nonviolence tend to leave discussions of self-suffering at this basic level. Training for nonviolent action may include exercises that deal with the risk of injury or suffering, but the training usually assumes that self-suffering is an integral part of nonviolent resistance and avoids facing the theoretical, personal, and

---

[12]King, "Pilgrimage to Nonviolence," *Strength to Love*, 154.

[13]Martin Luther King Jr., *Why We Can't Wait* (New American Library: New York, 1963), 37.

practical problematics that go with this assumption. Staying with these assumptions limits the reach of nonviolence and tends to leave it as the property of the already-convinced. I want to turn to an exploration of some of the fissures, gaps, and avoidances in dealing with self-suffering that I have experienced in my teaching and my activism.[14]

Awareness of Self-Suffering as a Process

Gandhi and many Christian theorists and practitioners of nonviolent resistance present the value of self-suffering as a theological given. For Gandhi self-suffering is a part of the religious asceticism needed to be a true *satyagrahi*. Many Christians see self-suffering as an appropriate imitation of Christ's suffering on the cross.

But many people committed to nonviolent resistance experience this "given" as a problem. Many of my students, especially those who are activists, question self-suffering as a threat to a fragile sense of self, and as societal forces asking them to accept a role that they have tried to escape. When I conducted training sessions for Middle East Witness (MEW), I found that even minimal role plays involving intervention in dangerous situations could create high levels of anxiety even though the "suffering" we enacted was that of Palestinians or Israelis rather than our own. When self-suffering raises such problems for committed activists, we need to look at the "givenness" of self-suffering present in much nonviolent training and teaching.

King provided another way to understand how people accept self-suffering. Although he approached it from his Christian perspective, he did not view self-suffering as a theological given. Instead, he

---

[14]By focusing on my personal engagement rather than theoretical writings, I am trying to avoid false universalizing and build an understanding of nonviolence rooted in "local knowledges." This approach is important in dealing with self-suffering because, at its core, the experience particular and internal. For more on the theoretical bases for this chapter, see Michel Foucault, *Power/Knowledge: Selected Interviews & Other Writings 1972-1977*, ed. Colin Gordon (New York: Pantheon Books, 1980), and Sharon Welch, *Communities of Resistance and Solidarity: A Feminist Theology of Liberation* (Maryknoll: Orbis Press, 1985).

experienced it as a process of self-discovery. He described the first twenty-four years of his life as "packed with fulfillment" and with "no basic problems or burdens." Only in the Montgomery bus boycott did he begin to face the "trials of life."[15] In *Stride Toward Freedom* he recorded in detail the threats on his life, the bombing of his house, his fear for himself and his family, his near-breakdowns under the intense pressure of sustaining the boycott. As he built the story of his growing awareness of the cost of nonviolent resistance and his new-found strength to continue, he unfolded a process that others needed to undergo if nonviolent resistance were going to change the South. He never returned to such a detailed account of his own experiences of self-suffering. Although he was frequently asked to recount them in print, he was reluctant because of the danger of a "martyr complex."[16] His final attitude was best summed up when he responded to a question about why he returned to Mississippi in spite of death threats:

> Because I have a job to do. If I were constantly worried about death, I couldn't function. After a while, if your life is more or less constantly in peril, you come to a point where you accept the possibility philosophically. I must face the fact, as all others in positions of leadership must do, that America today is an extremely sick nation, and that something could well happen to me at any time. I feel, though, that my cause is so right, so moral, that if I should lose my life, in some way it would aid the cause.[17]

In short, King discovered that self-suffering is a *process* in which one's ability to risk steadily grows. What, for King, drives this growth? It was fueled by ever deepening commitments to a cause or to other people, which led to the discovery of unknown strengths within one's

---

[15]King, "Our God is Able," *Strength to Love*, 112.
[16]King, "Suffering and Love," *A Testament of Hope*, 41.
[17]King, "Playboy Interview," *A Testament of Hope*, 355-356.

self or one's faith. These in turn led to conditions or opportunities that demand "the next step."

The K-Mart boycott in Greensboro illustrates that process. It began with a minimal commitment to civil disobedience from a number of fairly middle class African-American ministers. They were committed to a single arrest for trespassing, coordinated with the police, that would involve no jail time and a minimal fine. Even this level of engagement was new for most of them. After six months the civil disobedience had spread to the middle class white community (both Christian and secular) with over 200 arrests, with several people being arrested three times. The leaders were faced with a lawsuit for damages. Many of them were under a court injunction against future demonstrations and threatened with jail sentences of ten to ninety days for future arrests. If protesters had been faced with these penalties at the beginning, many would have hesitated to engage in civil disobedience. But after six months of involvement, some were willing to consider violating the court injunction and face jail time and unspecified penalties for contempt of court. The civil disobedience had developed its own momentum and the tactics employed by K-Mart required new, more risky actions in response. While there was a fair bit of talk about God and faith in moving to a willingness to accept more suffering, the central factor was a deepened commitment and relationship to the K-Mart workers, who were now friends and fellow arrestees for whom we were willing to take significant risks.

The members of the Christian Peacemaker Team in Palestine began with a deeper commitment, aware of the possibility of arrest, imprisonment, deportation, injury, even death. But their nonviolent intervention at first largely involved "public presence": standing with Palestinians when they were in danger, accompanying arrested Palestinians to detention, intervening between Palestinians and Israelis when violence was likely, teaching about nonviolence, and holding prayer vigils in public squares. As their friendships with Palestinians grew, and their understanding of the situation increased, more possibilities for action became possible. They began to engage in direct civil disobedience: tearing down the gates barring students and faculty from entering Hebron University; occupying Palestinians houses when the Israeli army came to demolish them; breaking the siege of refugee camps with food shipments; helping to replant olive trees that had been uprooted by the army. The Israeli response escalated to beatings by the army, arrests, imprisonments, accusations of membership in HAMAS, threats of deportation, prohibitions on returning to Hebron. The CPT members' response to being barred from Hebron in 1996 would not have been possible at an earlier juncture. At the urging of Palestinians, the team returned to Hebron in open defiance of the Israeli courts. They stated in a letter to Israeli authorities that under the Oslo agreement they do not recognize Israeli sovereignty over Hebron and will leave only if asked to do so by the Palestinian Authority.

All that may be present in the beginning of nonviolent resistance may be a willingness to make a commitment and to take a first, perhaps not well understood, first step. After that, the willingness and capacity to accept suffering emerges from a deepening commitment, not to abstract ideals, but to real people who are already taking risks, suffering, and in need. Only in this process does the true nature of the commitment and the full extent of the suffering become clear.

From the beginning of his work until his death, King wrote powerfully and perceptively about the trajectory of self-suffering. But the trajectory's arc is long and fragmented in his writings and readers tend to see the pain rather than the process. Teachers, organizers, and trainers tend to simplify by looking only at his basic conclusions. Not only does this cause us to miss his more complex exploration of self-suffering, but we also miss the way many activists take their own crucial step to accepting suffering in nonviolent resistance.

Understanding the Full Extent of Self-Suffering

When people think of self-suffering, the most likely images that come to mind are dramatic instances captured in photography or film: water cannon in Birmingham; beatings at the Pettus Bridge in Selma;

Gandhian *satyagrahi* being beaten with *lathis* at salt mines. These all deserve emphasis as pivotal incidents in swaying public sympathy and riveting examples of the courage of nonviolent resisters. In major, long-term nonviolent campaigns, such severe clashes are probably necessary and inevitable.

But having these examples as the primary or only images of self-suffering limits and distorts our understanding of the scope of nonviolence. Most contemporary examples of nonviolent resistance lack the scope and intensity of the civil rights and Indian independence movements. When campaigns are small, local, and distant (either in miles or in consciousness), suffering plays a different role and takes on different dimensions.

Sometimes the threat of severe suffering is still present. The CPT members in Hebron are engaged in confrontation and intervention with the Israeli army on a daily basis. Settlers have threatened them with death repeatedly. They have been roughed up by both settlers and soldiers. But the small number of peacemakers, the isolated location, the lack of media coverage, and antipathy in the Israeli and U.S. public toward the Palestinian cause create a different dynamic for the team. The serious injury, deportation, or the death of a team member might have a momentary impact in the media and in the consciousness of U.S. citizens and our government. But it lacks the possibility of being a pivotal moment. In the situation faced by CPT, severe suffering is to be avoided, not sought out.

In the Greensboro K-Mart boycott avoiding violent confrontation with the police and injury to the demonstrators became part of the strategy. Since the target was the K-Mart corporation, not city government or the police, violence from the police would have shifted the focus away K-Mart and on to the "rabble rousers" and the police. Furthermore, we were working in a context of violent police response to demonstrations.[18] We needed to show the police that they could handle nonviolent demonstrations with restraint.

The CPT work and our local boycott of K-Mart seem to be much more typical of contemporary nonviolent resistance than the work of King and Gandhi. But the absence of dramatic confrontations does not mean a lack of suffering. In the absence of physical injury the K-Mart boycott uncovered deeper, hidden levels of suffering, mostly psychological, that can occur in nonviolent resistance.

Externally, the legal system, the newspaper, and K-Mart all tried to bring as much psychological pressure as possible on the demonstrators, with some effect. When a magistrate placed most of the leadership under court injunction forbidding entry to K-Mart property, it raised the danger and anxiety level of the demonstrations. When the local newspaper began an editorial campaign demanding that the demonstrators pay $50,000 for police overtime for the demonstrations, the district attorney used it as a threat against us. In court the judge and the prosecutor made the proceedings as difficult and confusing as possible, stashing all the arrestees in an unoccupied, underlighted courtroom while the attorneys negotiated in the hall. K-Mart intensified the psychological pressure with a lawsuit designed to end demonstrations, place the leadership in financial hardship, and tie the campaign up in court. Workers in the K-Mart plant were subjected to spying from K-Mart security, harassment, confiscation of union literature, and random searches for stolen property.

The external pressures produced significant internal pressures of anxiety, anger, and frustration. Anxiety was far higher in the courtroom than during the arrests. In many ways the arrests were an emotional high point because of our singing, praying, marching, chanting in a common cause. When we faced criminal penalties and the power of the judiciary, however, our anxiety level soared,

---

[18]Police response to the Sit-In Movement in 1960, demonstrations at North Carolina A & T University in 1968, the Klan-Nazi shootings in 1979, and the K-Mart workers' sit-in at the K-Mart-Greater Greensboro Open Golf Tournament in 1994 all involved intimidation and excessive force. Our civil disobedience included participants from all of those movements.

particularly among middle class whites and students. The Reverend Nelson Johnson, one of the Greensboro Pulpit Forum leaders, explained the source of the anxiety in this way:

> You know, getting arrested and sitting in jail for a few hours on a physical level is really virtually nothing. I'm sitting here talking; we could be sitting in jail and have the same conversation. It's the association of that with criminality. That's what the powers ultimately hold over you. You are consciously breaking away from [societal] standards and saying that I'm willing to be thought of as a jailbird.[19]

The breaking of social norms, placing people in a situation of contradiction with their own social station and values, produced anxiety serious enough to impair their judgment and functioning. Finally, the strain of organization and leadership for people with jobs and families began to wear leaders out physically and emotionally. The ministers, in particular, came under mounting pressure from their parishioners to pay more attention to the work of the church.

These mundane, undramatic costs are the most common forms of self-suffering in nonviolent resistance. As King and Gandhi both emphasized, fear and anxiety are the primary weapons of oppressors, and the tools used to create and sustain fear are manifold. When an oppressor must resort to mass physical violence, fear has largely lost its grip. People are ready to face physical injury and possible death. But fear and anxiety can be effective in preventing a movement from getting started and they can maintain their grip on participants throughout a campaign. The everyday tactics of law suits, criminalization, threat of loss of job, community approbation, harassment, spying, police intimidation, and, at times, the quiet elimination of leaders produce suffering as surely as a police nightstick. They may well be more effective in undermining a

---

[19]Conversation with the Reverend Nelson Johnson about the theological bases for the K-Mart boycott, May 11, 1996.

campaign of nonviolent resistance and they must be a part of our contemporary discussions of self-suffering.

The Effects of Failure and Trauma.

Both Gandhi and King understood how great the immediate cost of nonviolent resistance could be in terms of lawsuits, lost jobs, physical injuries, and even death. But they tended to overlook much of the long-term cost of suffering, since it was not evident at the time. I know too little about contemporary India to make any assessment of the long-term cost of Gandhi's work. But in Greensboro I work in the shadow of the civil rights movement and see its effects on a regular basis. In Palestine I work in the wake of the *intifada*. In light of these two "aftermaths," I want to explore two elements of long-term cost: the effect of real and perceived failures in social transformation; the effect of long-term personal suffering.

The civil rights movement had notable successes, but today we live at the end of the "Second Reconstruction," with results that mirror the end of the First Reconstruction: rollback of economic gains, political disenfranchisement, and the stigmatization of many African-Americans as worthless and dangerous. In Greensboro this balance of gain and loss is a palpable presence every time we sit at the table to grapple with social change.[20] In the K-Mart protests, the real and perceived failures of the civil rights movement weighed more heavily than its gains. This assessment affected people's willingness to engage in nonviolent resistance modeled on King's work. Even though the civil disobedience actions were led by African-American

---

[20]Greensboro, one of the early centers of protest for civil rights, experienced its political gains mainly as the "last fruits" of the movement, well into the 1980s. In the K-Mart protests, we were joined or supported by four of nine City Council members (all of whom were elected in majority Black districts or by a Black-progressive white coalition), three state representatives (one of whom was arrested in the protests), a local Congressional Representative (representing a "majority-minority" district that has been declared unconstitutional), and the NAACP's representative on the governor's staff. All of these people but one is African-American. As recently as 1985, only one African American held any of those positions and none of the office holders would have supported our work.

ministers, when they asked parishioners to participate, the typical response was, "I'm with you all the way, pastor. I'll be praying for you when you're arrested." Some civil rights movement veterans did not see the arrests as true civil disobedience because terms of the demonstration and arrests were negotiated with the police. One friend, an activist leader in the Sixties, said, "You know what I gained from getting hit on the head in nonviolent demonstrations? A headache." She took no part in the demonstrations. Few African-American college students participated because the tactics were "old and tired" and tied to a "failed movement." These attitudes did not constitute a rejection of the K-Mart protests by the African-American community, as even the college students gave qualified support and occasionally came to a rally or meeting. But it constituted a significant distancing and non-involvement. The majority of the participants in the civil disobedience were African-American ministers who embraced King's work, K-Mart workers who had a direct stake in the protests, and white progressives and college students, who had a less critical and more romantic view of the civil rights movement.

A similar distancing is taking place among many Palestinian activists on the West Bank in the wake of the failure of the *intifada* and their disenfranchisement by the Oslo Accords. Some are becoming "entrepreneurs." Others are now "thieves with an ideology," or have contributed to the rising level of drug abuse and family violence. Many have turned away from direct action to building organizations for social support. Mahmud, an organizer in a refugee camp during the *intifada*, said, "I'm working with children to try to give them a chance at the life I've lost; I'm working for the release of refugees and the return of exiles. But I won't go back into the streets."

Although many Palestinian activists remain committed to rebuilding resistance, particularly nonviolent resistance, into a new *intifada*, the indications are that the former *shebab*, the school-age activists who carried the weight of unarmed resistance, and the children who would now take their place are skeptical about returning to the streets in protest. As Mahmud put it, "Why should they? The political factions took the *intifada* away from them and now just 'speak from the balcony.' Arafat has sold out. Why should they put their lives on the line like I did?"[21]

Four years after the Oslo Accords, while recognizing the *intifada*'s modest successes, most Palestinian activists view it as mostly a failure. As a result, I have seen a similar distancing from direct involvement in resistance and a lack of active support for those individual Palestinians who continue to challenge the authority of Israel and Arafat. Only in Hebron, where strong, direct oppression by the Israeli army continues unabated, does constant organized resistance carry forward. This retreat from action comes even though most Palestinians describe their situation under the Oslo Accords as worse than during the *intifada*. So even though some forms of suffering have escalated, the perceived and real failures of the *intifada* have made Palestinians reluctant to engage in further self-suffering.

But the distancing from self-suffering that I have seen has much deeper roots than just the perceived failure of movements or skepticism about the validity of suffering. In *her book, Trauma and Recovery*, Judith Herman makes persuasive links between the traumatic experience of women, war veterans, and political prisoners. One group that she does not discuss is political activists. In my work with Palestinian activists, however, the correlations are clear, with the trauma and subsequent post-traumatic stress syndrome (PTSS) manifesting a mixed set of symptoms from war veterans and political prisoners. Many of my students whose activism is rooted in work with abused women see the connections for themselves. Although I may be over interpreting, I see the similar reactions and patterns among many activists in Greensboro, particularly veterans of the civil rights movement.[22]

---

[21] All quotes from Mahmud are from two interviews during my visit to the West Bank and the Gaza Strip in September 1995, with a delegation from Grassroots International. All Palestinian names in the essay are pseudonyms.

[22] My theoretical understanding of trauma and post-traumatic stress syndrome (PTSS) is based on the work of Judith Herman in *Trauma and Recovery* (New York: Basic Books, 1992). But my practical understanding is as important. I have dealt with "activist-induced" PTSS in my own life for twenty-five years and my personal experience has made me aware of its presence in other people and in activist movements. Although this awareness may lead

Palestinian medical authorities have recognized the pervasive presence of PTSS among the thousands of Palestinian political activists who were held in administrative detention and are setting up programs to treat it. But, as Mahmud told me, "All 8,000 people in my refugee camp need treatment; we are a traumatized society." While many Palestinian activists experienced physical injury and torture from Israeli authorities during the *intifada*, it is the psychological pressure, humiliation, and abuse that all Palestinians experience on a daily basis that is virtually determinative in Palestinian PTSS responses. In the period following the Oslo Accords, many manifestations of PTSS are emerging in Palestinian society: numbness, disengagement from everyday life and political activity, inability to relate in group and family settings, incoherent rage, accompanied by a rise in crime, family violence, and drug use. Activists like Mahmud and Abbas who have turned to internal organizing, development of support services for prisoners and families, and quiet forms of resistance to the Palestinian Authority have not disavowed unarmed or nonviolent resistance. But they do not feel that they can go back into the streets and remain nonviolent.

At first my students would not express their opposition to self-suffering directly. Either through a process of self-discovery, or exasperation with my ability to hear what they were saying and move the class to an adequate resolution, they ended up giving direct voice to their concerns. Many of the women and some of the men had experienced and rejected Judeo-Christian-based injunctions to accept suffering and be martyrs. They had experienced or seen the long term effects of trauma on women who have been abused or raped. Having constructed a new and tentative sense of self that incorporated experiences of trauma (their own or others), they were not willing or able to jeopardize it for the sake of theories of self-suffering that gave little or no recognition to their experience. And for good reason. At age 18-21 they are far more aware of the profound long-term effects

---

me to "over interpret" the presence of PTSS in some instances, more frequently I think it enables me to see what others may miss.

of "self-suffering" than most theorists and practitioners of nonviolence, including Gandhi and King.

With Greensboro activists experienced in the civil rights movement and our ongoing local struggles, I can only intuit and extrapolate the experience of trauma. But I sense a pattern of response to trauma in my recent work in Greensboro. Our K-Mart boycott, especially with its invocation of King's work, called for a return to nonviolent civil disobedience. But for activists to put themselves back into a protest situation, even in relatively controlled and limited demonstrations, runs the risk of opening up old wounds, old experiences, old fears, and old angers. One of the effects among many people dealing with PTSS is that the body, mind, and emotions allow them to go only so far in terms of exposure, risk, and suffering. In an unconscious response to trauma they may give a rational explanation for their non-involvement. Or they may give a rational explanation that the listener can understand rather than voice the real reasons rooted in PTSS. In either case, the result is an oblique statement for noninvolvement rooted in self-imposed limits, exactly what we experienced with most of the Greensboro African-American community.

In all three of these cases, I think we are seeing a trauma-induced distancing from self-suffering. At our remove from Gandhi and King, such distancing seems reasonable. We understand more clearly now the instruments of repression that regimes are willing to use. In Central and South America and in many Middle Eastern countries (colonialist Algeria, Iran under the Shah, Iraq under Saddam, Palestine under the Israelis) we have seen the development and refinement of the physical and psychological torture techniques of the Nazis and the Stalinist Gulag. Regimes are able and willing to break the strongest resisters and frequently send them back into their communities as examples. I have seen the effects of Israeli occupation first hand: the "before and after" of Administrative Detention; Palestinian hospital wards full of children with arms or legs not just broken but shattered for throwing stones; the effects of everyday humiliation and psychological pressure. The unarmed resistance of the Palestinian *intifada* was not nonviolence as Gandhi or King would define it. But Israel's tactics would work against committed nonviolent resisters as well.

King said, "If physical death is the price that a man must pay to free his children and his white brethren from a permanent death of the spirit, then nothing could be more redemptive."[23] Perhaps so. But those who survive face long term costs: self-examination, questioning of the price, hesitation to be involved, and distancing. Gandhi and King missed an important element in self-suffering when they analyzed its role, because PTSS manifests itself only in the aftermath of nonviolent resistance. But we live in that aftermath and more than ever societies today have conscious and sophisticated mechanisms for traumatizing segments of their populations. Suffering and trauma may be no more prevalent now than they were for Gandhi and King's situation. But our understanding of their consequences is. Any understanding of the role of self-suffering in nonviolence today must take into account current knowledge about trauma and the effect of distancing in former and current activists.

Reprise

At this point academic norms and my own scholarly training push me to draw some relatively definitive conclusions. My desire to respond to my students' questions, to draw meaning out of Abbas' pain and anger, and to articulate the significance of the Greensboro protests pushes me in the same direction. But I resist that impulse because of the limited scope of this chapter. My "sample" is deliberately narrow, and I try to stay away from universalizing about the role of self-suffering. Here then are some suggestions that I hope are reasonably grounded in the experiences that I have tapped. They may or may not be generalizable to other situations of nonviolent resis-

---

[23]Martin Luther King Jr., "The Rising Tide of Racial Consciousness," *I Have A Dream: Writings and Speeches That Changed the World*, ed. James M. Washington (San Francisco: HarperCollins, 1992), 69.

tance. I offer them to provoke thought, conversation, and perhaps dissent.

Necessity, Rhetoric, and Realism.

My reprise revolves about the question of the necessity of self-suffering in nonviolent resistance. Both Gandhi and King affirm its necessity. If my explorations make any sense, I can't simply agree with them, no matter how central their work, no matter how nuanced a reading I give them. Nevertheless, in many ways the answer to the question of necessity is a simple and clear "yes." Unless resisters are willing to suffer blows without retaliation, then their actions are not nonviolent. But "willing" is an important qualifier, one that King often included. When we see self-suffering as part of a *process*, we can focus on the commitments that need to be made in the process. One central commitment is willingness to suffer rather than retaliate. But willingness is different from actuality, expectation, or necessity. King and Gandhi affirmed all of them, but we are not in their time and place. We have not been able to sustain the nonviolent mass movements that provided their inspiration, even though the need is as great. Our work for nonviolent social change is on a smaller scale and more fragmented, so an unqualified "yes" to the necessity for self-suffering is not self-evident.

While the lack of mass movements is the negative, there are also positives to our situation. The work of Gandhi, King, and others have enabled us to recognize instances of nonviolent resistance that have been unacknowledged for centuries.

As I try to look with new eyes, I return to King's statement, "unmerited suffering is redemptive." When I look more closely, I find that King offers some qualification. He variously introduces it as "the realization that . . . ," "the conviction that . . . ," "feeling that. . . . ," "faith that. . . . ," "history has proven that. . . . " But he never modifies the statement itself, never alters it to say that suffering might possibly not be redemptive. Especially when King's work is presented in summary fashion today, this central idea tends to be taken as an unqualified endorsement of unmerited suffering. My students' questions don't allow me to accept such an endorsement. King and Gandhi would not argue that the sexual abuse of children, rape, or battering would be redemptive. But regardless of the underlying assumptions, when we make a statement about unmerited suffering without qualification, it can produce a visceral rejection among many women and men who work with sexual abuse and trauma. We must take their responses into account.

I find that King points us in a useful direction through a contextual qualification. He frequently adds, "To suffer in a righteous cause is to grow to humanity's full stature."[24] Here King recognizes that the suffering he is describing is in the context of a nonviolent resistance movement. The suffering may be unmerited, but it is a suffering that the person chooses to risk. Suffering caused by robbery, murder, rape, sexual abuse, family violence, civil strife, or generalized repression are different from the chosen, "redemptive" suffering that occurs in a movement of nonviolent resistance. While the differences may seem obvious to people committed to nonviolence resistance, they are rarely made explicit. As a start in clearly formulating the role of self-suffering in nonviolent resistance, I suggest two qualifications: it involves a commitment to the willingness to suffer rather than strike back; it applies only in the context of a movement of nonviolent resistance.

Even these qualifications do not take seriously enough the visceral reaction against self-suffering that many have, especially people experienced in dealing with trauma. Choosing to risk suffering in a righteous cause is not necessarily redemptive. There are times, places, and circumstances today when suffering nonviolently in a righteous cause may not be redemptive.

I suggest that our rapid re-readings and summaries of King have become a misleading shorthand for a much greater complexity. To run the risk of further misrepresentation through shorthand, I want to reach for his deeper sense through a restatement: "We have the

---

[24]King, *Stride Toward Freedom*, 220.

opportunity to make the unmerited suffering that we are experiencing redemptive." As early as 1958, King said, "the Negro is in for a season of suffering . . . recognizing the necessity of suffering, the Negro will make it a virtue."[25]

Here he is linking the nonviolent resistance of the civil rights movement to the larger history of African-Americans. From slavery through segregation, unmerited suffering has been a defining element of African-American reality. Nonviolent resistance offered the opportunity to make that suffering (and the proven ability to survive it) redemptive.

But we no longer live in that moment of vision, optimism, and concerted action. Saying today that unmerited suffering is redemptive not only flies in the face of reality, but can undermine the hope that faith needs to cultivate. People can be destroyed by unmerited suffering as well as be redeemed. Movements can and do fail. In a skeptical time we need language that speaks to the realism of suffering and failure. Perhaps faith that nonviolent resistance can *sometimes* be redemptive is the best that its advocates can offer.

Necessity and Ritual.

The nature of the nonviolent protests in Greensboro and Palestine point me to Erik Erikson's discussion of the "ritualization" of nonviolence as a deeper reason for self-suffering.[26] Erikson posits nonviolence as a return to practices among earlier human societies and many animal species, in which situations of ambiguity and potential conflict over living space, possessions, sexual mates, or positions of dominance are resolved by contest rituals that involve little or no physical injury. Nonviolent resistance taps that lost ritualization at a time when the loss of ritual restraint is devastating the social and psychological fabric of our culture. Nonviolence offers an opportunity, perhaps a last, best

---

[25]King, *Stride Toward Freedom*, 220.

[26]Erik Erikson, *Gandhi's Truth: On the Origins of Militant Nonviolence* (New York: 1969), 429-436.

hope, to build a ritualization that can counter the devastation of violence.

But for the foreseeable future, we are faced with the necessity of enacting a ritual where only one side has accepted the ground rules. Whether in Greensboro or Palestine, police, army, business and political leaders all work on a model of intimidation and violence to suppress dissent and thwart unwanted change. If we enact a ritual of active nonviolent resistance in a situation where the opponent is socialized into the quick and easy use of violence, the opponent can be expected to respond with violence. Violent retaliation is central to the rules of our societal games. If nonviolent resisters refuse to play by the rules and the stakes are high enough, some of them will get hurt.

The only way, however, to change the rules, to create a ritualization that challenges the violence governing our social life, is to show that nonviolence works, to have people experience it as effective. More than a videotape from the past or words on a page, people need to have the experience of someone practicing nonretaliation, to feel in themselves or see in others the particular and unexplainable reactions that allow nonviolent resisters not only to avoid retaliation, but to not evince anger at their opponent. When this is experienced directly or indirectly, and the resisters can affirm its value, then an acceptance of nonviolent ritualization can grow.

Actions like the Greensboro K-Mart protests offer the best chance to begin to build such a ritual process. Palestinian activists have envisioned such rituals of protest, dialogue, and negotiation, but their efforts have been overwhelmed by forces committed to violence. My students experience the violence of our society in such myriad, fragmented, random forms that a process for overcoming it is virtually beyond envisioning. But our small, locally-based action in Greensboro enabled us to draw on local knowledge, personal connections, and social pressure to see and act in ways that moved beyond self-suffering. As a result, we created a small, successful campaign of nonviolent resistance with no physical violence and with the opportunity for ongoing community dialogue. It may be difficult to translate a ritualization so thoroughly grounded in local knowledge to larger societal structures, but small, local struggles are the place to begin developing ritualizations of nonviolent protest and negotiation.

We have reached the larger and deeper purpose of accepting the risk—and at times the actuality—of self-suffering. It is not an acceptance of suffering as good in and of itself, as Gandhi believed at some level. It is not just a process of discovery of the inner strength to engage in resistance and to accept violence without retaliating. The deeper purpose is to move toward a social system where violence is not the first answer, where opponents can disagree, and, through ritual processes that both sides recognize, resolve disputes without resorting to violence.

13

AFTERWORD

G. Simon Harak, S. J.

I t is surely impossible to recount all we have learned in this walk through the legacy to the future of nonviolence. Allow me then, instead, to suggest what we might have "unlearned" in the course of our journey.

I hope that we have unlearned the notion that nonviolence is the passive acceptance of harm. Unfortunately, that notion is omnipresent, especially in American culture. I recall that in December 1984, then-President Reagan was announcing the largest peacetime military build-up in the history of the world. He went to a VFW meeting and said, "We have tried our best to beat our ploughshares . . . uh, our swords into ploughshares, hoping that others will follow. Well . . . our time of weakness is now over." Ignoring his verbal (and more accurate) "slip," the audience cheered wildly. Though he received some criticism from theologians about his dismissive use of the Isaiah (2:4)/Micah (4:3) passage, his interpretation carried the day in American understanding, as evidenced by the massive military buildup that followed, and that, despite the collapse of the Soviet Union ten years ago, still continues largely unchallenged in our days of extreme budgetary cutbacks.

Some time ago, in a dinner conversation, one of my Jesuit brothers challenged me in the same way: "Of course, you would have allowed Hitler to do whatever he liked . . . ." My Jesuit brother, a very intelligent man, had mistaken nonviolence for nonresistance. He missed the point that nonviolence commits one to resist violence wherever it may be found—and primarily in one's own self. In my years as a pastor and teacher, I have invariably found the same dysfunctional interpretation of Jesus's injunction to "turn the other cheek."

I wonder if the word "nonviolence" (or its Hindu equivalent *a-himsa*) itself is to blame for such false interpretations, in that it is a verbal negation. It seems to imply only that, if someone strikes you, you will not strike back. To define nonviolence in that way, however, would be like defining marriage simply as, "You can't sleep with anyone else but your spouse." That is an accurate but surely a wholly inadequate description for marriage; so is "refraining from violence if struck" an accurate but wholly inadequate description of the nonviolent life.

More likely, though, is that the concept of "nonviolence" has been coopted by dominant cultural powers either to remove the people's most effective strategy for resistance to oppression, or else to foster subservience among oppressed peoples. I often use the celebration of "Mother's Day" to illustrate this process of co-optation. Let us conjure up for a moment what Mother's Day means to us. Flowers, cards, candy, something for Mom like breakfast in bed or dinner out.

But note to Julia Ward Howe's original Mother's Day proclamation from 1870:

> Arise then, women of this day! Arise, all women who have hearts, whether your baptism be that of water or of tears! Say firmly, "We will not have great questions decided by irrelevant agencies. Our husbands shall not come to us, reeking with carnage, for caresses and applause. Our sons shall not be taken from us to unlearn all that we have been able to teach them of charity, mercy and patience. We women of one country will be too tender to those of another country to allow our sons to be trained to injure theirs." From the bosom of the devastated earth a voice goes up with our own. It says, "Disarm! Disarm! The sword of murder is not the balance of

justice. Blood does not wipe out dishonor nor violence indicate possession." As men have often forsaken the plow and the anvil at summons of war, let women now leave all that may be left of home for a great and earnest day of counsel. Let them meet first, as women, to bewail and commemorate the dead. Let them then solemnly take counsel with each other as to the means whereby the great human family can live in peace, each bearing after his own time the sacred impress, not of Caesar, but of God.[1]

That is surely a far cry from hearts and flowers. It is a summons for peace of immense power, and a call to initiate a program of amazing scope. Now, however, that power is lost from our consciousness. In this dramatic case of coopting, we see a legitimization of the point that many feminist thinkers make: oftentimes "chivalry" is used to defuse a rightful and vital claiming of power. Moreover, the success of such a treacherous transformation is a further testimony in the ongoing (usually unconscious) cultural program to silence the calls for an end to violence.[2]

That then, is one reason why retrieving the legacy nonviolence is such an important task for us to undertake: we need to rescue the story of nonviolence from cultural forces that tend to minimize its power, trivialize it as "weak," and so either to dismiss or coopt it. Here

---

[1]Originally published as a pamphlet in September, 1870, "An Appeal to Womanhood throughout the World." The complete text is in Laura E. Richards and Maud Howe Elliott, *Julia Ward Howe, 1819-1910*, 2 vols. (Boston, MA: Houghton Mifflin, 1916), I:302-303. For a study of the period in Howe's activity (and of its ultimate failure), as she turned from the spirit which produced "The Battle Hymn of the Republic" toward the pacifism of this statement, see Deborah Pickman Clifford, *Mine Eyes Have Seen the Glory: A Biography of Julia Ward Howe* (Boston: Little, Brown and Company, 1978), 185-188.

[2]Valarie H. Ziegler admirably unites those two aspects—the silencing of women and dismissal of nonviolence in US culture—in her "Giving Peace a Chance: Feminist Historiography and Educating for Peace," *Nonviolent America: History through the Eyes of Peace*, Louise Hawlkey and James C. Juhnke, eds. (Newton, KS: Mennonite Press, 1993), 126-142. Her recounting of the struggles of Julia Ward Howe can be found on 128-133. I undertake a broad study of the strategies of the culture of violence in *Vicious Passions: The Deformation of Christian Character* (forthcoming).

is another reason: whenever we need to move forward, especially in a radical way, we need to reflect upon our roots (we get our word for "radical" from the Latin word for "root"). As with all good mining of history, we discover from our studies empowerments that help us move on in new ways. Further, by focusing as we do on the deeply personal struggle of particular people to become nonviolent, we find that we can no longer idealize and so dismiss nonviolence. Instead, the legacy and struggle of Gandhi, King, and their inheritors invite us to personalize and appropriate nonviolence ourselves.

In fact, I hope we have discovered from our journey by now that Gandhi drew "a distinction between passive resistance of the weak and active non-violent resistance of the strong."[3] Far from being tolerant of violence, *ahimsa* "is not merely a negative state of harmlessness but it is a positive state of love, of doing good even to the evildoer. But it does not mean helping the evildoer to continue the wrong or tolerating it by passive acquiescence. On the contrary, love, the active state of ahimsa, requires you to resist the wrong doer."[4]

In his own way, King arrived at a similar insight: "Yes, if the Negro accepts his place, accepts exploitation, accepts injustice, there will be peace. But it would be a peace boiled down to stagnant complacency, deadening passivity, and if peace means this, I don't want peace. If peace means accepting second-class citizenship, I don't want it. If peace means keeping my mouth shut in the midst of injustice and evil, I don't want it."[5] We can understand a similar injunction arising from Jesus's command to "love your enemy." If we

---

[3]Mohandas Gandhi, *Harijan*, 17 December, 1938, *The Collected Works of Mahatma Gandhi*, Vols. 1-90 (New Delhi, India: Publications Division, Government of India, 1958-85) [CWMG], 68:192.

[4]*Young India*, August 25, 1920, CWMG 18:195.

[5]"When Peace Becomes Obnoxious," *Louisville Defender*. Sermon preached on March 29, 1956. It is interesting to note that Gandhi had already had a profound influence on the African American community before the arrival of King. This familiarity with Gandhian thought and action enabled American blacks to embrace the nonviolence of the Civil Rights Movement all the more readily. The most revelatory research in this regard is to be found in Sudarshan Kapur, *Raising up a Prophet: The African-American Encounter with Gandhi* (Boston: Beacon Press, 1992). I highly recommend the book. Sadly, Dr. Kapur's schedule made him unable to contribute to this volume.

truly loved our enemy, we could never allow him to commit harm—since that would be for him to damage his own soul and risk permanent separation from the nonviolent reign of God.

Thus we know that our journey of peace must not only include confrontation with a violent power, but a long-term "constructive program" that might also be called peacebuilding. As we have said, it is insufficient to describe nonviolence merely as not using violence in response to violence. It requires a lifetime of special commitment and discipline. Gandhi's social equivalent of this personal lifetime commitment was the constructive program. In *Harijan* he wrote, "The best preparation for, and even the expression of, non-violence lies in the determined pursuit of the Constructive Programme. Anyone who believes that, without the backing of the constructive programme, he will show non-violent strength when the testing time comes, will fail miserably."[6] It is important to note that the constructive program was not only for personal training in nonviolence. It was intended to address the structural oppression of societal poverty and disenfranchisement.

Thus the "infrastructures of peace"—churches, local and regional civil groups, schools, health care centers, various community projects, local farming and economic ventures—must be the part of society upon which peace can be built and sustained. By their very nature such "infrastructures" train people in the art of acceptance and nonviolent cooperation. Johan Galtung identifies that activity as peace*building*, which is the necessary complement to peacemaking (a more immediate activity, such as intervention), and peacekeeping (such as the ongoing presence of mediators).[7] Along with our efforts for personal transformation, we must nurture those permanent structures of peace, if we wish to "fill up" the call to live a nonviolent life.

---

[6]*Harijan*, April 12, 1942, CWMG, 86:6.

[7]Johan Galtung, "Three Approaches to Peace: Peacekeeping, Peacemaking and Peacebuilding," in *Essays in Peace Research*, Vol. 2, *War, Peace ,and Defence*, ed. by Johan Galtung, (Copenhagen: Christian Ejlers, 1976), 282-304.

In our walk, we have met so many women and men and shared their struggles to build a world of peace. It remains for us to deepen our prayer to the God of nonviolence, to strengthen our personal commitment, and to expand our social action, so that the seeds of nonviolence, sown always with such suffering, can continue to bear fruit in the third millennium.

CONTRIBUTORS

Ira Chernus is professor of religious studies at the University of Colorado at Boulder. He is the author of *Dr. Strangegod: on the Symbolic Meaning of Nuclear Weapons* and *Nuclear Madness: Religion and the Psychology of the Nuclear Age*. He is currently studying the influence of the cold war on public discourse about war, peace, and foreign policy in the United States, with particular attention to the role of Dwight Eisenhower.

Paul R. Dekar is Professor of Evangelism and Missions at Memphis Theological Seminary, Memphis, Tennessee. For nineteen years, he taught at McMaster University, where he helped establish and direct the Centre for Peace Studies. He is author of *For the Healing of the Nations. Baptist Peacemakers* and a forthcoming book *Reconciliation*.

Shelley Douglass has been active in nonviolent movements since the 1960s and currently lives and works at Mary's House Catholic Worker in Birmingham, Alabama. With Jim Douglass, she co-authored *Dear Gandhi, Now What?* She and Jim have received The Adin Ballou Peace Award from the Unitarian Universalist Peace Fellowship, the Martin Luther King Award by the Fellowship of Reconciliation, the Paul Beeson Award from Washington PSR, and the Pope Paul VI Teacher of Peace Award from Pax Christi. She is active in efforts to bring about peace, justice, and racial reconciliation. In April 1997 Shelley received the "Woman of Justice" award from Network, the National Catholic Social Justice Lobby.

Arun M. Gandhi is the Founder-Director of the M. K. Gandhi Institute for Nonviolence, Christian Brothers University, Memphis, Tennessee, and a grandson of Mohandas K. Gandhi.

Joseph Groves is associate professor of religious studies and coordinator of peace and conflict studies at Guilford College, Greensboro, North Carolina. He has been active in Middle East peace efforts for twenty-five years and works with several organizations concerned about racial and economic justice in Greensboro. He is former co-chair of the Religion, Peace, and War Group of the American Academy of Religion.

Philip J. Harak earned his B.A. and M.A. (Professional Development) from Fairfield University. His previous published work includes the articles "The Professions In Connecticut: The Status of Public School Teaching and an Analysis of Existing Practitioner Governing Boards," and "Another Look At Iraq." He has also written several articles published in newsletters, and edited the booklet, *Backworks*, by Roman Slevinsky, P.T. He has been a licensed public school English teacher and varsity baseball coach in Connecticut since 1985. He has been trained in teaching conflict resolution, and is part of a team bringing nonviolent conflict resolution to his school. He has worked both in and outside of school in conjunction with peace and justice issues. He is a member of the Massachusetts Pax Christi Board of Directors. He lives in Massachusetts with his wife, Margaret.

G. Simon Harak, S. J. entered the Jesuits in 1970 and has served as a missionary in Jamaica and the Philippines. He has taught ethics at Fairfield University since 1986, and was John Early Visiting Professor at Loyola College in Baltimore in 1992-1993. He has written *Virtuous Passions: The Formation of Christian Character*, edited *Aquinas and Empowerment: Classical Ethics for Ordinary Lives*, co-edited *Beyond Boundaries: Student Volunteers in the Developing World*, co-edited the forthcoming book, *Riding on Faith: Essays in Disney, Culture, and*

Religion. He is currently working on *Vicious Passions: The Deformation of Christian Character*.

Kathy Kelly is a Chicago are educator and peace activist, active with the Catholic Worker movement and Christian Peacemaker Teams. She has participated in nonviolent direct action projects in the US, Haiti, Bosnia, Israel, Palestine, Nicaragua and Iraq. As a participant of Missouri Peace Planting, 1988, she spent nine months in Lexington Federal Prison for planting corn and flowers at nuclear missile silo sites in Missouri. She has an MA in Religious Education.

Sallie B. King is professor and head of the department of philosophy and religion at James Madison University. She is the author of *Buddha Nature* and *Journey in Search of the Way: The Spiritual Autobiography of Satomi Myodo* and co-editor with Christopher S. Queen of *Engaged Buddhism: Buddhist Liberation Movements in Asia*. She is active in national Buddhist-Christian dialogue.

Graeme MacQueen teaches in the department of religious studies at McMaster University in Hamilton, Canada. He is a specialist in Buddhism. He is a founding member, and former Director, of the Centre for Peace Studies at McMaster. He promotes nonviolence through teaching and research as well as through social activism.

David W. McFadden is associate professor of history and director of the Russian and East European Studies Program at Fairfield University (Connecticut). He is the author of *Alternative Paths: Soviets and Americans, 1917-1920* and the recipient of a Guest Fellowship for work in the Rufus Jones Papers, Quaker Collection, Haverford College. He is currently working on a book on Quakers in Soviet Russia, 1917-1931.

Anthony J. Parel is professor emeritus of political science in the University of Calgary, Canada. He is the author of *The Machiavellian*

Cosmos and he has recently published a critical edition of Gandhi's fundamental work, *Hind Swaraj* (1997)

Yeshua Moser-Puangsuwan has worked closely with Maha Ghosananda for years as his *kapia* (lay helper who takes care of money transactions) to India. He arranges and serves as secretary for meetings between Maha Ghosananda and such world peace leaders as Aung San Suu Kyi and H.H. the Dalai Lama. He has authored several articles on Maha Ghosananda and recently presented a paper at the International Peace Research Association (IPRA) in Brisbane Australia, analyzing the methodology and accomplishments of 5 years of the Dhammayietra movement in Cambodia, of which Maha Ghosananda is the titular head. His chapter is based both on research, and on interviews with Maha Ghosananda. He is currently writing a book on the movement.